Series in Asian Labor and Welfare Policies

Asia has been the new focus of global social sciences. One of the key features for the rise of Asia is the creation of the largest industrial workforce in the human history. China, India and many other newly industrialized countries in Asia have been transformed as 'world factories' for the global capitalism in the past four decades. This development involves both extensive and intensive migration of labour across Asia. Massive populations in the Asian countries, who formerly involved in traditional self- subsistence activities, have become wage labourers. In China itself, more than 260 million of rural-urban migrant labours have been created in the past three decades. The production and the reproduction of labour in Asia have therefore become the major research themes in a wide range of disciplines such as gender studies, development studies, policies studies, employment relations, human resource management, legal studies as well as sociology, politics and anthropology.

More information about this series at
http://www.springer.com/series/14486

Elaine Sio-ieng Hui

Hegemonic Transformation

The State, Laws, and Labour Relations in Post-Socialist China

palgrave
macmillan

Elaine Sio-ieng Hui
School of Labor and Employment Relations
Pennsylvania State University
University Park, PA, USA

Series in Asian Labor and Welfare Policies
ISBN 978-1-349-70019-6 ISBN 978-1-137-50429-6 (eBook)
DOI 10.1057/978-1-137-50429-6

Library of Congress Control Number: 2017938132

Printed on acid-free paper

This Palgrave Macmillan imprint is published by Springer Nature
The registered company is Nature America Inc.
The registered company address is: 1 New York Plaza, New York, NY 10004, U.S.A.

For my parents

Acknowledgements

This book is based on my Ph.D. dissertation, submitted in October 2014 to the Department of Social Sciences at the University of Kassel under the title 'Hegemonic Transformation: The State, Laws, and Labour Relations in Post-Socialist China'. Some parts of my dissertation have been revised and published in *China Quarterly* and *Journal of Contemporary Asia* under the titles "The Labour Law System, Capitalist Hegemony and Class Politics in China" and "Putting the Chinese State in Its Place: A March from Passive Revolution to Hegemony" respectively. The idea of investigating the hegemonic capacity of the Chinese state first came to mind in 2008 while I studied for a Masters in the Labour Policies and Globalization program at the Global Labour University (GLU). I wanted to make it a research topic for my thesis, but, after talking to my supervisor Prof. Christoph Scherrer, I found it would be too ambitious. However, I did not put the topic out of my mind. After graduating from GLU, I decided to pursue a Ph.D. and wrote a proposal on this topic that I had been thinking about for some time.

I could not have finished this book without the aid and encouragement of numerous persons and organizations. Most importantly, I have to thank my mom and dad. They offered me everything that they had without asking for anything in return. Words fail to convey my deepest gratitude to and my love for them. I would also like to thank my two brothers and sisters-in-law for their support and tolerance in my never-ending studies.

I am deeply grateful to Prof. Christoph Scherrer, my masters and Ph.D. supervisor. He is one of the key people that have inspired me to embark on this research on capitalist hegemony in China. He has given me much room for formulating my own research while offering me invaluable advice when needed.

I am indebted to Prof. Simon Clarke, Prof. Andreas Bieler, Dr. Lee Chun Wing, Ms. Ellen David Friedman, Dr. Boy Lüthje, Dr. Christa Wicherich and Dr. Bernd Reiter. They patiently read through drafts of parts of my thesis, offering me highly constructive comments. I would like to thank Prof. Jude Howell, a respectable expert in China Studies, for being my examiner. I would also like to express my gratitude to Prof. Gordon Mathews, the supervisor for my M.Phil. thesis. He patiently showed me what writing a dissertation really means. I have to thank Ah So and my friends from the Grassroots College, who first enlightened me on the issue of hegemony and its relationship to social and labour movements.

Numerous people have given substantial support to my fieldwork, without which I could hardly have completed this research. They include Dr. Chris Chan, Ellen, Ms. Li, Francine, YY, Pat, Ah Ki, Little Chu, SW, Tong Tong, April, all of the worker-informants and other interviewees. I deeply appreciate their kindness, generosity and trust.

I am thankful to Heinrich Boell Stiftung for awarding me a full scholarship for three years, without which my Ph.D. life would have been much more difficult. I must also thank those who made my Ph.D. life in Germany enjoyable and inspiring—my Ph.D. colleagues in the Kolleg of Global Social Policies and Governance, the coordinators of the Kolleg, Yuan Ming, Luciana, Miao Miao, and my friends from Hong Kong, including Ah Keung, Kit Sum, Ah Kin, and Ah Wing, who rendered me all kinds of support during my life in Germany. Last, but not least, I have to thank Jason and Bryce for kindly proofreading my Ph.D. dissertation and this book manuscript.

Contents

Abbreviations

ACFTU	All-China Federation of Trade Unions
ACWF	All-China Women's Federation
CCP	Chinese Communist Party
CCYL	China Communist Youth League
FIEs	Foreign-Owned Enterprises
NGOs	Non-governmental Organizations
NPC	National People's Congress
PLC	CCP Politics and Law Commission
PRC	People's Republic of China
PRD	Pearl River Delta
SOEs	State-Owned Enterprises
TVEs	Township and Village Enterprises

List of Graphs

List of Tables

CHAPTER 1

Putting the Chinese State in Its Place: The March from Passive Revolution to Hegemony

1 Research Question and Overarching Framework

The Chinese party-state has been studied in a wide range of academic fields. Usually employing a comparative approach, transition studies is interested in China's state-socialist history, its path of socio-political and economic reform, and the role of the state in the transition to a market economy (Gallagher 2005b; McMillan and Naughton 1992). The Chinese state's significant capacity to maintain steady economic growth has attracted attention from economics and development studies (Oi 1995; Wu et al. 2013). Its authoritarian features and the possibilities of democratic transition are the foci of political science (McCormick 1990; Goldman 1994). The poor working conditions in China's global factories and the rise of the new working class and its relations with the party-state are regularly debated in the field of sociology and labor studies (Pun and Chan 2012; Pun et al. 2010). Beyond the national level, China's growing influence in the international realm has driven international relations scholars to delve into the characteristics of its party-state (Beeson 2009; Zheng 2005). Like these investigations, the Chinese state is one of the key subjects of inquiry in this book. I argue that *the Chinese economic reform begun in 1978 is a top-down passive revolution, to borrow the words of Italian Communist theoretician Antonio Gramsci* (1971, 1988), *and that after almost four decades of capitalist reform, the post-socialist Chinese state has been transforming from forcefully steering the country's passive revolution into assisting the capitalist class to build up hegemony (i.e., cultural, moral,*

E.S.I Hui, *Hegemonic Transformation*, Series in Asian Labor and Welfare Policies, DOI 10.1057/978-1-137-50429-6_1

and political leadership). Within this framework, I further argue that *the labor law system, which has undergone substantial reform, is a crucial means through which the Chinese party-state has attempted to secure the working class's consent to the ruling class.*

The shift from the socialist mode of production to the capitalist mode of production in China should be understood as a 'passive revolution' or 'revolution from above'. The term was coined by Gramsci to understand the differences between the French revolution and the Italian Risorgimento. Gramsci points out that the former was actively initiated by the popular masses and led by the bourgeois, and that it resulted in a transition into a capitalist state; but the Italian Risorgimento came about through a passive revolution that was marked by state-engineered social and political reform built upon the ruling class's domination rather than popular support, which led to 'an institutional framework consonant with capitalist property relations' (Morton 2007, 610). According to Gramsci, a passive revolution leading to a capitalist social formation is usually backed by the domination of and forces possessed by the ruling class, which occurs, however, without much capacity to acquire the subaltern's consent to capitalist development. Gramsci argues that passive revolution is usually concurrent with two other political phenomena: trasformismo and caesarism. Trasformismo refers to co-opting the working class's leaders in such ways that the exploited class is put into a politically passive position (Merrington 1968). Caesarism refers to a situation in which a strong individual political figure intervenes to resolve conflicts between antagonistic social forces (Buci-Glucksmann 1980).

Passive revolutions that have taken place in various economic and political settings have been examined in detail, including Mexico (Morton 2003), Russia (Van der Pijl 1993), South Korea (Moore 2007), Japan (Kelly 2002), Turkey (Hendrick 2009), and Senegal (Fatton 1986). Cox (1983) highlights that passive revolution is a concept that is 'particularly apposite to industrializing Third World countries', wherein a hegemonic dominant class that is supported by the subordinate class is usually absent. I find this concept useful for analyzing China, which has been in a similar situation that Cox has described. In fact, Gray suggests that post-socialist China has been experiencing a passive revolution in which the Chinese party-state 'took upon itself the leading role in the reorganization of social relations commensurate with a restoration of capitalism' (Gray 2010, 456). My position aligns with Gray's, holding that China's economic reform is a passive bourgeois revolution, which has been guided by strong state intervention. However, as will be explained, I go beyond Gray's argument to suggest that the Chinese ruling class has been seeking to acquire workers' consent to its rule, i.e., constructing capitalist hegemony. Moreover, my approach to the Chinese state also transcends the perspectives of the authoritarian state, developmental state, and corporatist state, as will be explicated in Sect. 2, by taking the ideological role of the Chinese state seriously.

During the state-socialist period, Marxism–Leninism and Maoism were the ruling ideologies; they served as the sources of political legitimacy for the Chinese Communist Party (CCP) and helped mobilize the working class and peasants to support the state. Some scholars even suggest that the Maoist state was hegemonic in the sense that many people bought into the socialist ideas (Chau 2005). However, to cope with economic stagnation and declining political legitimacy of the state in the aftermath of the Cultural Revolution, Deng Xiaoping, from the second generation of leadership in the People's Republic of China (PRC), kicked off the top down capitalist revolution in 1978, or what he called the second revolution of China.[1] At the national level, the party-state forcefully dismantled work units (*danwei*) and rural communes (*renmin gongshe*), rolling back workers' and farmers' welfare provision such that they were forced into the capitalist market to sell their labor power. Thus, the socialist working class was decomposed and then remade into the exploited class of the capitalist system (see Chap. 3). At the international level, understanding China's passive revolution against 'a world-historical context of uneven and combined development' (Morton 2007, 612–613), its open door policies and incorporation into global capitalism were concurrent with the overproduction crisis that occurred during the 1970s in the West. Attempting to boost their profits, many foreign corporations adopted the 'spatial fix' strategy (Silver 2003) by investing in China. As a result, the capitalist class, composed of foreign capitalists, cadres-turned-capitalists, private domestic capitalists, and state-capitalists, all of whom were absent in the state socialist era, were gradually recreated in the reform period and become key market players (see Chap. 3).

Despite lingering official slogans and rhetoric, Marxism–Leninism and Maoism are no longer the CCP's dominant ideologies; they are neither put into real practice, nor does the general populace still believe in them. Since its ideological capacity has been shrinking and no capitalist class has been ready to exercise ethico-political leadership during the early stage of this passive revolution, the party-state has relied mainly on domination and naked power to steer the capitalist reform; the most prominent example being its use of grave violence to clamp down on the Tiananmen democratic movement in 1989 and the autonomous workers' organizations formed around that period, such as the Workers' Autonomous Federation, Free Labour Union of China, the League for the Protection of the Rights of Working People, the Workers' Forum, and the Chinese Workers' Autonomous Alliance (Warner 1996; Lau 1997).

However, the implementation of capitalist reform for close to four decades has resulted in the exploitation of workers on an unheard-of scale (Chan 2001; Pun 2005), which in turn has triggered tremendous labor unrest (Lee 2007); to continue ruling mainly through coercion will be politically hazardous for the party-state. Labor protests against unfair treatment in the workplace, protests against land expropriation and housing demolition, and protests over environmental issues are three principal forms of social unrest in contemporary China.[2] It was estimated that as of May 2014 the total number of mass incidents, the official government term for peoples' protests, was above one hundred thousand per year, among which labor and environmental protests altogether constituted approximately 30%.[3] According to a labor advocacy group, there were 1171 strikes and protests in the 18 months leading up to December 2013[4]; that amounts to more than 2 strikes taking place every day. In the past, worker grievances were mainly concerned with managerial corruption, layoffs by state-owned enterprises (SOEs), wage defaults, compensation for workplace injuries, overtime payments, corporal punishment and so forth (Chan 2001; Lee 2007; Chen 2003). Recently, democratic elections in enterprise trade unions, reasonable wages above the minimum wage rate (Chan and Hui 2012), compensation related to factory closures or relocations, and social insurance have also become important concerns of workers.

In light of the escalating social and labor discontent, the party-state has started to assist the fledgling capitalist class in constructing hegemony in order to elicit the consent of the popular masses. Going beyond Gray's argument that the Chinese state has navigated the country's passive revolution (2010), I propose that the Chinese state does not simply seek to retain its role of engineering the passive revolution through coercion, but has manifested signs of undergoing a hegemonic transformation—endeavoring to secure the peoples' consent to its cultural and ethico-political leadership as well as to the leadership of the new-born capitalist class in order to avoid the subordinate classes rising up against the state–capital nexus. What I mean by hegemony here is in the strict Gramscian sense. Instead of stretching the concept to include every relation between the oppressor and the oppressed,[5] this book focuses on *the Chinese party-state's hegemonic capacity with regard to state–capital–labor relations in the country*. In *Prison Notebooks*, Gramsci (1971) advances the idea that the ruling class's power is organized by the state in both political society and civil society through 'coercion' plus 'hegemony'. On the one hand, following Marx and Engels' arguments, he contends that the coercive machinery of the state—the army, the police, the prisons and so forth—helps sustain the domination of the capitalist class. On the other hand, the dominant class has to acquire the active consent of the working class by establishing 'its own moral, political and cultural values as conventional norms of practical behavior' in order to sustain its class rule (Femia 1987, 3). This ideological ascendency of the capitalist class over the subordinate classes is what Gramsci calls hegemony. This condensed explanation of hegemony will be further elaborated in Chap. 2.

Rising worker discontent has made it imperative for the Chinese party-state to cope effectively with labor unrest so as to maintain political stability and a stable environment for capital accumulation. Over the past few decades, the party-state's strategy in handling labor protests have shifted from suppression to tolerance, and now to partial acknowledgment. While trade unions independent from the party-led All-China Federation of Trade Unions (ACFTU) and associations challenging the CCP's political monopoly were heavily clamped down upon in the 1990s and are still banned, during the 2000s, the party-state became less harsh towards worker protests (Chen 2006; Tanner 2005). Some local government officials have taken active roles in pacifying angry protestors or mediating between employers and workers. Instead of suppressing protestors in the first instance, police forces are now deployed to talk them into dropping their collective actions.[6] My interviews with trade union officials in Guangdong province reveal that in the past few years, the provincial government's attitude towards labor demonstrations has changed even further: it has started to regard labor protests with economic demands as a normal part of society.[7] One trade union official noted that 'any intelligent government would not resort to violence to quash strikes. As long as worker strikes do not aim to overthrow the regime and are economic in nature, most governments would not suppress them'.[8] In addition, some labor practitioners and labor rights lawyers noted that the party-state is, in fact, more tolerant with labor demonstrations than other kinds of social protests, such as those related to land and human rights issues.[9] It would be naïve, however, to assume that the party-state in any hegemonic social formation has forsaken coercive measures to cope with labor protests (Gramsci 1971; Poulantzas 1969, 1978). Indeed, none of the Western countries, where capitalist hegemony prevails, have ever abandoned coercive tactics. In China, the party-state remains harsh with worker leaders in strikes,[10] but it now simultaneously tries to acquire worker allegiance to capitalist moral and ethico-political leadership. The changing strategies from suppression to tolerance to partial acknowledgement over time should thus be assessed seriously. If forceful crackdown is no longer its predominant tactic, then how does the party-state reduce labor unrest, contain it within the economic arena, and build up capitalist leadership over workers? I argue that *the labor law system serves these purposes by endorsing, inculcating, and reproducing capitalist hegemony, and that it is a crucial point of departure to anatomize the hegemonic power of the Chinese state* due to theoretical reasons, lessons from other countries, and the development of legal apparatuses in China.

First, as Gramsci has pointed out, laws serve a hegemonic purpose by creating and sustaining 'a certain type of civilization and of citizen', eliminating 'certain customs and attitudes', and promoting certain values (Gramsci 1971, 246). The legislative and judicial branches of the state are 'organs of political hegemony' (Gramsci 1971, 246). Many contemporary scholars have used Gramsci to highlight the hegemonic characteristics of laws; for example Litowitz (2000), Culter (2005), Kennedy (1982), and Buckel and Lescano (2009). Second, the experience of Western countries shows that labor laws are an ideology (Klare 1980) and that they can negatively affect worker activism. For instance, the Wagner Act in the USA deradicalised the labor movement by instilling a legal consciousness into workers premised upon contractualism and private property rights, and by confining their actions within existing legal institutions and practices (Klare 1978, 1982).

Third, within the Chinese context the labor law system is one of the vital means through which the post-socialist party-state has constructed capitalist hegemony in order to avert revolutionary labor insurgency. During the Maoist era, the legal system was completely marginalized (Potter 1999), but it has gained greater weight in the reform period, as will be explained in Chap. 3. During the 1980s, the labor contract and economic contract systems were introduced into the legal system and private property rights were constitutionally endorsed. The 1992 Trade Union Law, the 1994 Labour Law, and the 1995 Arbitration Law were enacted to regulate the newly emerging capitalist labor relations (Liebman 2007). Moreover, the concept of '*yifa zhiguo*' (rule of laws) was added to the Chinese constitution in 1999 and the notion of '*yifa weiquan*' (defending rights according to laws) has been widely promoted by the party-state. During the 2000s, the intensification of labor–capital conflicts and the proliferation of strikes prompted the party-state to pass three new laws in 2007: the Labour Contract Law, the Employment Promotion Law, and the Labour Dispute Mediation and Arbitration Law. The 18th CCP National Congress in 2012 endorsed the deepening of judicial reform,[11] which continues to occupy an important place on the agenda of the new Chinese leaders, Xi Jinping and Li Keqiang, and their government.[12]

Scholars widely agree that the labor law system in China is an important vehicle for the state to channel worker grievances to the regulated, individualized, and officially-sanctioned procedures so as to forestall radical actions (Lee 2007; Gallagher 2007; Wang et al. 2009; Friedman and Lee 2010; Chen and Tang 2013). However, at the same time, some scholars reiterate that labor laws are poorly enforced and ill respected by local governments and businesses (Lee 2007; Cooney 2007; Ngok 2008; Wang et al. 2009). If both of these arguments hold true, then an intriguing puzzle arises: how is it possible that an often-criticized labor law system is capable of persuading workers to utilize legal vehicles for redressing their grievances or to abide by legal principles when taking actions, thus channeling their activism into the legal realm? If the labor law system fails to perform its mediating or mitigating functions, workers would likely have become more rebellious and subversive. But workers have not become insurrectionary. Given that, how has the labor law system, however flawed, managed to contain labor activism within the legal boundaries? To my knowledge, little is known about this grievance-diversion mechanism inherent in the labor law system: *how has the party-state made many workers believe that the labor law system can protect their interests so that they do not take to the streets? In what ways does the labor law system help resolve the capital–labor conflict? To what extent do workers trust it and why? Under what circumstances would workers be willing to bypass it?* Drawing on Gramsci's theory of hegemony, *my research seeks to solve the aforementioned puzzle and provide a deeper understanding of the grievance-diversion capacity of the labor law system, which I call legally-mediated hegemony or legal hegemony.* In addition, as previous research on the Chinese labor law system seldom explored workers' views on the laws, I have spent tremendous effort to make their voices heard in this book (see Chaps. 4–6).

My argument that the Chinese party-state has been undergoing hegemonic transformation (i.e., shifting its role from forcefully carrying out the passive revolution without popular support to acquiring workers' consent to the ruling class through the labor law system) should be seen in the context of greater socio-political and economic development that have taken place in China over the past four decades. During the early stage of China's passive revolution, capitalist economic growth was a cardinal agenda forcefully put forward by Deng Xiaoping and Jiang Zemin, the second and third generation of the Chinese leadership, who supported a version of the trickle down thesis promoted by neoliberal economics (Gray 2010). This was well captured by Deng's famous saying 'black cat or white cat, it is a good cat if it catches the mouse', 'to get rich is glorious' (Tok and Zheng 2007, 5) and Jiang's idea of the Three Representatives (which led to the admission of capitalists into CCP). However, when the labor share of GDP plummeted from 51.4% in 1995 to 42.4% in 2007 (Hao 2014) and China's Gini coefficient reached a new height of 0.47 in 2010,[13] social protests triggered by serious social inequality and a wide wealth gap became as important a concern as economic growth for Hu Jintao and Wen Jiaobao, the fourth generation of China's leadership. They realized that the legitimacy of the party-state and the capitalist economy was being tested increasingly. They thus emphasized the construction of a 'harmonious society' and granted greater material concessions to the working class in the form of more generous social policies and labor law legislation, including the 2008 Labour Contract Law and the 2011 Social Insurance Law. Post-Mao China has initiated numerous economic policies, but its social policies were mainly implemented after the mid-1990s, and most of them were put into place by the Hu-wen regime (Wang 2008). 'Harmonious society' is thus regarded as a hegemonic project of the party-state to curb labor discontent (Hui and Chan 2012). The newly formed Xi-Li government continues to use the rhetoric of a 'harmonious society'. It has also attempted to mobilize the popular masses to support capitalist development through propagating discourses such as building up a 'moderately prosperous society' (*xiaokang shehui*) by 2020 and pursuing 'China's dream'. The party-state's increasing effort to elicit the consent of the popular masses for capitalist development has resulted in greater popular support for the party-state. Research conducted in 2013 showed that 85% of the citizenry was satisfied with the country's direction, ranking it first out of 39 countries. It had increased by 37% when compared to 2002.[14]

In a nutshell, both national development (i.e., economic stagnation, declining legitimacy of the political regime and etc.) and international political-economic dynamics (i.e., the overproduction crisis occurred in the West during the 1970s) have fuelled a passive revolution in China. This has consequently put a strain on capital–labor relations in post-socialist China; labor protests have burgeoned over the past few decades. Instead of primarily turning to coercive measures to maintain industrial peace and social stability as in the early phase of the passive revolution, the Chinese party-state has increasingly sought to strengthen its hegemonic capacity, especially through the labor law system and the 'harmonious society' project, to secure the working class's consent to its rule. Section 2 reviews current studies on the Chinese state in order to expound on how my approach fills up the intellectual gap. Section 3 clarifies the methods deployed to conduct this research. The last section explains the organization of this book and the theme of each chapter.

2 Literature Review

Contrary to Stern and O'Brien's (2012) opinion that current literature on China has a tendency to sidestep the issue of the state, I notice that research on the Chinese state has actually been proliferating in the past few decades; indeed, to the extent that it is imperative to further structure and analyze them if we are to gain a more thorough understanding of the Chinese state. This book aims to conduct a systematic review of the literature on the Chinese state to provide a new point of departure for comprehending it. I contend that the Chinese state has emerged in this literature in three major forms, pertinent to its *political*, *economic*, and *social* characteristics. Politically, it largely appears as an authoritarian state. Economically, it is commonly considered a developmental state or another related form. Socially, state–society relationship in China has been largely understood through the concept of a corporatist state or civil society. All of these conceptualizations have made significant contributions to our understanding of the Chinese state, but, as will be revealed, *its ideological characteristics are largely overlooked and these three dominant perspectives hardly grasp the Chinese state in its totality.* Although I divide the current literature into three categories—those stressing the political, economic and social facets of the Chinese state respectively, there by no means exist stiff boundaries between them. I consider these categories analytical rather than rigid and discrete divisions. These studies are classified according to their main attributes, but they may, at the same time, involve elements from the other categories.

2.1 The Political Facet: Various Forms of the Authoritarian State

Since the founding of the Peoples' Republic of China (PRC), the CCP has been the ruling party, monopolizing the government machinery with Leninist practices. The Chinese government is not popularly elected. Any attempt to challenge the CCP's political power will be met with suppression as in the case of the 1989 Tiananmen Democratic Movement. No freedom of association is allowed in the country; only social organizations and trade unions that are subordinate to the CCP or its authorized bodies are legally permissible. Due to this political reality, many scholars have taken the authoritarian state thesis as the premise when studying the reform China.[15] During the 1980s, there were many discussions in China on 'neo-authoritarianism'—strongman politics (see Sautman 1992; Petracca and Xiong 1990). However, Perry (1993) argues that, unlike the Four Asian Tigers (South Korea, Singapore, Taiwan, and Hong Kong), neo-authoritarianism is hard to take root in China. This is because, firstly, tight centralization, which is an indispensable foundation for strongman politics, is not truly possible in China, given its sheer size and the great diversity across the country. Secondly, political acquiescence to the authoritarian rule is not so readily secured, Perry holds, because communication technology has substantially advanced in the contemporary world. The other experts, such as Lieberthal and Lampton (1992), Oksenberg (2001), and Goldstein (1994) conceptualize the Chinese political system during the 1980s as 'fragmented authoritarianism' due to its high degree of decentralization in terms of government structures and decision making processes. However, that concept was later criticized for being static and unable to capture the forces propelling changes within the political system. Subsequently, scholars have started to investigate two important types of questions: (1) why has the CCP's rule remained relatively stable or, alternatively, why is it in jeopardy? (2) Is democratic transition of the Chinese authoritarian regime possible? If yes, what are the driving forces?

Regarding the first question, some specialists advocate the idea of 'resilient authoritarianism' to underline the Chinese state's ability to acclimatize to changing socio-political and economic development through implementing different institutional adaptations, allowing it to maintain political stability and a thriving economy (Nathan 2003; Shambaugh 2008; Miller 2008). However, this conceptualization is not without contestation (Shirk 2007; Gilley 2003). For instance, Li (2012) argues that the resilient authoritarian thesis cannot capture the paradoxical and transformative development of the country, which is simultaneously characterized by 'weak leaders, strong factions', 'weak government, strong interest groups', 'weak Party, strong country' (Li 2012, 595). He holds that the CCP has to implement democratic changes if it is to maintain political legitimacy and forestall bottom-up insurgency.

Other terms are also used to explicate Chinese politics. Perry (2007) categorizes the Chinese state as a 'revolutionary authoritarian' state because its durable rule is largely attributed to its continuous recollection and reinvention of the socialist heritage. 'Populist authoritarianism' (Saich 2004; Dickson 2005) and 'authoritarian populism' (Gallagher 2005a, 26) are employed to grasp the political trend where the Hu-Wen regime placed growing emphasis on reducing social inequality but retained tight control over society. Landry (2008) describes the Chinese party-state as 'decentralized authoritarianism' for it has been able to maintain an authoritarian system while at the same time allowing room for economic and administrative decentralization, a strategy that is associated with democracy; it is also a strategy that other authoritarian regimes in history have not pursued. Mertha (2009) revitalizes the concept of 'fragmented authoritarianism', arguing that the policy-making process in China is still shaped by the fragmented authoritarian framework, but the party-state has become more malleable for interest groups and social actors, who manage to shape policy outcomes within structural constraints. Similarly, Lee and Zhang (2013) use the notion 'bargained authoritarianism' to highlight the room for social actors to bargain and maneuver within the authoritarian political regime.

Concerning the second question about the possibility of democratic transition, some experts see a glimmer of hope in grassroots elections, which were first introduced in two counties in Guangxi in the early 1980s and in the legislation of the Organic Law of the Villagers Committees. Xu asserts that grassroots elections have empowered different social forces, yet it 'does not necessarily weaken the capacity of the state to govern society' (1997, 1431). Hence, the party-state would be relatively open to these elections. She is positive that in the long run this type of election will lead to a peaceful democratic transition in China. However, other scholars have a bleaker view of grassroots elections. Jakobson (2004) points out bluntly that the purpose of village elections is not to achieve democracy but to promote better governance and stability in remote rural areas. That said, she does not totally dismiss the long-term impacts of these elections on educating rural dwellers and instilling a checks and balance system at the grassroots level. Shi (2000) concludes that people's attitudes towards political reform have not changed much as a result of grassroots elections. Referencing the case of Chiang Kai-shek in Taiwan, she, instead, places hope on the political elites to initiate democratic changes. O'Brien and Li (2000) argue that grassroots democracy in China can hardly be realized unless the Party cadres are subjected to democratic monitoring. They are of the view that in China, '[e]lections are designed to increase mass support for the Party, and grassroots democracy is understood [by the state] to be fully compatible with strong state control' (O'Brien and Li 2000, 488–489).

Despite the differences among them, all the literature of Chinese authoritarianism possess one common feature. Echoing neo-statist theory (Evans et al. 1985; Skocpol and Amenta 1986),[16] their approach is state-centered and explains Chinese politics by paying primary attention to the political regime and the political system. The Chinese state is, in varying degrees, treated as an actor that is free-standing from society. Their focus rests upon the power of the Chinese state to regulate the society, its ability to act independently from social forces, how political institutions have influenced the party–state's governing capacities and, so forth. The state–society relationship has become secondary, if not marginalized, in ways that non–state forces, such as social movements, classes, and pressure groups have receded into the background of their analysis. However, as stressed by Jessop (2008), a sophisticated theory of the state should be a theory of society because the state is socially embedded. If we seek to understand the Chinese state in a comprehensive and profound manner, then it should be examined in relation to the society, the economic and social relations of the country.

Another deficiency of the literature of Chinese authoritarianism is that it delivers the incorrect impression that the Chinese state has not undergone any significant changes because it has remained authoritarian after almost 40 years of economic reform. However, Howell is correct in stating that 'China remains authoritarian, but it is an authoritarianism that is increasingly, albeit haltingly, opening up, allowing the expansion of spaces for self-regulation and intellectual reflection, and even the competitive contestation of power at lower levels' (Howell 2004a, 17). We thus need a more sophisticated analytical framework, which is able to underscore concurrently both the authoritarian characteristics of the Chinese state and the crucial changes it has been undergoing (especially those pertinent to its ideological and hegemonic capacity) in order to comprehend it accurately.

2.2 *The Economic Facet: Developmental State or Not?*

The pre-reform economy in China has been characterized as neo-traditionalist (Walder 1986), state paternalist (Chen 2000), or as a moral economy (Wang 2008). However, due to the CCP's declining legitimacy in the aftermath of the Cultural Revolution and the long-stagnant economy marked by serious unemployment and huge population growth (McNally 2008; Gray 2010), Deng Xiaoping initiated the passive revolution in the era of global capitalism. China's capitalist economic reform has been conducted in a piecemeal manner as captured by Deng's famous slogan 'let some people get rich first' and 'groping for stones to cross the river'. The economic reform was considered a 'segmented deregularization' (Gallagher 2004, 17). The years from 1979 to 1984 were a period of insulated laboratory, and from 1986 to 1992, the economic reform was markedly controlled liberalization (Gallagher 2004); both periods focused on reforming SOEs and attracting foreign investment into the country. In the wake of the Tiananmen democratic movement, opposition to economic reform emerged within the CCP, with cadres from the leftist faction arguing that the open door policies had led to serious corruption, social inequality, and widespread discontent. However, Deng Xiaoping's Southern Tour in 1992 was seen as reflecting the party-state's full endorsement of the economic reform. Afterwards, more reforms were put into place, and foreign trade was promoted widely.

From 1993 to 1998, China's economic reform concentrated mostly on the fiscal, financial, and corporate realms. Its accession to the World Trade Organization in 2001 further incorporated the country into global capitalism. Its banking system was restructured from 1998 to 2006 (Naughton 2008). And since 2013 the Xi-Li government has initiated a deepening of reform. Driven by its export-oriented model, China's GDP has grown tremendously (see Graph 1), and it is now the second largest economy in the world. After the 2008 economic crisis, the party-state sought to reduce reliance on overseas markets, especially the USA and Europe,

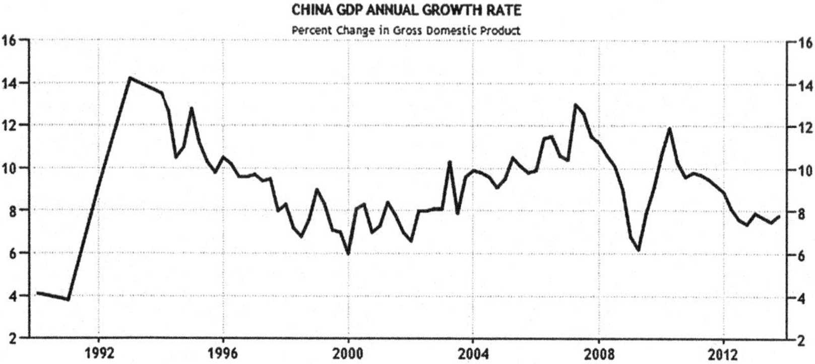

Graph 1 China's GDP growth rate (1992–2013). *Source* http://www.tradingeconomics.com/china/gdp-growth-annual (compiled from data of National Bureau of Statistics of China)

hoping to transform the country's economy into one based on domestic consumption.

Contrary to the neo-classical viewpoint that the state should not intervene in the market, the Chinese state has played a crucial role in restructuring and boosting the economy in such ways that China's economy may be viewed as a miracle. Regarding the economic role of the Chinese state, there are at least three major debates: (1) Should the Chinese state be categorized as a developmental state or is it pursuing another economic route? (2) Apart from the central government, what are the roles of local government in China's developmental process? (3) How is China different from or similar to other developmental countries in Asia?

The developmental state perspective gives weight to the role of the state in organizing and facilitating economic development during industrialization and modernization.[17] Many studies uphold the Chinese developmental state thesis (Oi 1995, 1999; Blecher 1991; Wade 2005). For instance, Baek (2001) explicates that China has followed the same developmental model pursued by Taiwan, Japan, and South Korea. It has exercised strict control over the financial sector, provided tremendous support to the SOEs, and strongly promoted export industries. Gallagher (2005b, 6, 7) calls China's economic model as 'state-led capitalist developmentalism', but argues that its developmental path differs from other East Asian countries as they have not depended on FDI as much as China has. Extending the concept of the developmental state beyond the capitalist paradigm, White and Wade maintain that China, unlike its Asian counterparts, in its early reform era was a 'socialist developmental state' because it retained certain socialist elements in its economic reform (White 1984; White and Wade 1988).

While many of the early studies drawing on the developmental thesis concentrate on the central Chinese state, later research starts to take China's local diversity into consideration (see Segal and Thun 2001; Blecher and Shue 1996). Oi (1992, 1998) uses the concept of 'local state corporatism' to account for the developmental role of the local state vis-à-vis the central state. She highlights that the fiscal reform started in the 1980s allowed local governments to submit only a proportion of their revenue to the central government, thereby providing great incentives for local governments to pursue local economic development. As a consequence of this, many local governments acted as entrepreneurs to 'coordinate economic enterprises in its territory as if they were a diversified business corporation' (Oi 1992, 100–101). Echoing this local state approach, various terms have been coined to elucidate the local state's economic role, but they usually do not lie within the developmental state paradigm. With the idea of the 'entrepreneurial state', Blecher and Shue analyze the profit-seeking behaviour of local governments which act as economic players rather than trying to provide a conducive environment for local economic development (as in the case of the local developmental state) (Blecher and Shue 1996; Blecher 1991). The 'clientelist state' is deployed to investigate how local government officials gained economic benefits from personalized ties to enterprises in their local areas (rather than directly engaging in running businesses) (Pearson 1997; Ruf 1999). The 'predatory state' is used to describe local governments that extracted heavy rents from peasants, producers, and businesses in the form of taxes, fees, and fines (Bernstein and Lu 2000). Other concepts, such as the 'regulatory state' (Shue 1995), 'dual developmental state' (Xia 2000), 'market facilitating state' (Howell 1993), 'diffuse developmental state' (McNally and Chu 2006), and 'rent-seeking state' (Wedeman 2003) are also applied to illuminate the economic behaviour of local governments.

However, Howell contends that the developmental state thesis and the other competing concepts cannot capture the real dynamics in China. The co-existence of these concepts and corresponding empirical evidence, in her opinion, expose the 'contradictory features of developmentalism and predation, rivalry and unity, autonomy and clientelism, efficiency and inefficiency, across time and space' (Howell 2006, 278). She proposes the concept of the 'polymorphous state' to account for the diversified economic policies, strategies, and outcomes across the country (Howell 2006, 278).

Notwithstanding the differences among these competing theorizations of the Chinese state, they share a similar ground by principally focusing on the economic sphere. They fail to provide a profound account of the state's activities in the social, political, and ideological domain, and, most importantly, for the connection between its social, political, ideological, and economic roles. The economic arena in any society is neither isolated from nor unrelated to the social, political, and ideological terrain (Jessop 2008; Poulantzas 2000). The developmental state thesis and the other aforementioned approaches fall short of addressing one key question: how has the Chinese party-state mediated conflicting social relations and maintained its political power so that it could push capitalist economic reform through?

2.3 *The Social Facet: Civil Society or Corporatist State?*

The Chinese party-state exercises tight control over social organizations. The CCP has established so-called mass organizations in the field of labor, women, and youth, which are the ACFTU, All-China Women's Federation (ACWF), and China Communist Youth League (CCYL) respectively. While business and commercial associations are encouraged by the government for the sake of promoting foreign investment (Kang and Han 2008, 47), all the other social organizations and trade unions that are not under the CCP or its authorized bodies' leadership are forbidden. Until recently, grassroots NGOs wishing to register as social organizations must find an administrative supervising agency from the government as required by the Regulations on the Registration and Management of Social Organizations; this has always been difficult, if not impossible. As a result, many NGOs simply register as business enterprises, which is much easier procedurally (Kang and Han 2008).

Concerning the state–society relations, the current literature has at least two foci: (1) are Chinese social organizations autonomous from the state, as in the case of western civil society, or are they incorporated into the Chinese state? (2) How does the state deal with dissidents and the discontented? Let's begin with the first point. During the 1980s, as noted earlier, most studies of Chinese politics focused on the political regime; many of them were grounded in theories of neo-authoritarianism and democratism (Kang and Han 2008). However, after the 1989 Tiananmen democratic movement and the collapse of communist regimes in Eastern Europe (in which a sign of civil society emerged), academic attention has shifted towards the social realm outside of the Chinese state by adopting a civil society framework (Chamberlain 1993; Wakeman 1993). The major concern is whether civil organizations independent from the state were emerging in China, and whether this autonomous social sphere would weaken the state's authoritarian rule. Some scholars advocate that civil society is in the process of formation in China (White 1993; White et al. 1996). According to Chamberlain (1993), studies of Chinese civil society can be classified into three types. First, civil society is treated as a 'product of a revolutionary moment' (Chamberlain 1993, 200), as in the case of the Tiananmen democratic movement, and it is seen in opposition to the state (Gold 1990; Sullivan 1990). The second type of scholarship sees it as germinating from intellectuals and students (Nathan 1990; Bonnin and Chevrier 1991). The third kind considers civil society to have existed in China since at least a century ago, but it was suppressed during the periods of Nationalist and Maoist rule, and has reasserted itself in the reform era (see Gold 1990).

Twenty years after Chamberlain's investigation, I maintain that a fourth type of scholarship of Chinese civil society has come into existence, which concentrates on burgeoning social organizations ranging from labor organizations, business associations, religious groups, to locality-based organizations. White (1993) holds that some elements characterizing civil society in the weak sense can be identified in intermediate social organizations in Xiaoshan; he is optimistic that the corporatist traits of social organizations will gradually transform into that of civil society. Howell (2004b, 143) underscores two new developments in Chinese civil society, including the emergence of new types of autonomous organizations focusing on marginalized social groups (rather than those initiated by social elites such as intellectuals, businessmen and professionals as in the earlier period), and the increasing social space for independent organizations. Chan (2013) highlights that labor NGOs in South China have contributed to the formation of relatively independent civil society, but they have not yet become democratic labor organizations.

The civil society perspective is not without contention in the field of China Studies. Recognizing the Chinese state's authoritarian control, some scholars contend that social organizations are only partially independent from the state, and thus the notion 'semi-civil society' is more appropriate in the Chinese context (He 1997). Pushing the argument even further, Frolic (1997) argues that civil society under authoritarian China is state-led because many social organizations are top-down creations that assist the state in managing a changing society and economy.

Some scholars have totally abandoned the civil society framework to analyze state–society relations in China; they have, instead, adopted the corporatist perspective (Saich 2004; Chan 1993; Unger and Chan 1995).[18] The state corporatist model assumes that diverse and conflicting social and political interests exist in the society, and that the state is 'the guardian of the common good, of a national interest that supersedes the parochial interests of each sector' (Unger 2008, 49).[19] Some scholars note that the ACFTU is a part of the state corporatist structure (Chan 2008), which is designated as the only legitimate organization representing labor under state corporatism. It must, on the one hand, help the party-state to (dis)organize workers and keep them under control, while, on the other, protecting the interests of these same workers (its constituents). Dickson also notes that this corporatist tactic has been applied to the organizing of professional, industrial, and commercial associations in China (2003 and 2004).

The state corporatist approach has made substantial contributions to the examination of the Chinese state. However, it is problematic for treating the state as positioned above sectoral interests in society with the capability to mediate those interests, while in fact, the state is both a condensation and reflection of social relations, as Poulantzas (2000) indicates. The Chinese state is neither detached nor independent from these social relations. Besides, by concentrating on the state corporatist structure and corporatist actors, this approach overlooks social forces that are highly active in contemporary China but kept outside of the corporatist structure, such as labor NGOs, international organizations, human and labor rights lawyers and so forth. Given the fact that many social organizations outside the corporatist structure have mushroomed in the past few decades, the state-corporatist approach falls short of accounting for their relations with the state.

2.4 *The Missing Ideological Link*

All of the above-elaborated concepts enhance our knowledge of the Chinese party-state, but they do not fill certain lacunae. Poulantzas (1973), an influential post-war state theorist in Europe, contends that the capitalist state should be examined at three levels: political, economic, and ideological (though he neglects the social dimension of the state, as will be explained in Chap. 2). Its economic function, he maintains, is to organize and supervise the labor process, whereas its political function is to maintain the political order and contain political class conflict. Its ideological function is to educate the popular masses and create social consensus (Poulantzas 1973). These three types of state activities combined are aimed at maintaining the conditions of production, preventing the bursting apart of the capitalist system, and forestalling the outbreak of political class conflict. Seen in this light, current studies on the Chinese state separately shed light on the political, social, and economic dimensions of the Chinese party-state, but they are not sufficient to grasp its full dynamics since its ideological and hegemonic capacities have not been satisfactorily examined.

One of the reasons for the inadequate analysis of the Chinese state's ideological role is the predominance of the authoritarian framework, which gives overwhelming attention to the Chinese state's coercive capacity (rather than its soft ideological tactics) to deal with social organizations, and the acts of advocacy and dissent. Gries (2004, 3) correctly remarks that "[i]nfluenced by a Liberal fear of the state, it had long been common among Western observers to depict Chinese politics as a simple matter of coercion: the 'butchers of Beijing'...imposing their will upon a submissive people". Here are but a few examples of research centering on the coercive features of the Chinese state. Kang and Han propose an ideal type called 'system of graduated controls' to theorize the Chinese state (Kang and Han 2008, 36), suggesting that it deploys five grades of control over social organizations. Stern and O'Brien (2012) maintain that besides the clearly defined forbidden zones, the Chinese state sends mixed signals concerning its limit of tolerance on acts of advocacy and dissent. Not knowing whether the state's mixed signals are intentional or unplanned, they nonetheless serve as low-cost policing for the state because political uncertainty drives people towards self-censorship and self-control.

In spite of its insights, the authoritarian approach leads to serious neglect of the Chinese state's ideological traits. However, it would be an exaggeration to claim that there is no research on these ideological characteristics at all. In fact, there exist scattered studies of this type. Taking Jiang Zemin's 'Three Representatives' and Hu Jintao's 'harmonious society' as examples, Holbig (2006) contests the view that economic reform has marginalized the role of ideology in China. She holds that the ideology has key roles in maintaining the Post-Maoist state's legitimacy. Breslin argues that nationalism has taken the place of socialism as the ideology legitimizing the party-state, which often presents itself as defending 'national interests' against the 'hostile west' (Breslin 2007, 43). Zhao (1998, 290) notes that the CCP has endeavored to build up 'performance legitimacy' (with regard to economic development) and 'nationalist legitimacy' by invoking Chinese culture and warning against hostile foreign forces. It also tries to construct state-led nationalism as the official ideology through the education system.

These studies are useful for comprehending the Chinese state's ideological potency, especially how it justifies and legitimizes its rule. However, they cannot answer one deeper question: while legitimacy is not identical to popular consent and ideology is not necessarily the same as moral, cultural, and political leadership,[20] how does the Chinese state, which pursues capitalist economic reform, obtain the consent of workers that are usually victims of this reform? To put it in Gramscian terms, how does it produce, transmit, and reproduce capitalist hegemony in such ways that the working class has not staged any political uprising, while ruling class's leadership has been sustained or even strengthened over the past few decades?

When Burawoy examined how hegemony was manufactured at the point of production in US factories, most of the studies in his time focused on hegemony reproduced in the political arena (1979, XII). The reverse has been taking place in the field of China Studies. There exist abundant intellectual discussions on whether the Chinese labor regime is hegemonic, despotic, or despotic hegemonic, most of which are influenced by Burawoy's insights (Lee 1998, 1999; Zhang 2008; Peng 2011),[21] but only a few scholars have attempted to theorize the hegemonic capacity of the Chinese party-state at the national level. Ling (1994, 393) suggests that the Chinese state is able to justify its application of violence to dissenters with Confucian hegemony which emphasizes parental governance. The dissenters, playing the role of children, have appealed to morality and shame in their discourse to discredit the state, but 'filial piety inherently favours the authority of the parent-state over its children-subjects' (Ling 1994, 393), and thus rationalizes the former's violence inflicted on the latter. Ling's endeavor to connect the coercive and hegemonic sides of the Chinese state is insightful as they are hardly isolated from each other. However, her focus lies on the political dissent movement, rather than on the state–capital–labor relations in the reform era. In other words, she does not take capitalist hegemony and capitalist labor relations into account.

Blecher (2002, 2004) explains that the laid-off urban Chinese workers used to be exposed to socialist ideologies, but they have come to accept the market ideologies in the post-Maoist era. Many of his interviewees are victims of economic reform, but they surprisingly think that the market economy is more effective than the planned one. Some workers feel the unfairness of the economic reform, but they believe it is natural and inevitable. Therefore, many of them are unmotivated to struggle for labor rights through collective action. This is, Blecher argues, a testimony to workers' acceptance of common sense created by the ruling class. Blecher sheds light on the study of the Chinese state by deploying a Gramscian perspective. However, his research is inadequate in accounting for recent developments in China because, firstly, it was conducted almost 20 years ago during the late 1990s. Substantial socio-political and economic changes have taken place in both the national and international arena in the past two decades; therefore, the Chinese state's hegemonic power needs to be revisited. Second, Blecher's study only focuses on laid-off urban workers; the substantial migrant workforce from rural areas is left out. Nothing is known regarding their attitude towards capitalist development; for instance, what do they think about unfair treatment in the workplace? Have capitalist ideologies become common sense for them? Have they given any consent to the ruling class's leadership? Third, Blecher's study portrays a gloomy picture for the working class's future since his interviewees were submissive and unmotivated to carry out resistance. However, after the publications of Blecher's works, there has been an explosion of workers' protests. My research aims not only to shed light on ruling class's leadership over migrant workers, but also to investigate the precariousness of legal hegemony in China; this helps us explore the possibility of staging counter-hegemony in the country.

Another study of the Chinese state's hegemonic power was conducted by Hui and Chan (2012). They contend that 'harmonious society' is not simply a political slogan propagated by the Hu-Wen regime; it is the party-state's hegemonic project to tame restive labor and secure acquiescence to the ruling class's leadership. Examining the state–capital–labor relationship during the period from 2004 to 2011, they propose that the harmonious society project aims to shape the political and moral worldviews of migrant workers, and to safeguard the ruling class's dominance by incorporating the working class's short-term concern into social policies. Their findings centering on migrant workers in the 2000s supplement Blecher's study on laid-off SOE workers conducted in the 1990s. Nonetheless, as no worker voices are included in their study, little is revealed regarding to what extent migrant workers' worldviews have been shaped by capitalist hegemony, under what circumstances they will act within the hegemonic boundaries, and when they are willing to transgress it. I seek to answer these unattended questions in this book.

2.5 *Filling the Lacunae*

In summary, there are two major problems with the approaches assuming an authoritarian state, a developmental state (and other similar perspectives), and a corporatist state. First, they delve separately into the Chinese party-state's political, economic, and social traits while its ideological and hegemonic capacities are under-examined. It is true that the state-socialist ideology is declining, but this by no means weakens the party-state's ideological and hegemonic potency. While it retains some authoritarian practices, the Chinese state has increasingly strengthened its hegemonic capacity to guide capitalist development and to persuade the working class of the political, cultural and moral values of the ruling class. My research seeks to fill this intellectual gap by studying the hegemonic mechanisms vested in the labor law system, i.e., legal hegemony. I investigate questions such as: *through what mechanisms has the post-Maoist state reproduced legal hegemony? How do workers perceive capitalist common sense? To what extent have they surrendered consent to the ruling class? Under what situations will they confine themselves within hegemonic boundaries, and under what circumstances would they be willing to challenge and transgress legal hegemony? What social forces can help cultivate workers' class consciousness to offset the hegemonic impact of the labor law system? What makes legal hegemony fragile and unstable?*

The second problem with the three predominant approaches to the Chinese state is that, in spite of their insights, they merely disjointedly grasp one dimension of the state, and thus fail to comprehend it in its totality. I seek to go beyond their limitations with the Gramscian approach that puts the political, economic, social, and ideological traits of the Chinese state under careful scrutiny. First, unlike the authoritarian perspective, my conceptual approach does not focus narrowly on the Chinese political regime, the political system, or the legal system; nor do I see them as autonomous from society. Instead, I consider the Chinese state and the law to be embedded in wider social and economic relations, and thus cannot be studied in isolation from broader society and economics. Furthermore, arguing that the Chinese state has been transforming from engineering the passive revolution with coercion to establishing capitalist hegemony, I simultaneously examine the manoeuvres of coercion and hegemony imbued within the Chinese labor law system so as to illuminate how force and persuasion back and supplement each other when the state mediates capital–labor relations. Second, instead of only stressing the Chinese state's economic function, as the developmental approach does, I posit that its economic performance is hinged on its political, social and hegemonic capacities. China's GDP could not have been maintained at such a high level if workers' consent had not been secured by the state's political power and capitalist hegemony. Third, unlike the state corporatist approach, I do not view the Chinese state as neutrally positioned or situated above sectoral interests in society. Instead, I hold that it is socially-embedded, is a condensation of social relations, and seeks to sustain capital accumulation in the society. Also, I do not simply stress the state corporatist structures or turn a blind eye to social forces external to the state. Acknowledging that the ACFTU is part of the state corporatist structure, I also dissect the role of civil society actors, such as labor NGOs, in promulgating or debilitating capitalist common sense.

Alongside contributing to a better understanding of the Chinese party-state undergoing hegemonic transformation, my research, from a broader conceptual perspective, is related to the issue of how a state's ideological project changes within the context of a radical transformation of the economic (and political) system. Many former socialist and communist countries have been facing this ideological challenge subsequent to the demise of soviet communism, the ideological decline of socialism, and their incorporation into global capitalism. The ruling class's hegemonic capacity in stabilizing social relations of production and facilitating capital accumulation in many post-socialist countries have aroused great concern and been frequently examined. At the regional level, scholars adopting the Gramscian approach emphasize that neoliberalism has overtaken communism as a hegemonic ideology in the formerly communist

Eastern Europe. In addition, neoliberal hegemony has been strengthened by the 'changing structures of capital, states and international relations' (Stuart 2012, 362; also see Bohle 2006). At the national level, Slovenia's state hegemony is built upon a model of managerial capitalism in which the state and corporatist actors play a strong role in economic and social development, while in Estonia it is based on a model of liberal capitalism with the state playing a minimal role (Adam et al. 2009). In Hungary, the hegemonic growth machine promoted by a class coalition between the state and big businesses has legitimatized the pro-growth agenda in society (Kulcsar and Domokos 2005). In Poland, neoliberal hegemony has induced populist resistance led by nationally conservative social forces; but this resistance was restricted by the state and has now been co-opted by neoliberal hegemony (Stuart 2012). My research on the Chinese party-state's hegemonic capacities will add further knowledge to the conceptual issue of the ideological role of the post-socialist state during economic (and political) transition.

3 Methods

I conducted the first major phase of my fieldwork research over eight months from September 2012 to April 2013. During the period of October 2013 to July 2014, I carried out the second phase of my fieldwork to gain updated knowledge on the socio-political and legal developments in China. My fieldwork was conducted in 5 of the 9 cities in the Pearl River Delta (PRD) in Guangdong Province. These include Shenzhen, Dongguan, Foshan, Huizhou, and Guangzhou. I chose the PRD in Guangdong as the site of my fieldwork for both socio-economic and political-legal reasons. The cities in the PRD were among the first to be opened up to foreign investment in the 1980s. The PRD has been undergoing a process of rapid industrialization and urbanization, and is economically strong.[22] Its growing labor-intensive and export-oriented manufacturing industries (such as automobiles, electronics, and textiles) have attracted many migrant workers from rural areas (where there are not many jobs available). This 'agrarian-industrial mobility' is not specific to post-Mao China, having also taken place in Europe and elsewhere (Leggett 1963, 684).

The Chinese migrant workers are usually not well–educated; many of them are in their teenage years and are female.[23] Because of the area's reliance on cheap migrant labor and foreign investment, labor exploitation is commonplace, and a culture of labor protest has been cultivated in the PRD. In comparison to the other regions in the country, labor relations in the PRD are exceptionally tense, and worker strikes are an everyday occurrence. Endeavoring to pacify the aggrieved workers, the central government, Guangdong provincial government, and Shenzhen municipal government (which enjoys administrative autonomy and legislative power) have enacted many labor legislations and social policies, such as the 2008 Labour Contract Law, the 2008 Regulations of the Shenzhen Special Economic Zone on the Promotion of Harmonious Labor Relationships, and the 2011 Social Insurance Law. The booming economy, high concentration of global capital, abundance of migrant workers, governmental concern about antagonistic labor–capital relations, and a growing emphasis given to labor laws in the area makes the PRD an ideal place for investigating capitalist hegemony vested in the labor law system, particularly regarding migrant workers (rather than SOE workers that were already studied by Blecher).

My research focusing on capitalist hegemony and worker class consciousness, an issue closely related to hegemony, is qualitative in nature. Some western studies on class consciousness have been conducted with a quantitative approach (Wright 1989; Marshall et al. 1988; Evans 1992; Western 1999). They use workers' attitudes and opinions on various issues, such as capitalist economic institutions, markets, and labor rights, as indicators of the level of class consciousness of workers. In the field of China Studies, some research studies on rights consciousness were conducted quantitatively (Wong 2011; Li 2010). However, the quantitative approach to consciousness has been criticized for being ahistorical with a lack of context (Brooks 1994; Fantasia 1988; Marshall 1983; Carchedi 1989), and for treating class consciousness as 'a static, individuated phenomenon, abstracted from social action and the context of class practices' (Fantasia 1995, 269). Aligning with these critiques, I have, therefore, employed qualitative methods to investigate hegemony and class consciousness in this book.

My research has relied on a triangulation of sources: participant observation, in-depth interviews, and documentary research, which permits me to verify information collected from one source against other sources, therefore, the issues of invalidity and bias of using only one source can be overcome (Blaikie 1991; Berg and Lune 2004). Participant observation was done on occasions including workers' collective actions,[24] academic seminars,[25] NGO activities,[26] trade union activities,[27] worker gatherings,[28] legal clinics hosted by universities, and so forth.

Besides, I conducted interviews with various kinds of informants (see Appendix 1). For interviews with workers, I conducted 40 informal interviews and 75 semi-structured interviews. Informal interviews were done on occasions such as NGO outreach activities in industrial zones, NGOs' visits to workers in hospitals, trade unions' and workers' activities, etc. Among the 75 semi-structured interviews with workers, one-third of them had encountered no labor disputes previously, one-third had individual experiences of labor disputes, and the last third had run into collective labor disputes. Workers' experiences of labor disputes (especially those of a collective nature) are highly relevant to the development of workers' class consciousness and their resistance to legal hegemony (Thompson 1978; Fantasia 1988, 1995; Langford 1994). As the emergence of capitalist labor relations during the reform of China is my research focus, this interview design permits me to dissect how experiences of labor–capital conflicts have shaped workers' worldviews, their class consciousness, and their susceptibility to ruling class's hegemony. In addition to their experience in labor disputes, I tried to select interviewees with diverse backgrounds, for example, different ages, education, gender, positions in factories, and experience working in different cities and industries.

In addition to workers, I also interviewed 16 trade union officials at the provincial, city, district, and enterprise level.[29] Seven legal and labor scholars teaching in Guangzhou, Hong Kong, and Shenzhen were also interviewed. Three of them were also lawyers, while one was a former arbitrator. Additionally, I also conversed with five full-time lawyers and legal practitioners in Shenzhen, Guangzhou, and Hong Kong. Moreover, I consulted three judges from Dongguan who had experiences hearing labor dispute cases. And I talked to four government and party officials. Two were from the city-level CCP Politics and Law Commission while the other two informants were a current and a retired town-level government official. Furthermore, 19 NGO staff from Shenzhen, Dongguan, Guangzhou, Huizhou, and Hong Kong were also interviewed. Lastly, three employers and one Human Resources manager from the furniture, electronics, and watch industry were interviewed.

Alongside in-depth interviews and participant observation, I also conducted documentary research. I have analyzed the websites of various government and party organs, including the State Council, the Politics and

Law Commission, the ACFTU, the Bureau of Public Security, the Procuratorate, the Courts, the Bureau of Justice, the National Bureau of Statistics and so forth. Various government reports have been examined too, including the annual report of the State Council from 1994 to 2013, the annual report of the Guangdong government from 2003 to 2012. Numerous orders, circulars, and notices issued by the central and local governments, the ACFTU, the Courts, the Procuratorate, the Bureau of Justice, etc. were carefully reviewed. In addition, I studied printed materials produced by trade unions and NGOs, workers' discussions in *Weibo* and workers' online blogs. Review of news reports on labor relations, labor laws, and worker protests was also conducted.

4 Organization of the Book

This book is organized as follows. Chapter 2 elucidates my theoretical approach to the Chinese party-state, which integrates Gramsci and Poulantzas's theories. In addition, this chapter summarizes how the notion of hegemony has been used, although ambiguously, by scholars in the field of China Studies. Subsequently, it explicates how I understand hegemony and the party-state in the Chinese context.

Chapter 3 explains how the party-state has utilized the labor law system to promote the Chinese passive revolution. For example, it has helped create a rising capitalist class that was non–existent in the Maoist era, establish private property rights which are a prerequisite for the development of capitalism, legitimize the selling and buying of labor power, and endorse the market wage system which prioritizes wage flexibility and labor productivity. In addition, this chapter examines the party-state's relative autonomy from capital, which is newly developed. In the reform era, it has stepped back from direct production and acted as an impartial mediator of industrial relations; but it is by no means classless. Similarly, the legal system has developed relative autonomy from the state and capital.

Chapter 4 constructs a typology of worker susceptibility towards legal hegemony. I contend that the labor law system has exercised varying degrees of hegemonic effects on workers. The affirmative workers have granted active consent to legal hegemony whereas the indifferent, ambivalent, and critical workers have conferred passive consent. The radical workers have given no consent to legal hegemony at all. Furthermore, this chapter studies the affirmative workers in great depth. I conclude that the labor law system exercises double hegemony on the state–labor and capital–labor relations in such ways that the affirmative workers have not come to challenge the capitalist economy and party-state fundamentally.

Chapter 5 investigates the indifferent, ambivalent, and critical workers, as well as in what ways they have conferred passive consent to legal hegemony. Due to labor and social policies in China, the indifferent workers feel detached from the cities and consider their working life there transitory; therefore, they see labor laws and the socio-economic development as irrelevant to them. Although both critical and ambivalent workers criticize the labor law system and do not place full trust in it, it is still able to impose a minimal degree of hegemonic effect on them because their values and actions are still constrained by legal boundaries and capitalist common sense.

Chapter 6 analyzes the radical workers who are quite unsusceptible to legal hegemony. The labor law system fails to shape their worldviews or actions in favor of capital accumulation; they have formulated radical challenges to both the capitalist economy and the party-state.

Chapter 7 summarizes the major arguments of this book. It highlights the characteristics of legal hegemony in China, as well as factors contributing to its fragilities. Finally, it points to different directions for future research about capitalist hegemony in China.

Notes

1. See http://theory.people.com.cn/BIG5/n/2012/1026/c350765-19398348.html and http://www.wtoutiao.com/a/426494.html, both accessed on 21st August 2014.
2. http://www.ibtimes.com.cn/trad/articles/18068/20121219/group-events.htm, accessed on 24th May 2014.
3. http://news.sina.com.hk/news/20121218/-9-2851316/1.html, accessed on 24th May 2014. 50% of these mass incidents were related to land expropriation and another 20% were related to other issues. It should be noted that official statistics on mass incidents are not always accurate, see http://www.ft.com/intl/cms/s/0/9ee6fa64-25b5-11df-9bd3-00144feab49a.html#axzz2uhQS1Qnn, accessed on 25th May 2014.
4. http://www.worldfinance.com/markets/ibm-strikes-shine-light-on-chinas-labour-laws, accessed on 24th May 2014.
5. Some scholars apply the idea of hegemony to study gender relations (Connell and Connell 2005; Connell and Messerschmidt 2005); some use it to analyze linguistic relations (Shannon 1995; Woolard 1985); some

applies the concept to examine racial inequality (Hall 1986; Crenshaw 1987).

6. http://www.china-labour.org.hk/en/node/100376, accessed on 24th May 2014.
7. Interview G1, G2 and G3.
8. Interview G1. Chen Weiguang, the former president of the Guangzhou Federation of Trade Unions revealed a similar point in an interview, noting that "[t]he Guangdong provincial government basically did not view these strikes negatively. We, as a trade union, found the workers' demands just and reasonable...We therefore believe that the demands of the workers were justified. But we hope that such economic disputes do not develop into political incidents and will not disrupt social order; this is our bottom line", see http://column.global-labour-university.org/2011/01/trade-unions-and-worker-struggles-in.html, accessed on 12th December 2011.
9. Interview F1, F4 and D10.
10. Solinger writes that "the general pattern, extending back to the first outbreaks of worker protest right up to the present, is to arrest, detain and imprison the leaders at protests, while distributing token cash hand-outs or partial back-pay to the masses" (2006, 191).
11. http://usa.chinadaily.com.cn/opinion/2014-01/30/content_17265942.htm, accessed on 11th May 2014
12. http://www.china.org.cn/china/2013-11/07/content_30525464.htm, accessed on 11th May 2014
13. China Daily. 12 May 2010. "Country's Wealth Divide Past Warning Level."
14. http://www.pewglobal.org/database/indicator/3/country/45/, accessed on 19th June 2014.
15. Political science scholars that consider the Chinese state authoritarian include Landry (2008), Pei (2006), Stockmann and Gallagher (2011). Studies within the field of labor studies adopting the authoritarian state approach include Friedman and Lee (2010, 514), Perry (2001, 175), Lee (2007, XI). Socio-legal studies that accept the authoritarian state thesis include Gallagher (2006), Chen and Xu (2012). Economic scholars that see the Chinese state as an authoritarian one include Naughton (2008). For the theorization of authoritarianism, see Linz (2000) and Tarrow (1994).
16. Inspired by the Weberian tradition and neo-institutionalism, the neo-statist theorists have adopted a state-centered approach to explain political outcomes; they claim that the state is an independent actor and is free-standing and autonomous from society (Hay and Lister 2006; Jessop 2008).
17. Howell (2006) has conducted a comprehensive review of the development of developmental state theories. Other important works on the

developmental state include, Leftwich (1996), Wade (2005), Weiss (2000), White and Wade (1988).

18. Corporatism consists of two types: societal corporatism and state corporatism; the former has given citizens substantial rights, including the right of association, while the latter only allows citizens limited rights. For more on the theory of corporatism, see Schmitter (1974).
19. The corporatist state discussed in this sub-section is different from Jean Oi's concept of local state corporatism as explained in the previous sub-section. The former refers to a particular pattern of relations between the state and social organizations, while corporatism as used by Oi highlights that local states act like corporations.
20. Legitimacy is a concept usually associated with political regimes, focusing on the political relations between the govern and the governed but without considering the relationship between the state and the capitalist class and the relations between the political and the economic. For example, Max Weber's understanding of legitimacy is "the belief that someone's position and the system incorporating it are right and proper" (Wallace and Wolf 2006, 74); for Habermas, it is "a political order's worthiness to be recognised" (Habermas 1979, 178). However, from the Gramscian perspective the concept of hegemony concerns both political and economic relations, as well as the state–capital–labor relations. It focuses on how the state and the capitalist class try to obtain worker consent and allegiance to the leadership of the ruling class so as to sustain the long-term dominance of the capitalist system. Due to their conceptual differences, it is inappropriate to equate hegemony with legitimacy.
21. Adding to this, studies on China's hegemonic power in the international arena have also mushroomed (Li 1996; Woo 1994; Weede 1999).
22. In 2012, the overall foreign trade of Guangdong Province was US$ 9838.2 billion, constituting 25.4% of the country's total foreign trade. In fact, its total exports increased 7.9% to US$ 5741.4 billion, making up 28% of total exports from China (http://www.gd.gov.cn/gdgk/gdyw/201301/t20130116_173592.htm, accessed on 1st January 2014). The PRD is an important engine of economic growth in Guangdong Province. In 2009, the PRD's GDP jumped by 9.4% to $32105.88 billion, which constituted 82.2% of the total GDP of the province. And the PRD's total exports and imports comprised 95.7% of the provincial total in 2009 (http://www.gd.gov.cn/govinc/nj2010/01qsgk/010202.htm, accessed on 1st January 2014).
23. For demographic details of Chinese migrant workers, see government information at http://www.gov.cn/gzdt/2013-05/27/content_2411923.htm and http://www.moh.gov.cn/ldrks/s7847/201309/12e8cf0459de42c9-81c59e827b87a27c.shtml, accessed on 1st January 2014.

24. For instance, worker strikes and actions to demand proper compensation for occupational diseases, terminations, raises, etc.
25. Including seminars where worker activists, trade unionists, government officials were invited to attend.
26. For example, worker meetings, visits to work injury victims in hospitals, outreach activities in industrial zones, staff meetings, legal consultations for workers, retreat meetings, training for worker activists, and handling of collective labor disputes.
27. For instance, Worker Congresses, meetings of enterprise trade union officials, spring festival dinner for union members, dinner meetings between enterprise trade union officials and management.
28. Such as having meals in workers' dormitory and homes, shopping, dancing, singing karaoke and so forth.
29. Eleven of them are also counted as worker-interviewees as they were workers elected to be enterprise trade union officials.

References

Adam, Frane, Primož Kristan, and Matevž Tomšič. 2009. Varieties of Capitalism in Eastern Europe (with Special Emphasis on Estonia and Slovenia). *Communist and Post-Communist Studies* 42 (1): 65–81.

Baek, S.W. 2001. Does China Follow the East Asian Development Model? *Journal of Contemporary Asia* 35 (4): 485–498.

Beeson, Mark. 2009. Hegemonic Transition in East Asia? The Dynamics of Chinese and American Power. *Review of International Studies* 35 (1): 95–112.

Berg, Bruce Lawrence, and Howard Lune. 2004. *Qualitative Research Methods for the Social Sciences*, vol. 5. Boston: Pearson.

Bernstein, Thomas P., and Xiaobo Lu. 2000. Taxation Without Representation: Peasants, the Central and the Local States in Reform China. *China Quarterly* 163: 742–763.

Blaikie, Norman W.H. 1991. A Critique of the Use of Triangulation in Social Research. *Quality & Quantity* 25 (2): 115–136.

Blecher, Marc. 1991. Development State, Entrepreneurial State: The Political Economy of Socialist Reform in Xinji Municipality and Guanghan County. In *The Chinese State in the Era of Economic Reform: The Road to Crisis*, ed. Gordon White. Basingstoke: Macmillan.

Blecher, Marc. 2002. Hegemony and Workers' Politics in China. *China Quarterly* 170: 283–303.

Blecher, Marc. 2004. The Working Class and Governance. In *Governance in China*, ed. Jude Howell. Lanham, MD: Rowman & Littlefield Publishers, Inc.

Blecher, Marc, and Vivienne Shue. 1996. *Tethered Deer: Government and Economy in a Chinese County*. Stanford: Stanford University Press.
Bohle, Dorothee. 2006. Neoliberal Hegemony, Transnational Capital and the Terms of the EU's Eastward Expansion. *Capital & Class* 30 (1): 57–86.
Bonnin, Michel, and Yves Chevrier. 1991. The Intellectual and the State: Social Dynamics of Intellectual Autonomy During the Post-Mao Era. *China Quarterly* 127: 569–593.
Breslin, Shaun. 2007. *China and the Global Political Economy*. New York: Palgrave Macmillan.
Brooks, C. 1994. Class Consciousness and Politics in Comparative Perspective. *Social Science Research* 23 (2): 167–195.
Buci-Glucksmann, Christine. 1980. *Gramsci and the State*, trans. David Fernbach. London: Lawrence and Wishart Ltd.
Buckel, Sonja, and Andreas Fischer Lescano. 2009. Gramsci Reconsidered: Hegemony in Global Law. *Leiden Journal of International Law* 22: 437–454.
Burawoy, Michael. 1979. *Manufacturing Consent: Changes in the Labor Process Under Monopoly Capitalism*. Chicago: University of Chicago Press.
Carchedi, Gulielmo. 1989. Classes and Class Analysis. In *The Debate on Classes*, ed. Erik Olin Wright. New York: Verso.
Chamberlain, Heath B. 1993. On the Search for Civil Society in China. *Modern China* 19: 199–215.
Chan, Anita. 1993. Revolution or Corporatism? Workers and Trade Unions in Post-Mao China. *The Australian Journal of Chinese Affairs* 29: 31–61.
Chan, Anita. 2001. *Chinese Workers Under Assault*. Armonk, NY: M.E. Sharpe.
Chan, Anita. 2008. China's Trade Unions in Corporatist Transition. In *Associations and the Chinese State: Contested Spaces*, ed. Jonathan Unger. New York: M. E. Sharpe Inc.
Chan, King Chi Chris. 2013. Community-Based Organizations for Migrant Workers' Rights: The Emergence of Labour NGOs in China. *Community Development Journal* 48 (1): 6–22.
Chan, King-Chi Chris, and Sio-Ieng Elaine Hui. 2012. The Dynamics and Dilemma of Workplace Trade Union Reform in China: The Case of the Honda Workers' Strike. *Journal of Industrial Relations* 54: 653–668.
Chau, Adam Yuet. 2005. *Miraculous Response: Doing Popular Religion in Contemporary China*. Stanford: Stanford University Press.
Chen, Feng. 2000. Subsistence Crises, Managerial Corruption and Labour Protests in China. *China Journal* 44: 41–63.
Chen, Feng. 2003. Industrial Restructuring and Workers' Resistance in China. *Modern China* 29 (2): 237–262.
Chen, Feng. 2006. Privatization and Its Discontents in Chinese Factories. *China Quarterly* 185: 42–60.

Chen, Feng, and Mengxiao Tang. 2013. Labor Conflicts in China: Typologies and Their Implications. *Asian Survey* 53 (3): 559–583.

Chen, Feng, and Xin Xu. 2012. "Active Judiciary": Judicial Dismantling of Workers' Collective Action in China. *China Journal* 67 (January): 87–107.

Connell, Robert W., and James W. Messerschmidt. 2005. Hegemonic Masculinity Rethinking the Concept. *Gender & Society* 19 (6): 829–859.

Connell, Robert William, and Raewyn Connell. 2005. *Masculinities.* Berkeley: University of California Press.

Cooney, Sean. 2007. China's Labour Law, Compliance and Flaws in Implementing Institutions. *Journal of Industrial Relations* 49: 673–686.

Cox, Robert. 1983. Gramsci, Hegemony and International Relations: An Essay in Method. *Millennium: Journal of International Studies* 12 (2): 162–175.

Crenshaw, Kimberle Williams. 1987. Race, Reform, and Retrenchment: Transformation and Legitimation in Antidiscrimination Law. *Harvard Law Review* 101: 1331.

Culter, A.Claire. 2005. Gramsci, Law and the Culture of Global Capitalism. *Review of International Social and Political Philosophy* 8 (4): 527–542.

Dickson, Bruce. 2003. *Red Capitalists in China: The Party, Private Entrepreneurs, and Prospects for Political Change.* New York: Cambridge University Press.

Dickson, Bruce. 2004. Dilemmas of Party Adaptation. In *State and Society in 21st-Century China: Crisis, Contention, and Legitimation*, ed. Peter Hays Gries and Stanley Rosen. New York: RoutledgeCurzon.

Dickson, Bruce. 2005. Populist Authoritarianism: The Future of the Chinese Communist Party. In *"Chinese Leadership, Politics, and Policy" Carnegie Endowment for International Peace.* George Washington University.

Evans, Geoff. 1992. Is Britain a Class-Divided Society? A Re-Analysis and Extension of Marshall et al'.s Study of Class Consciousness. *Sociology* 26 (2): 233–258.

Evans, Peter B., Dietrich Rueshemeyer, and Theda Skocpol. (eds.). 1985. *Bringing the State Back In.* Cambridge: Cambridge University Press.

Fantasia, Rick. 1988. *Cultures of Solidarity: Consciousness, Action, and Contemporary American Workers.* Berkeley: University of California Press.

Fantasia, Rick. 1995. From Class Consciousness to Culture, Action, and Social Organization. *Annual Review of Sociology* 21: 269–287.

Fatton, Robert. 1986. Gramsci and the Legitimization of the State: The Case of the Senegalese Passive Revolution. *Canadian Journal of Political Science* 19 (4): 729–750.

Femia, Joseph V. 1987. *Gramsci's Political Thought: Hegemony, Consciousness, and the Revolutionary Process.* Oxford: Clarendon Press.

Friedman, Eli, and Ching Kwan Lee. 2010. Remaking the World of Chinese Labour: A 30-Year Retrospective. *British Journal of Industrial Relations* 48 (3): 507–533.

Frolic, B. Michael. 1997. State-Led Civil Society. In *Civil Society in China*, ed. Timothy Brook and B. Michael Frolic. Armonk, NY: M.E. Sharpe.
Gallagher, Mary E. 2004. "Time is Money, Efficiency Is Life": The Transformation of Labor Relations in China. *Studies in Comparative International Development* 39 (2): 11–44.
Gallagher, Mary E. 2005a. China in 2004: Stability Above All. *Asian Survey* 45 (1): 21–32.
Gallagher, Mary E. 2005b. *Contagious Capitalism: Globalization and the Politics of Labor in China*. Princeton, NJ: Princeton University Press.
Gallagher, Mary E. 2006. Mobilizing the Law in China: "Informed Disenchantment" and the Development of Legal Consciousness. *Law & Society Review* 40 (4): 783–816.
Gallagher, Mary E. 2007. 'Hope for Protection and Hopeless Choices': Labour Legal Aid in the PRC. In *Grassroots Political Reform in Contemporary China*, ed. Elizabeth J. Perry and Merle Goldman. London: Harvard University Press.
Gilley, Bruce. 2003. The Limits of Authoritarian Resilience. *Journal of Democracy* 14 (1): 18–26.
Gold, T. 1990. The Resurgence of Civil Society in China. *Journal of Democracy* 1: 18–31.
Goldman, Merle. 1994. *Sowing the Seeds of Democracy in China: Political Reform in the Deng Xiaoping Era*. Cambridge: Harvard University Press.
Goldstein, Avery. 1994. Trends in the Study of Political Elites and Institutions in the PRC. *China Quarterly* 139: 714–730.
Gramsci, Antonio. 1971. *Selections from the Prison Notebooks*, trans. and ed. Q. Hoare and G.N. Smith. New York: International Publishers.
Gramsci, Antonio. 1988. *A Gramsci Reader: Selected Writing 1916–1935*, ed. D. Forgacs. New York: New York University Press.
Gray, Kevin. 2010. Labour and the State in China's Passive Revolution. *Capital and Class* 34 (3): 449–467.
Gries, Peter Hays. 2004. Popular Nationalism and State Legitimation in China. In *State and Society in 21st-Century China: Crisis, Contention, and Legitimation*, ed. Peter Hays Gries and Stanley Rosen. New York: RoutledgeCurzon.
Habermas, Jürgen. 1979. Legitimation Problems in the Modern State. In *Communication and the Evolution of Society*, ed. Jürgen Habermas. London: Heinemann Education Books.
Hall, Stuart. 1986. Gramsci's Relevance for the Study of Race and Ethnicity. *Journal of Communication Inquiry* 10 (2): 5–27.
Hao, Qi. 2014. The Labor Share Question in China. *Monthly Review* 65 (8).
Hay, Collin, and Michael Lister. 2006. Introduction: Theories of the State. In *The State: Theories and Issues*, ed. Colin Hay, Michael Lister, and David Marsh.
He, Baogang. 1997. *The Democratic Implications of Civil Society in China*. New York: St. Martin's Press.

Hendrick, Joshua D. 2009. Globalization, Islamic Activism, and Passive Revolution in Turkey: The Case of Fethullah Gülen. *Journal of Power* 2 (3): 343–368.

Holbig, Heike. 2006. Ideological Reform and Political Legitimacy in China: Challenges in the Post-Jiang Era. In *Program: Legitimacy and Efficiency of Political Systems*, ed. G.I.G.A. Research. Hamburg: German Institute of Global and Area Studies.

Howell, Jude. 1993. *China Opens its Doors: The Politics of Economic Transition*. Boulder, CO: Lynne Rienner Inc.

Howell, Jude. 2006. Reflections on the Chinese State. *Development and Change* 37 (2): 273–297.

Howell, Jude. 2004a. Governance Matters: Key Challenges and Emerging Tendencies. In *Goverance in China*, ed. Jude Howell. Lanham, MD: Rowman & Littlefield Publishers, Inc.

Howell, Jude. 2004b. New Directions in Civil Society: Organizing Around Marginalized Interests. In *Governance in China*, ed. Jude Howell Lanham, MD: Rowman & Littlefield Publishers, Inc.

Hui, Sio-Ieng Elaine, and King Chi Chris Chan. 2012. The “Harmonious Society” as a Hegemonic Project: Labour Conflicts and Changing Labour Policies in China. *Labour, Capital and Society* 44 (2): 153–183.

Jakobson, Linda. 2004. Local Governance: Village and Township Direct Elections. In *Governance in China*, ed. Jude Howell. Maryland, MD: Rowman & Littlefield Publishers, Inc.

Jessop, Bob. 2008. *State Power: A Strategic-Relational Approach*. Oxford: Polity Press.

Kang, Xiaoguang, and Heng Han. 2008. Graduated Controls: The State-Society Relationship in Contemporary China. *Modern China* 34 (1): 36–55.

Kelly, Dominic. 2002. Japan and World Order. *New Political Economy* 7 (3): 397–414.

Kennedy, Duncan. 1982. Antonio Gramsci and the Legal System. *ALSA Forum* 6 (1): 32–37.

Klare, Karl E. 1978. Judicial Deradicalization of the Wagner Act and the Origins of Modern Legal Consciousness, 1937–1941. *Minnesota Law Review* 62: 265.

Klare, Karl E. 1980. Labor Law as Ideology: Toward a New Historiography of Collective Bargaining Law. *Industrial and Labor Relations Review* 4: 450.

Klare, Karl E. 1982. The Public/Private Distinction in Labor Law. *University of Pennsylvania Law Review* 130: 1358.

Kulcsar, Laszlo J., and Tamas Domokos. 2005. The Post-Socialist Growth Machine: The Case of Hungary. *International Journal of Urban and Regional Research* 29 (3): 550–563.

Landry, Pierre F. 2008. *Decentralized Authoritarianism in China: The Communist Party's Control of Local Elites in the Post-Mao Era*. Cambridge: Cambridge University Press.

Langford, Tom. 1994. Strikes and Class Consciousness. *Labour/Le Travail* 33: 107–137.

Lau, Raymond W.K. 1997. China: Labour Reform and the Challenge Facing the Working Class. *Capital and Class* 21: 45–80.

Lee, Ching Kwan. 1998. *Gender and the South China Miracle: Two Worlds of Factory Women*. Berkley: University of California Press.

Lee, Ching Kwan. 1999. From Organized Dependence to Disorganized Despotism: Changing Labour Regimes in Chinese Factories. *China Quarterly* 157: 44–71.

Lee, Ching Kwan. 2007. *Against the Law: Labor Protests in China's Rustbelt and Sunbelt*. Berkeley: University of California Press.

Lee, Ching Kwan, and Yonghong Zhang. 2013. The Power of Instability: Unraveling the Microfoundations of Bargained Authoritarianism in China. *American Journal of Sociology* 118 (6): 1475–1508.

Leftwich, Adrian. 1996. Two Cheers for Democracy? Democracy and the Developmental State. In *Democracy and Development*, ed. Adrian Leftwich. Cambridge: Polity Press.

Leggett, John C. 1963. Uprootedness and Working-Class Consciousness. *American Journal of Sociology* 68 (6): 682–692.

Li, David D. 1996. A Theory of Ambiguous Property Rights in Transition Economies: The Case of the Chinese Non-state Sector. *Journal of Comparative Economics* 23 (1): 1–19.

Li, Lian Jiang. 2010. Rights Consciousness and Rules Consciousness in Contemporary China. *China Journal* 64: 47–68.

Li, Cheng. 2012. The End of the CCP's Resilient Authoritarianism? A Tripartite Assessment of Shifting Power in China. *China Quarterly* 211: 595–623.

Lieberthal, Kenneth G., and David M. Lampton. 1992. *Bureaucracy, Politics, and Decision Making in Post-Mao China*, ed. Kenneth G. Lieberthal and David M. Lampton. Berkeley: University of California Press.

Liebman, Benjamin. 2007. China's Court: Restricted Reform. *China Quarterly* 191: 620–638.

Ling, L.H.M. 1994. Rationalizations for State Violence in Chinese Politics: The Hegemony of Parental Governance. *Journal of Peace Research* 31: 393–405.

Linz, Juan J. 2000. *Totalitarian and Authoritarian Regimes*. Boulder: Lynn Reinner.

Litowitz, Douglas. 2000. Gramsci, Hegemony, and the Law. *Brigham Young University Law Review* 2: 515–551.

Marshall, Gordon. 1983. Some Remarks on the Study of Working-Class Consciousness. *Politics & Society* 12 (3): 263–301.

Marshall, Gordon, Howard Newby, David Rose, and Carol Vogler. 1988. London: Hutchinson.

McCormick, Barrett L. 1990. *Political Reform in Post-Mao China: Democracy and Bureaucracy in a Leninist State*. Berkeley: University of California Press.

McMillan, John, and Barry Naughton. 1992. How to Reform a Planned Economy: Lessons from China. *Oxford Review of Economic Policy* 8 (1): 130–143.

McNally, Christopher A. 2008. The Institutional Contours of China's Emergent Capitalism. In *China's Emergent Political Economy: Capitalism in the Dragon's Lair*, ed. Christopher A. McNally. London: Routledge.

McNally, Christoph A., and Y. Chu. 2006. Exploring Capitalist Development in Greater China: A Synthesis. *Asian Perspective* 30 (2): 31–64.

Merrington, J. 1968. Theory and Practice in Gramsci's Marxism. *Socialist Register* 5: 145–176.

Mertha, Andrew. 2009. Fragmented Authoritarianism 2.0: Political Pluralization in the Chinese Policy Process. *China Quarterly* 200: 995–1012.

Miller, Alice. 2008. Institutionalization and the Changing Dynamics of Chinese Leadership Politics. In *China's Changing Political Landscape: Prospects for Democracy*, ed. Cheng Li. Washington DC: The Brookings Institution Press.

Moore, Phoebe V. 2007. *Globalisation and Labour Struggle in Asia: A Neo-Gramscian Critique of South Korea's Political Economy.* London: Tauris Academic Studies.

Morton, Adam David. 2003. Structural Change and Neoliberalism in Mexico: 'Passive Revolution' in the Global Political Economy. *Third World Quarterly* 24 (4): 631–653.

Morton, Adam David. 2007. Waiting for Gramsci: State Formation, Passive Revolution and the International. *Millennium-Journal of International Studies* 35 (3): 597–621.

Nathan, Andrew J. 1990. *China's Crisis: Dilemmas of Reform and Prospects for Democracy.* New York: Columbia University Press.

Nathan, Andrew J. 2003. Authoritarian Resilience. *Journal of Democracy* 14 (1): 6–17.

Naughton, Barry. 2008. *A Political Economy of China's Economic Transition*, ed. Loren Brandt and Thomas G. Rawski. Cambridge: Cambridge University Press.

Ngok, Kinglun. 2008. The Changes of Chinese Labor Policy and Labor Legislation in the Context of Market Transition. *International Labor and Working-Class History* 73: 45–64.

O'Brien, Kevin J, and Lian Jiang LI. 2000. Accommodating "Democracy" in a One-Party State: Introducing Village Elections in China. *China Quarterly* (162): 465–489.

Oi, Jean. 1992. Fiscal Reform and the Economic Foundations of Local State Corporatism in China. *World Politics* 45 (1): 99–126.

Oi, Jean. 1995. The Role of the Local State in China's Transitional Economy. *China Quarterly* 144: 1132–1149.

Oi, Jean. 1998. The Evolution of Local State Corporatism. In *Zouping in Transition: The Process of Reform in Rural North China*, ed. Andrew Walder. Cambridge, MA: Harvard University Press.

Oi, Jean. 1999. *Rural China Takes Off.* Berkeley: University of California Press.

Oksenberg, Michel. 2001. China's Political System: Challenges of the Twenty-First Century. *China Journal* 45: 21–35.

Pearson, Margaret M. 1997. *China's New Business Elite*. Berkeley: University of California Press.

Pei, Minxin. 2006. *China's Trapped Transition: The Limits of Developmental Autocracy*. Cambridge: Harvard University Press.

Peng, Thomas. 2011. The Impact of Citizenship on Labour Process: State, Capital and Labour Control in South China. *Work, Employment and Society* 25 (4): 726–741.

Perry, Elizabeth J. 1993. China in 1992: An Experiment in Neo-Authoritarianism. *Asian Survey* 33 (1): 12–21.

Perry, Elizabeth J. 2001. Challenging the Mandate of Heaven: Popular Protest in Modern China. *Critical Asian Studies* 33 (2): 163–180.

Perry, Elizabeth J. 2007. Studying Chinese Politics: Farewell to Revolution? *China Journal* 57: 1–22.

Petracca, Mark P., and Mong Xiong. 1990. The Concept of Chinese Neo-authoritarianism: An Exploration and a Democratic Critique. *Asian Survey* 33 (11): 1099–1117.

Potter, Pitman B. 1999. The Chinese Legal System: Continuing Commitment to the Primacy of State Power. *China Quarterly* 159: 673–683.

Poulantzas, Nicos. 1969. The Problem of the Capitalist State. *New Left Review* I (58): 67–78.

Poulantzas, Nicos. 1973. *Political Power and Social Classes*. London: New Left Review and Sheed and Ward.

Poulantzas, Nicos. 1978. *Classes in Contemporary Capitalism*. London: Verso.

Poulantzas, Nicos. 2000. *State, Power, Socialism*. London: Verso.

Pun, Ngai. 2005. *Making in China: Women Factory workers in a Global Workplace*. Durham: Duke University Press.

Pun, Ngai, and Jenny Chan. 2012. Global Capital, the State, and Chinese Workers: The Foxconn Experience. *Modern China* 38 (4): 383–410.

Pun, Ngai, King Chi Chris Chan, and Jenny Chan. 2010. The Role of the State, Labour Policy and Migrant Workers' Struggles in Globalized China. *Global Labour Journal* 1 (1): 132–151.

Ruf, Gregory A. 1999. Collective Enterprise and Property Rights in a Sichuan Village: The Rise and Decline of Managerial Corporatism. In *Property Rights and Economic Reform in China*, ed. Jean Oi and Andrew Walder. Stanford: Stanford University Press.

Saich, Tony. 2004. *Governance and Politics of China*. Basingstoke: Palgrave Macmillan.

Sautman, Barry. 1992. Sirens of the Strongman: Neo-Authoritarianism in Recent Chinese Political Theory. *China Quarterly* 129: 72–102.

Schmitter, Philippe. 1974. Still the Century of Corporatism? *Review of Politics* 36 (1): 85–131.

Segal, Adam, and Eric Thun. 2001. Thinking Globally, Acting Locally: Local Governments, Industrial Sectors, and Development in China. *Politics & Society* 29 (4): 557–588.

Shambaugh, David. 2008. *China's Communist Party: Atrophy and Adaptation.* Berkeley, CA: University of California Press.

Shannon, Sheila M. 1995. The Hegemony of English: A Case Study of One Bilingual Classroom as a Site of Resistance. *Linguistics and Education* 7 (3): 175–200.

Shi, Tianjian. 2000. Cultural Values and Democracy in the Peoples' Republic of China. *China Quarterly* 162: 540–559.

Shirk, Susan L. 2007. *Fragile Superpower: How China's Internal Politics Could Derail Its Peaceful Rise.* New York: Oxford University Press.

Shue, Vivienne. 1995. State Sprawl: The Regulatory State and Social Life in a Small Chinese City. In *Urban Spaces in Contemporary China*, ed. Deborah S. Davis, Richard Kraus, Barry Naughton, and Elizabeth J. Perry. Cambridge: Cambridge University Press and Woodrow Wilson Center Press.

Silver, Beverly. 2003. *Forces of Labor: Workers' Movements and Globalisation Since 1870.* Cambridge: Cambridge University Press.

Skocpol, Theda, and Edwin Amenta. 1986. States and Social Policies. *Annual Review of Sociology* 12: 131–157.

Solinger, Dorothy J. 2006. The Creation of a New Underclass in China and Its Implications. *Environment and Urbanization* 18 (2): 177–193.

Stern, Rachel E., and Kevin J. O'Brien. 2012. Politics at the Boundary: Mixed Signals and the Chinese State. *Modern China* 38 (2): 174–198.

Stockmann, Daniela, and Mary E. Gallagher. 2011. Remote Control: How the Media Sustain Authoritarian Rule in China. *Comparative Political Studies* 44 (4): 436–467.

Stuart, Shields. 2012. Opposing Neoliberalism? Poland's Renewed Populism and Post-communist Transition. *Third World Quarterly* 33 (2): 359–381.

Sullivan, Lawrence. 1990. The Emergence of Civil Society in China, Spring 1989. In *The Chinese People's Movement: Perspectives on Spring 1989*, ed. Tony Saich. Armonk, NY: M. E. Sharpe.

Tanner, Murray Scot. 2005. *Chinese Government Responses to Rising Social Unrest.* Santa Monica: Rand.

Tarrow, Sidney. 1994. *Power in Movement: Social Movements, Collective Action and Politics.* New York: Cambridge University Press.

Thompson, E.P. 1978. *The Poverty of Theory and Other Essays.* London: Merlin.

Tok, Sow Keat, and Yonggian Zheng. 2007. *"Harmonious Society" and "Harmonious World": China's Policy Discourse Under Hu Jintao*, ed. Briefing Series. Nottingham: China Policy Institute, University of Nottingham.

Unger, Jonathan. 2008. *Chinese Associations, Civil Society, and State Corporatism: Disputed Terrain*. In *Associations and the Chinese State: Contested Spaces*, ed. Jonathan Unger. New York: M. E. Sharpe Inc.

Unger, Jonathan, and Anita Chan. 1995. China, Corporatism and the East Asian Model. *The Australian Journal of Chinese Affairs* 33: 29–53.

Van der Pijl, Kees. 1993. State Socialism and Passive Revolution. In *Gramsci, Historical Materialism and International Relations*, ed. Stephen Gill. Cambridge: Cambridge University Press.

Wade, Robert. 2005. Bringing the State Back In: Lessons from East Asia's Development Experience. *Internationale Politik und Gesellschaft* 8 (2): 98–115.

Wakeman, Frederic J.R. 1993. The Civil Society and Public Sphere Debate: Western Reflections on Chinese Political Culture. *Modern China* 19 (2): 108–138.

Walder, Andrew. 1986. *Communist Neo-Traditionalism: Work and Authority in Chinese Industry*. Berkeley: University of California Press.

Wallace, Ruth A., and Alison Wolf. 2006. *Contemporary Sociological Theory: Expanding the Classical Tradition*. Englewood Cliffs, NJ: Prentice Hall.

Wang, Shaoguang. 2008. The Great Transformation: The Double Movement in China. *boundary 2* 35 (2): 15–47.

Wang, Haiyan, Richard P. Appelbaum, Degiuli Francesca, and Nelson Lichtenstein. 2009. China's New Labour Contract Law: Is China Moving Towards Increased Power for Workers? *Third World Quarterly* 30 (3): 485–501.

Warner, Malcolm. 1996. Chinese Enterprise Reform, Human Resources and the 1994 Lahour Law. *The International Journal of Human Resource Management* 7 (4): 779–796.

Wedeman, Andrew. 2003. *From Mao to Market. Rent Seeking, Local Protectionism, and Marketisation in China*. Cambridge: Cambridge University Press.

Weede, E. (1999). *Future Hegemonic Rivalry between China and the West?* London: Sage.

Weiss, Linda. 2000. Developmental States in Transition: Adapting, Dismantling, Innovating, not "Normalising". *Pacific Review* 13 (1): 21–55.

Western, Mark. 1999. Who Thinks What About Capitalism? Class Consciousness and Attitudes to Economic Institutions. *Journal of Sociology* 35: 351–370.

White, Gordon. 1984. Developmental States and Socialist Industrialisation in the Third World. *Journal of Development Studies* 21 (1): 97–120.

White, Gordon. 1993. Prospects for Civil Society in China: A Case Study of Xiaoshan City. *Australian Journal of Chinese Affairs* 29: 63–87.

White, Gordon, and Robert Wade. 1988. Developmental States and Markets in East Asia: An Introduction. In *Developmental States in East Asia*, ed. White Gordon. Basingstoke: Macmillan Press.

White, Gordon, Jude Howell, and Xiaoyuan Shang. 1996. *In Search of Civil Society: Market Reform and Social Change in Contemporary China*. New York: Oxford University Press.

Wong, Linda. 2011. Chinese Migrant Workers: Rights Attainment Deficits, Rights Consciousness and Personal Strategies. *China Quarterly* 208: 870–892.

Woo, Wing Thye. 1994. The Art of Reforming Centrally Planned Economies: Comparing China, Poland, and Russia. *Journal of Comparative Economics* 18 (3): 276–308.

Woolard, Kathryn A. 1985. Language Variation and Cultural Hegemony: Toward an Integration of Sociolinguistic and Social Theory. *American Ethnologist* 12 (4): 738–748.

Wright, Erik Olin. 1989. The Comparative Project on Class Structure and Class Consciousness: An Overview. *Acta Sociologica* 32 (1): 3–22.

Wu, Fulong, Jiang Xu, and Anthony Gar-On Yeh. 2013. *Urban Development in Post-reform China: State, Market, and Space*. New York: Routledge.

Xia, Ming. 2000. *The Dual Developmental State: Development Strategy and Institutional Arrangements*. Brookfield, VT: Ashgate.

Xu, Wang. 1997. Mutual Empowerment of State and Peasantray: Grassroots Democracy in Rural China. *World Development* 25 (9): 1431–1442.

Zhang, Lu. 2008. Lean Production and Labor Controls in the Chinese Automobile Industry in An Age of Globalization. *International Labor and Working Class History* 73 (1): 24–44.

Zhao, Suisheng. 1998. A State-Led Nationalism: The Patriotic Education Campaign in Post-Tiananmen China. *Communist and Post-Communist Studies* 31 (3): 287–302.

Zheng, Bijian. 2005. China's" Peaceful Rise" to Great-Power Status. *Foreign Affairs* 84 (5): 18–24.

CHAPTER 2

The Gramscian Approach to the Chinese State

1 Introduction

As explained in Chap. 1, the approach of the authoritarian state, developmental state, and corporatist state have failed to offer a sufficiently sophisticated conceptualization of the Chinese party-state. Building largely upon the theoretical insights of Gramsci, complemented by those of Poulantzas, in this book I propose the Gramscian approach to investigate the Chinese state. I maintain that the Chinese party-state has been transforming from ruling principally with coercion to drive the country's passive revolution into governing with both persuasion and domination. That being said, I do not claim that the Chinese state has become fully hegemonic. Instead, it is undergoing a hegemonic transformation, moving slowly but significantly towards that direction. In other words, my approach underscores the broader trend of its socio-political and economic development, rather than merely analyzing a stationary moment within this trend.

In the next section, I first highlight the critical state theories developed by Gramsci and Poulantzas, which have inspired my conceptualizations of the Chinese state. In Sect. 3, I expound on the theoretical benefits of integrating Gramsci and Poulantzas' intellectual insights, Sect. 4 elaborates on how scholars in the field of China Studies have used the concept hegemony, and my hegemony approach to the Chinese state.

E.S.I Hui, *Hegemonic Transformation*, Series in Asian Labor and Welfare Policies, DOI 10.1057/978-1-137-50429-6_2

2 Gramsci and Poulantzas' Critical State Theories

To understand Gramsci and Poulantzas' theories, we have to first grasp the development of state theories prior to their time as their aims were to advance the Marxist state theories prominent at that time that suffered from a few theoretical deficits. Due to his death, Marx did not have a chance to complete a systematic theory of the state (Miliband 1969). However, the state is not a missing focus from his work; it is discussed in his writings, such as *The Eighteenth Brumaire of Louis Bonaparte* (Marx 1973) and *The Civil War in France* (Marx 1974). Commenting on the coup d'état of Bonaparte, Marx argues that the bourgeoisie's interest is 'most intimately imbricated precisely with the maintenance of that extensive and highly ramified state machine' (Marx 1973, 186). He and Engels contend in the *Communist Manifesto* that the modern state is the management committee for the bourgeoisie (Marx and Engels 1978). They see different modes of production as requiring different forms of state intervention and argue that 'the nature of the state power is determined by the changing needs of the economy and/or by the changing balance of class forces at the economic level' (Jessop 1982, 10). By underscoring the class character of the state, Marx and Engels lay down a significant foundation for critical state theories that refuse to regard the state as representing the entire society or serving the national interests.

Since Marx and Engels do not formulate a definitive theory of the state and politics, there is great room for interpretation of their ideas. As a result, state theories drawing upon their work but with diverse positions have come into existence, and there are no unitary or coherent Marxian state theories. Some interpretations of their ideas, especially dogmatic Marxism, are criticized for their instrumentalist tendency because they tend to view the state as a 'thing' or an 'entity' that can be taken over by any class (Jessop 1990). This criticism is one of the major premises for the subsequent debates about the state. Furthermore, dogmatic and orthodox Marxism are also disapproved for their economic reductionist orientation as they consider the state (the superstructure) to be a mere epiphenomenon of the economic structures. Hobsbawm has pointed out that they focus on 'the derivation of political, juridical and other ideological conceptions from the basic economic facts' (1977, 207).

Lenin regards the state as an instrument of class rule and as a machine for class oppression, holding that 'it [the state] is the creation of "order", which legalizes and perpetuates this oppression by moderating the conflict between classes' (Lenin 1969). He believes that the state is a thing that any class can take over and that the proletarian revolution has the potential to smash the bourgeois state apparatus to bring about a socialist state (Wright 1979). This kind of Marxism-Leninism characterized by instrumentalism and epiphenomenalism was once quite influential, especially in the Second and Third International. However, it lost its predominance in the 1960s when many Marxians in Europe became disillusioned with Stalinism and the authoritarian socialism of the Soviet Union. Marxism-Leninism then came under attack by invigorated theoretical endeavors in different countries, including Althusserian structuralism in France which later spread to Britain and the USA, the Gramscian schools of thought in Italy and beyond, and the capital logic school (*Staatsableitung debatte*) in West Germany.

Gramsci's state theory represents a crucial break from Marxism-Leninism due to his rejection of instrumentalism and crude economic reductionism. He is considered the first Marxian to produce a 'full political theory' (Hobsbawm 1977, 208) that neither treats the political structures as mere reflections of the economic base, nor views the state as an instrument for class rule.[1] The political and socio–economic circumstances of the times drove Gramsci to create a state theory that surpasses Marxism-Leninism in a number of ways.[2] First, vulgar Marxism in Gramsci's time was marked by evolutionary determinism; it viewed the development of history and society as guided by objective laws and as 'beyond the scope of active human intervention' (Merrington 1968, 146). Many of its proponents believed that proletarian revolution and the demise of capitalism would come inevitably and automatically due to its inherent contradictions. Gramsci contests this mechanistic position, seeking to examine, with his own theories, why the working class in Western Europe, unlike their Russian counterparts, had not developed a class consciousness or risen up against capitalism automatically in times of economic and political crisis (Burawoy 2003; Salamini 1974). By introducing the dimension of worker subjectivities and consciousness into his social and political inquiries, as will be elucidated, Gramsci is able to convincingly explain why revolution did not take place in Europe.

Second, Gramsci circumvents the trap of reducing the superstructures into the economic base by paying legitimate attention to the former. He enriches Marxian state theories by proposing that civil society is part of the state. He regards the state not simply 'as the apparatus of government operating within the "public" sphere (government, political parties, military) but also as part of the "private" sphere of civil society (for instance, church, media, and education) through which hegemony functions' (Bieler and Morton 2003, 483). Building upon this broadened concept of the state, or what he calls the 'integral state', Gramsci further sheds light on how class power is organized by the state in political society and civil society with his ideas of 'coercion' and 'hegemony'. Following the arguments of Marx, Engels, and Lenin, he holds that the coercive machinery of the state (political society) helps maintain the capitalist class's domination (Gramsci 1971). At the same time, the dominant class seeks to acquire the active consent of the working class for its leadership by establishing 'its own moral, political and cultural values as conventional norms of practical behavior' in order to sustain its class superiority (Femia 1987, 3). This capitalist class's ideological ascendency over the subordinate class is what Gramsci calls hegemony. He maintains that a state is ethical if it helps organize capitalist hegemony:

> [The] state is ethical in as much as one of its most important functions is to raise the great mass of the population to a particular cultural and moral level, a level (or type) which corresponds to the needs of the productive forces for development, and hence to the interests of the ruling classes. (Gramsci 1971, 258)

The ethical state reproduces capitalist hegemony through civil society (and political society). Because of the intricate power mechanism of coercion and hegemony, Gramsci reveals that the working class's consciousness and its rebellions against capitalism do not appear automatically as vulgar Marxism predicts.

As explained in Chap. 1, hegemony is a concept in contrast to passive revolution. In a hegemonic social formation, the subordinate class's consent to capitalist development is elicited largely through persuasion. In some non-hegemonic Western societies, capitalism was introduced through state-engineered social and political reforms rather than through the initiative of the popular masses and capitalist class. The absence of a hegemonic class in these societies dictated that the state had to resort to domination and force to drive a top–down capitalist revolution.

Third, due to his renunciation of evolutionary and mechanistic Marxism, Gramsci endeavors to explore strategies for working class struggles in Western Europe. He observes that the state in Russia was strong and its civil society was 'primordial' and 'gelatinous', whereas the state and civil society in the West has a more balanced relation and its civil society is comparatively 'developed' and 'sturdy' (Gramsci 1971, 238). Because of these substantial differences, Gramsci advocates that working class revolution, or what he calls the war of manoeuvre, that had taken place in Russia could not be copied in Italy or Western Europe. He argues that in the West, where hegemony, instead of coercion, is the prevalent form of class control, the exploited classes should deploy the strategy of war of position to accomplish 'steady penetration and subversion of the complex and multiple mechanisms of ideological diffusion' in order to stage counter-hegemony (Gramsci 1971, 232).

Because of restrictions in prison, Gramsci's ideas could only be indirectly expressed in his work. This has created room for diverse or sometimes contradictory interpretations of his theories by different political forces in post-war Italy. For example, Togliatti's interpretation of Gramsci's insights is in line with the Marxist-Leninist political views held by the Italian Communist Party (PCI) while opponents of the PCI presented Gramsci as an unorthodox thinker who offers alternative theoretical resources to Leninism and Stalinism. Moreover, Gramsci is simultaneously criticized by some PCI supporters as a reformist and by some on the right and the left as a Stalinist (Mouffe and Sassoon 1977; Femia 1987). His major works were written during the 1920s and 1930s, but they were widely published in Italy only after the 1950s. Since the late 1960s, his intellectual contribution started to gain attention in countries beyond Italy, inspiring many subsequent theorists, such as Poulantzas, Laclau, Jessop, and Foucault.

Poulantzas was one of the most notable post-war critical state theorists. He adopts a structural approach in his counter-reductionist and counter-epiphenomenalist theorizations.[3] In his first book published in English, *Political Power and Social Classes* (1973b), Poulantzas puts forward three propositions on the capitalist state: (1) the economy determines the political and the ideological only in the last instance; (2) the state enjoys relative autonomy from the dominant class; (3) the state performs a cohesive function in a capitalist formation. For Poulantzas, the capitalist social formation consists of three levels—the economic, the political, and the ideological. Following Althusser's contention that the economic level is determinant in the last instance, Poulantzas argues that the political and the ideological cannot be reduced to the economic, though the economic level determines them in the last instance. Instead of focusing only on one's position in relations of production, his theory concentrates on the overdetermined effects of the ensemble of these three instances and the dynamics between them in social class formation (Poulantzas 1969, 1973a). This is what he first calls 'overdetermination of class' in *Political Power and Social Classes* (1973b, 54) and later calls 'structural determination of class' in *Classes in Contemporary Capitalism* (1978, 29).

Within this conceptual framework, Poulantzas contends that the state is relatively autonomous from the dominant class due to the specificity of capitalism. In feudalism, elaborates Poulantzas, the serfs exercised some degree of control over the means of production and the object of labor because they still 'had possession of his [their] parcel of land, which was protected by custom' (Poulantzas 1978, 19). In other words, while the exploiting class had the economic ownership of the land, the exploited class was to a certain degree engaged in relations of economic possession. Under these circumstances, the feudal state had to exercise political force and legitimate violence over the serfs in order to secure the extraction of surplus labor from them. As a consequence, the state and the economy were intricately linked in feudal society. However, this kind of 'overlapping' or 'mixedness' (Poulantzas 2000, 18) between the economic and the political has been replaced by the relative separation between the two spheres in capitalism. Workers in capitalist societies, who are completely deprived of control over the means of production and the labor object, appear to be 'free labourers' in a double sense. First, unlike the serfs who were bounded to the land owned by their landlords, the working class is not legally or politically tied to the capitalist class. Second, workers are juridically free to sell their labor power in the market and to enter into labor contracts with capitalists. Direct political coercion of the state is unnecessary for the conversion of surplus labor into surplus value. Instead, the state's intervention takes an indirect and legal-political form by creating the formal and abstract equality among exchangers of labor power (or other commodities) in the market (Poulantzas 1973a, 2000). Poulantzas sees the relative separation between the state and the economy as an inherent characteristic of capitalism. This relative autonomy of the state from the capitalist class has enabled the former to reproduce the latter's long-term dominance by offering short-term benefits to the exploited class so that they will not revolt against the capitalist system.

The relative autonomy of the capitalist state does not mean that it is neutral or classless in nature. In contrast, Poulantzas argues in *Political Power and Social Classes* that the capitalist state is a cohesive factor in maintaining the unity between the economic, political, and ideological instances in capitalist societies. As explained in Chap. 1, Poulantzas proposes that the state has three kinds of functions: economic, ideological, and political. Separate as these functions might seem, they together help prevent political conflicts from breaking out and the capitalist social formation from bursting apart, thereby maintaining the conditions for production. These functions of the capitalist state are interrelated in the sense that they all serve the purpose of upholding the unity of a capitalist formation.

After the release of his first book, Poulantzas's state theory changed over time in at least four respects. First, while his theorizations on the final determinant role of the economic and the relative autonomy of the state remain in his later writings, the idea that the state serves a cohesive function in capitalist societies has become less prominent, if not totally displaced. In his two other books, *Classes in Contemporary Capitalism* (1978) and *State, Power, Socialism* (2000), Poulantzas proposes that the capitalist state is the materialization and condensation of class relations. No longer stressing the role of the state in organizing the capitalist class's interests and unity, he advances that class contradictions and social relations of production are inscribed, crystallized, and condensed in the state. He writes that

> …the state crystallizes the relations of production and class relations. The modern political state does not translate the 'interest' of the dominant classes at the political level, but the relationship between those interests and the interests of the dominated classes—which means that it precisely constitutes the 'political' expression of the interests of the dominant classes. (2008, 80)

Many political scientists in Poulantzas's time interrogated the state from an institutional perspective (Hay and Lister 2006). Poulantzas's argument that the state is a condensation of class relations is therefore novel and insightful.

Second, in his later publication Poulantzas better portrays the dynamics between the state and class struggles. Building upon his thesis that the state is a condensation of class relations, in *State, Power, Socialism* he holds that even though class struggles take place beyond the state, they are not external to it; class struggles are inscribed in the institutional and material structures of the state (2000). Third, in his first book on the capitalist state, structures assumed primacy over class struggles, but in his later writings Poulantzas gradually shifted from structuralist formalism to asserting primacy of class struggles over the structures (Jessop 1982).

The fourth shift of focus in Poulantzas's writings concerns the weight he attributes to economic materiality. While the role of the economic instance is not explored so much in his early work *Political Power and Social Classes*, it is given greater attention in Poulantzas's two later books. This is probably due to the accusation of overpoliticizing the state in his early works (Poulantzas 2000). *Classes in Contemporary Capitalism* has a more discernible 'economic framework' (Hall 1980); it delves into such questions regarding whether the role of the capitalist state changes during the transition from competitive capitalism to monopoly capitalism and whether the capitalist state still possesses relative autonomy vis-à-vis the dominant classes. In *State, Power, Socialism*, Poulantzas further restores the importance of the economic to his state theory with the concept of 'institutional materiality' (2000, 14). He stresses that the state manifests a material framework which is irreducible to political or ideological domination.

Despite his theoretical contribution, Poulantzas's state theory is not without criticism. To name a few examples, he has been accused of 'structural super-determinism' and 'structuralist abstractionism' by his opponent in the famous Poulantzas-Miliband debate (Laclau 1982). Ellen Meiksins Wood (1986) asserts that Poulantzas is the 'forerunner' in embarking on a retreat from class and leading to the complete autonomization of ideology and politics from economic materiality. Holloway and Picciotto (1977) disagree with Poulantzas's postulation that the separation between the state and the economy is an inherent characteristic of capitalism, arguing that such a separation is the product of continuous struggles by the ruling class to uphold its domination. Simon Clarke (1991) criticizes Poulantzas's structural determinism for underemphasizing the role of class struggle and assuming the predominance of structures.

These criticisms contain some truth. However, if we examine Poulantzas's theory within the historical and intellectual milieu of his time, his contributions to rebutting the instrumentalist and epiphenomenalist tendency of Marxism-Leninism should be rightfully acknowledged.[4] Due to his premature death, Poulantzas's state theory was mainly developed during the 1960s and 1970s, and he was not able to respond to many criticisms against him. However, many contemporary theorists still find his theories relevant and stimulating. Within the British tradition, Jessop (1985) has dedicated a whole book to exploring Poulantzas's theories; and Poulantzas is a vital reference in much of his work (Jessop 1982, 1990, 2008). Within the US tradition, Aronowitz, and Bratsis (2003) have taken the Poulantzas–Miliband debate and Poulantzas's theories as points of departure in reasserting the relevance of the state in the globalized era. Within the German tradition, Gallas et al. (2011) have offered an acute reading of Poulantzas's writings and explored how his theories should be applied and further developed in the contemporary context; Brand et al. (2011) have reformulated Poulantzas's theories to analyze the international political economy.

3 Integrating Gramsci and Poulantzas' Insights

My theorization of the Chinese state is largely inspired by Gramsci's theory of hegemony (and passive revolution) with additional insights from Poulantzas. Gramsci and Poulantzas share some vigorous ideas, yet differ in other areas. As will be explicated, this has made their intellectual contributions complementary. Against the mainstream perception that Poulantzas inherits his ideas from Althusserian structuralism, Jessop maintains that Poulantzas actually adopts a neo-Gramscian approach in his work (1982). He writes:

> But, if we ignore his earliest studies of law and the juridical system with their strongly Sartrean overtones...and his obvious flirtation with Althusserian structuralism in his first major work on the capitalist state (PPSC) and its residues in his subsequent analyses..., it is apparent that his principal sources of inspiration among twentieth-century Marxists are Gramsci and Lenin and that Gramsci is the more influential in many respects. (Jessop 1982, 154)

Gramsci's influence on Poulantzas is evident in the latter's emphasis on ideologies. As emphasized, Gramsci's concept of two modalities of class power (coercion and hegemony) is a breakthrough for Marxian state theory. With the ideas of hegemony, he convincingly illustrates how the capitalist class remains dominant by gaining cultural, political and moral leadership. Following in Gramsci's footsteps, Poulantzas elucidates that to sustain capitalist structures and the capitalist class's superiority, the state does not simply rule with its repressive apparatuses (such as police, army, judiciary and so forth) whose major functions are to maintain political order, it also rules with ideological apparatuses that elaborate and inculcate its ideologies (Poulantzas 1969, 1973a, b, 1978). Furthermore, Poulantzas extends Gramsci's concept of hegemony to analyze internal factions within the capitalist class (Poulantzas 1967, 1973b, 1978). The bourgeoisie is the dominant class in a capitalist formation and, according to Poulantzas, within the dominant class there exist hegemonic classes that exercise dominance over the other dominant factions and unify them under its leadership.

In addition, both Gramsci and Poulantzas hold that capitalist hegemony and ideologies are rooted in economic materiality while scholars like Laclau and Mouffe have denied their relations to the economic. Gramsci believes that 'if hegemony is ethico-political, it must also be economic' (Femia 1987, 24). For him, in order to sustain the bourgeoisie's dominance, the ruling class has to absorb the antagonism of the dominated class by addressing their concerns with short-term material measures. Similarly, Poulantzas (2000, 31) maintains that '...in working for class hegemony... the state...continually adopts material measures which are of positive significance for the popular masses...' The fact that the capitalist state often forces concessions from the dominant class for the subordinate class has inspired Poulantzas to put forward the concept of the relative autonomy of the state.

Despite their common analysis on certain issues, Gramsci and Poulantzas' thoughts have differences; these make their theories complementary to each other. Poulantzas puts flesh on the bones of some of Gramsci's ideas. For instance, Gramsci does not clearly outline the mechanisms through which the state builds up and maintains capitalist hegemony (Poulantzas 2000),[5] but Poulantzas fills the gap by highlighting the dual role of the state in organizing the power bloc and disorganizing the dominated class. On the one hand, it attempts to forestall working class struggles by producing effects of isolation at the ideological level, concealing the class nature of social relations of production from workers. On the other, the state seeks to unify the dominant class and help them overcome the isolation of their economic struggles by, for example, articulating their interests as the universal interests of society (Poulantzas 1973b). Furthermore, borrowing from Althusser, Poulantzas utilizes the concept of ideological apparatus to explain how the state elaborates upon and inculcates capitalist ideologies to maintain class hegemony. Examples of such apparatuses are churches, political parties, schools, mass media, and unions (Poulantzas 1969, 1978).

Moreover, influenced by Althusser, Poulantzas considers Gramsci's understanding of hegemony subjectivist as he reduces ideology and consciousness to the subjectivity of class agents and does not analyze class subjects' consciousness against economic and social structures.[6] Criticizing Gramsci for conceptualizing the political and the economic as 'moments' (rather than structures) which is an expression of subjectivism (Poulantzas 2008, 163), Poulantzas argues that ideologies should be located within 'an objective system of relations' in a social formation (2008, 94). For him, the capitalist social formation consists of three instances: the economic, the political, and the ideological. Ideologies function within this ensemble of structures to shape social class formation, but the economic plays a determinant role in the last instance.

In addition, Gramsci has been criticized for insufficient attention to the economic and the economic role of the state (Hawley 1980; Anderson 1976). He surely does not deny the importance of economic materiality in class reproduction and social formation, but due to his central focus on hegemony, he does not explain the economic role of the state adequately. With his structuralist perspective, Poulantzas brings the economic structures, which Gramsci does not elaborate on much, back to the center of Marxian state theory.

However, there are two problems with Poulantzas's structuralist approach to which Gramsci's theories offer solutions. First, as mentioned in Chap. 1, Poulantzas's political-ideological-economic structural concept lacks a social dimension. Influenced by Althusser (1971), Poulantzas tends to conceive of civil society as not enjoying any autonomy from the state. In his opinion, the actions of civil society institutions are determined by the repressive apparatuses of the state. Therefore, 'the destruction of the ideological apparatus has its precondition in the destruction of the State repressive apparatus which maintains it' (Poulantzas 1972, 252–253). Having conflated the state and civil society, Poulantzas does not pay adequate attention to the latter in his work.[7] Gramsci's emphasis on civil society and its relative autonomy from the state can compensate for the lack of a social dimension in Poulantzas's state theory.

Second, Poulantzas has been criticized for overemphasizing structures at the expense of class agency. This perspective has a certain degree of validity, especially concerning his early writings, but it is not applicable to his later work which starts to emphasize the primacy of class struggles over structures (Jessop 1982, 156). Nevertheless, when compared to Gramsci's theory, it is true that the strength of Poulantzas's theory lies in its structural conceptualization, and that he has not shed much light on the role of social forces and class agents in transforming the structures. In contrast, Gramsci takes class actors, class organizations and class struggles more seriously. In his conceptualization, class agents play a crucial role in building hegemony and working class revolution. For instance, the factory council was once conceived of as a platform through which workers can practise real democracy and self-autonomy; political parties are considered a modern 'collective prince' capable of revolutionizing the working class; organic intellectuals are regarded as vital in assisting the working class to overcome capitalist common sense. In brief, both theorists' insights do not only share commonalities, but also help overcome each other's weaknesses in different respects.

4 The Gramscian Approach to the Chinese Party-State

Although capitalist hegemony in China has received inadequate intellectual attention, scholars in the field of China Studies frequently refer to the term 'hegemony'. It is, however, often used vaguely and ambiguously; and its meaning is always unspecified. According to my own analysis, hegemony is understood in at least four different undefined ways in the literature relating to the Chinese state, laws, and labor.

First, some scholars have equated hegemony with legitimacy. For instance, in his writing entitled *Contesting State Legitimacy in the 1990s*, Wright (2004) uses the term hegemony and legitimacy interchangeably when discussing to what extent the Chinese Democratic Party and China Labour Bulletin (a NGO led by overseas dissidents) can challenge the legitimacy of the Chinese state. Without defining what these two terms mean, the confusion between them manifests in his conclusion that 'decentralized CCP control provides openings that may be probed by groups challenging CCP *legitimacy*...the political atmosphere on the mainland remains extremely constricted, such that only groups that pose a limited threat to CCP *hegemony* (such as the CLB) may be allowed to persist' (Wright 2004, 137–138).[8] Legitimacy is a concept usually associated with political regimes, but without considering its relationship with the economic. For example, Max Weber's understanding of legitimacy is 'the belief that someone's position and the system incorporating it are right and proper' (Wallace and Wolf 2006, 74); for Habermas, it is 'a political order's worthiness to be recognised' (Habermas 1979, 178); for Jessop, it is 'the socially acknowledged character of its [the state's] political functions' (Jessop 2008, 10). However, from the Gramscian perspective the concept of hegemony concerns both political and economic relations. Due to their conceptual difference, it is inappropriate to equate hegemony with legitimacy.

Second, hegemony is used by some scholars to indicate ideological influence or dominance. Gries argues that the Chinese state's 'hegemony over national discourse' (2004, 187) has been challenged by the popular notion of nationalism, which criticizes the state's nationalist discourse and foreign policies for failing to protect national interest. He suggests that '[s]truggling to keep up with popular nationalist demands, the Party appears to be losing its hegemony over Chinese nationalism' (Gries 2004, 183). Comparing it to the production regime characterized by localistic despotism in Shenzhen, Lee (1995) advances that the production regime in Hong Kong is based on 'familial hegemony', which refers to the managerial control of labor relying on discourses and ideologies related to the Chinese family and the domestic responsibilities of women. Although this kind of usage of hegemony concerns values and ideologies, it is different from the Gramscian notion of hegemony. These authors use hegemony to refer broadly to ideological domination rather than specifically to acceptance by the subaltern class of capitalist worldviews concerning the state and the economy.

Third, hegemony is treated as a synonym for domination, power or control. Solinger (1993, 93) emphasizes the Chinese state's 'socioeconomic domination' over floating migrant workers, arguing that they have been 'absorbed into the state's hegemony'. Potter examines how Chinese economic reform has strengthened the party-state's reliance on the legal system, which in turn has restrained state power and challenged 'party hegemony' (Potter 2004, 480). He highlights that '...once policies are publicly articulated in law, the regime loses important degrees of *control* over the content and interpretation of these new norms. Instead, *hegemony* is protected by preserving the party's authority over personnel...the regime has attempted to maintain *hegemony* over legal reform through *control* over personnel' (Potter 2004, 482).[9] Like most of the scholars who have used the term hegemony, Potter does not define precisely what it means. The meaning of the above quotation does not change much if 'hegemony' is replaced by 'domination' or 'power'.

Fourth, some scholars in the field of China Studies have used hegemony in the Gramscian fashion and understood it as moral and political leadership of the capitalist class. As elaborated in Chap. 1, Blecher (2002), and Hui and Chan (2012) clearly spell out their Gramscian approach when studying the acceptance of market ideologies by urban workers, and the party-state's hegemonic project of a harmonious society. Capitalist hegemony is a clear and principal theme of their research.

Some scholars do not make hegemony their subject of inquiry, but use the concept in a Gramscian sense or in connection to class relations. Friedman and Lee (2010, 528, 530) suggest that the response of the Chinese party-state to the 2008 economic crisis shows that it 'has accepted the interests of capital as hegemonic' and workers were 'forced to confront the hegemonic power of state and capital as individuals'. Pun and Chan (2008, 91) hold that the new working class in China has been undergoing a process of unmaking under 'the hegemonic project undertaken by a "quest for globality" driven by neoliberal political ideologies'. Pun suggests that in China, capitalism has to prevail over 'noncapitalist reasoning in order to assert its hegemony' (1999, 6), and she argues that the hegemonic bloc in China has tried to decry class politics with the neoliberal discourse of modernity (2005). These scholars, however, have employed the term hegemony too readily and casually, which has led to confusion and loss of precision. Without providing an unequivocal definition, some authors associate hegemony with differing ideas in the same piece of work. For instance, Pun, at one point in her book, refers to hegemony as the dominance of the capitalist system over non–capitalist reasoning (Pun 2005, 119–120, also see 22, 24, 28); but when discussing the politics of dialects at the workplace, she uses hegemony to indicate the cultural superiority of Cantonese, remarking that Mandarin has lost its 'hegemonic position' (Pun 2005, 128). Friedman and Lee basically employ hegemony in a Gramscian sense (2010, 531); but when they note that Chinese rule by law has become a 'hegemonic discourse' (2010, 519), they do not explain its relationship with capitalist ethico-political leadership. They simply use hegemony to express the general acceptance by workers of handling labor disputes through the legal system.

The lack of clarity and coherence in deploying the term hegemony has hindered constructive debates on the concept and created intellectual confusion. In order to avoid theoretical ambiguity and incoherence, in the following, I expound on my theoretical approach to the Chinese state by critically engaging with Gramsci and Poulantzas's theories, as well as a wider range of scholarship in regards to the concept 'hegemony'.

First, following Gramsci, I see the Chinese state undergoing hegemonic transformation as an integral state that does not merely include the government apparatus, but also civil society. Class power is organized by the

Chinese state in both political and civil society. Anderson (1976) disagrees with Gramsci's ideas of the state for entailing certain antinomies. On some occasions, Gramsci considers the state a combination of civil and political society, but on others he defines it either as equivalent only to political society or only to civil society (Hawley 1980). Defending Gramsci, Jessop argues that these antinomies are not significant as long as they are interpreted with reference to the exercise of state power, instead of to the definition of state apparatuses. I agree with Jessop that it is more crucial to pay attention to Gramsci's analysis of 'the modalities of state power and the periodisation of forms of state than to consider his various definitions of the state' (Jessop 1982, 147). Therefore, despite the 'antinomies', in this book I adhere to Gramsci's idea of integral state and conceptualize the Chinese state as a combination of political society and civil society.

Second, I maintain that the Chinese state rules with both coercion and persuasion (Gramsci 1971; Poulantzas 1969). The long-term ascendency of the Chinese ruling class is not simply buttressed by the coercive capacity of the party-state, as the authoritarian thesis claims (see Chap. 1). It also relies on the state's hegemonic endeavour to promote and reproduce capitalist commonsensical worldviews among the Chinese working class.

Although I argue that hegemony is a rising modality of power exercised by the Chinese party-state, in no way do I imply that it now rules without coercion. Some scholars advocate that hegemony and coercion form two discrete modes of class power and counterpoise each other; if hegemony is predominant then coercion will decline proportionately in significance (for example, Gwyn 1960). Some of the writings of Gramsci, in fact, can lead to such an interpretation (Anderson 1976). However, his later elaboration on the relations between consent and force changes to one that does not view hegemony as '"consent" in contrast to another of "coercion", but as itself a synthesis of consent and coercion' (Anderson 1976, 22). Poulantzas (2000) also maintains that the ruling class's power is rooted in both hegemony and violence and that hegemony is not a replacement of coercion. In this book, hegemony is not simply taken as ideological and cultural leadership of the capitalist class; I adopt the view that hegemony is always bulwarked by the application of state coercion (Burawoy 2003; Merrington 1968). Even the most hegemonic state cannot rule without the support of military and physical forces. This is what Gramsci calls 'hegemony protected by the armor of coercion' (Gramsci 1971, 263).

Considering the Chinese party-state's application of force to ensure worker compliance and its reliance on political control to forestall the formation of independent worker associations, some people may doubt the hegemonic capacity of the Chinese party-state. I contend that this type of opinion has polarized the modality of hegemony and domination, assuming that they are mutually exclusive. As explained, hegemony is, here, understood as the synthesis of consent and force. Under normal circumstances, the reign of the state–capital nexus in China is largely built upon the consent of the working class, with coercion receding into the background, but by no means eliminated. In a moment of crisis, the role of control and force in securing conformity of the subaltern will become more palpable and will prevail over consent.

Third, concerning the question about where the site of practice of hegemony is, the predominant opinion is that in addition to the points of production (Gramsci 1971; Burawoy 1979; Merrington 1968), it is mainly exercised through private organizations in civil society, such as churches, schools and trade unions (Femia 1987). However, Anderson (1976) reminds us that hegemony is exercised not only in civil society, but also in political society. He and other scholars, such as Hobsbawm (1977) and Jessop (2008), argue that the parliamentary democratic system performs a hegemonic function in convincing the subordinate class that they are in control of the government; it thus helps dampen their motivation to rebel against the socio–economic system. Supporting this argument, Buckel and Lescano (2009, 444) assert that '[i]n the political and legal apparatuses the leadership personnel act not only repressively but also hegemonically'. In fact, Gramsci (1971, 246) advances that the legislature, judiciary, and executive are 'organs of political hegemony'.

Unlike their Western counterparts, social organizations in China are not completely autonomous from the party-state in terms of their structures and operations. Some scholars hold that only state-led civil society (Frolic 1997) or semi-civil society (He 1997) exists in China. The strong government control over social organizations in China may weaken the conditions for exercising hegemony in the civil arena. Under these circumstances, I contend that the labor law system in China acts as a crucial organ of hegemony by endorsing, inculcating, and transmitting capitalist common sense. Moreover, as parliamentary democracy is absent in China, the rule of law through the legal system, which is increasingly emphasized by the party-state, is an even more critical site for the reproduction of hegemony.

Fourth, concerning the relationship between the economic structures, and the political and ideological superstructures, I propose that the socio–economic structures in China and the global economic setting have constituted the terrain within which the mode of governance and mode of regulation by the Chinese party-state develop. Yet the Chinese state is not unilaterally shaped by the economic structures; it still plays a vital role in reproducing the conditions that sustain capitalist social relations of production (Poulantzas 1973b, 1978).

There is no doubt that Gramsci places an emphasis on the superstructural elements, such as hegemony, values, ideas, and cultures, but different interpretations of his views on the relationship between ethico-political superstructures and economic structures exist. Scholars, such as Bobbio and Jean-Marc Piotte, argue that Gramsci puts primacy on the superstructures over the structures (Mouffe and Sassoon 1977). Contesting this super-structural reading of Gramsci, Texier contends that the superstructures and the base have a dialectical relation 'in which each element can in turn assume the role of conditioner or conditioned' (Mouffe and Sassoon 1977, 45), and that the economic structures are determinant in the last instance because they limit the possibilities of the development of superstructures. Portelli has a third opinion, holding that Gramsci attributes equal weight to both the economic base and ideological superstructures (Mouffe and Sassoon 1977, 46). Glucksmann considers Gramsci a theorist of superstructures, for he livens up historical materialism by delving into questions of the state and ideology/hegemony. However, she warns that we should avoid an 'excessively super-structural' reading of Gramsci, which regards the superstructures/state/ideology both as unrelated to specific relations of production and as 'independent variables' (Mouffe and Sassoon 1977, 48).

In this book, I discard the purely super-structural reading of Gramsci and align more with Texier and Glucksmann who adopt a non–economistic and non–reductionist interpretation of Gramsci's ideas. Instead of seeing the Chinese state as mechanically determined by the base or manipulated by the bourgeoisie class, I maintain that the superstructural elements are highly relevant to the reproduction of social relations of production in China. Yet, the economic base is determinant in the last instance as it shapes the possible forms of superstructure development (Poulantzas 1973b, 1978). Social reproduction should be analyzed

> ...from the point of view of the articulation of the whole ensemble of the various levels of society. The economic aspect remains, in the last instance, as the final determinant but politics may now play the dominant role since it is through politics that a historical bloc is created or destroyed. (Mouffe and Sassoon 1977, 51)

Fifth, the capitalist class in China will become hegemonic only when it is able to create a national-popular appearance for its parochial interests (Gramsci 1971; Poulantzas 2008; Culter 2005). The formation of this trans-class interest is in no way equivalent to the imposition of false consciousness on the working class; it has to take account of and incorporate some of their interests and demands in order to gain universal appeal (Poulantzas 2008). In the country, only when the interests of the dominant Chinese class are successfully articulated and taken as national interest will the subordinate class render its consent to the leadership of the dominant class.

Moreover, the hegemonic class in China needs to grant economic concessions to the working class so as to maintain its support and allegiance (Femia 1987). These concessions are usually short-term in nature, related to secondary issues and do not endanger the long-term dominance of the capitalist class. Burawoy underscores that

> To be an effective hegemonic force, a dominant or potentially dominant class must make economic concessions to elicit the consent of a subordinate or allied class. But these concessions must not touch the essential, and in the case of capitalists they must leave profit intact. (Burawoy 2003, 225)

These concessions, however, should not be seen as granted readily or willingly to the working class. In fact, they are often 'imposed by the struggle of the subordinated classes' (Poulantzas 2000, 31). In Western societies, minimum wages, standard working hours, rights to organize and collective bargaining, social welfare and universal suffrage are all hard-won concessions gained by the working class. Similarly, in China, concessions to the working class in the form of labor and social policies, and labor laws should be understood as the products of working class struggle.

Sixth, for the Chinese capitalist class to become hegemonic, it has to naturalize its moral, ethico-political, and intellectual worldviews; and they must turn these worldviews into a 'common sense' held by the Chinese popular masses so that they will endorse the capitalist logics and not challenge the leadership of the dominant class. This common sense is usually mixed with scientific and philosophical ideas; they are 'half-way between folklore properly speaking and the philosophy, science, and economics of the specialists' (Gramsci 1971, 326).

This common sense is transmitted and reinforced by organic intellectuals that are allied with the capitalist class (Femia 1987; Adamson 1980), as well as by the state's ideological apparatuses in civil society and political society (Poulantzas 1969, 1978). They are not stable, coherent, or comprehensive thoughts, but are 'fragmentary, incoherent and inconsequential' in nature; they usually do not serve the interests of the exploited class who come to accept 'common sense' (Adamson 1980, 150). To overcome the hegemony of the ruling class, the working class, and its organic intellectuals must build up 'good senses' that meet their interests and needs (Gramsci 1971, 326).

Seventh, in this book, hegemony is not seen as a *thing*. Instead, it is conceptualized as a *historical process of class struggles* through which the ruling class continuously reinforces and reproduces their ideological ascendency, and through which the working class resists capitalist hegemony (Benney 1983; Mouffe 1979; Culter 2005). *Hegemony is 'historical'* because class agents are born into societies that are shaped by class struggles of the past. As a result of these past struggles, some class agents take up hegemonic and dominant positions in social relations of production, and they will need to strive to sustain their control and hegemony (Adamson 1980, 149). *Hegemony is a 'process'* because it does not only concern 'the fact of consent', but, more importantly, it is related to the process of creating and mobilizing that consent (Hunt 1993, 20).

Hegemony is 'class struggles' between the capitalist and the working class because the former needs to maintain its ideological, intellectual, and moral leadership continuously so as to pre-empt revolt by the working class, while the working class and its class organizations strive to develop stronger class consciousness among workers in order to transgress capitalist hegemony. In other words, hegemony is not equal to complete submission of the working class or total domination of the capitalist class; instead, it is only an 'unstable equilibrium of compromises between capital and labor' (Poulantzas 2000, 31). How hegemonic a social class is, how much consent is given by labor to the capitalist class, and how much concession is wrung from capital is not definite or stable; rather, they result from class struggles in the economic, political, and ideological terrain at various particular historical moments of a social formation.

Understanding hegemony as a historical process of class struggles, rather than merely as a mode of power exercised by the ruling class, offers two theoretical benefits. First, it does not only focus on how the dominant class reproduces and stabilizes the current socio-economic system, but also opens up the possibility of conceptualizing how this system can be transformed. By inserting class agency and struggle into the analysis, capitalist hegemony is no longer perceived as stationary or insuperable. Instead, the unstable and fragile nature of hegemonic labor–capital relations can be sophisticatedly conceptualized, and the possibility of carrying out subaltern projects of counter-hegemony is not conceptually denied.

Moreover, viewing hegemony as a historical process of class struggles allows us to do away with a zero-sum understanding of hegemony when studying state–capital–labor relations in China. Capitalism has been introduced into China through the passive revolution since 1978 and has a short history in the country. Therefore, in comparison with its Anglo-Saxon and European counterparts, the process of building hegemony in China is still in the infant stage. Seen from a wider historical-temporal perspective, the Chinese capitalist class is in the initial *process of building up* their moral and intellectual leadership, and the Chinese state is in the early process of transforming the basis of its governance from one that relies principally on coercion to one that combines persuasion and force. As elucidated in Chap. 1, if we adopt the authoritarian perspective to analyze the Chinese state, we would overlook the sprouting of an important mode of power exercised by the Chinese ruling class. Conceptualizing hegemony as a historical process allows us to capture the critical transformation of the Chinese state 'within capitalism from political dictatorship to political hegemony' (Burawoy 2003, 220).

Eighth, hegemony has a praxis dimension. As Buckel and Lescano point out, '...hegemony is not some metaphysical subject, but a permanent practice, a world-view fought out in struggles for recognition, through which moral, political, and intellectual leadership is established' (2009, 442). Since hegemony is a historical process of class struggles, the construction of hegemony in China involves 'permanent practice' carried out by the hegemonic class in the socio–economic and political domain to continually reacquire the consent of the Chinese working class to capitalist leadership. The commonsensical worldviews of the Chinese dominant class need to be continuously promulgated and reproduced through their class practices. In addition, hegemony also has an institutional dimension. The ideological apparatuses of the Chinese state, such as the legal system, trade unions, and schools, help transmit, inculcate, and reproduce capitalist hegemony.

Finally, although Gramsci has shed light on how the state helps organize class power, he does not discuss much about what the state is. On this issue, it is useful to apply Poulantzas's insight about the state as a condensation and materialization of social relations to analyze the Chinese party-state. The Chinese state does not translate the interests of the capitalist class onto the political level, but 'the relationship between those interests and the interests of the dominated classes' (Poulantzas 2008, 80). Therefore, class contradictions and social relations of production are inscribed, crystallized, and condensed in the Chinese party-state. The mode of governance, the social and labor policies, and the labor law system are a condensation and crystallization of class relations, an unstable equilibrium of class forces, and products of class struggle.

5 Conclusion

My theorization of the Chinese state is substantially different from the authoritarian, corporatist, and developmental state perspectives outlined in Chap. 1. I conceptualize the Chinese party-state as undergoing a hegemonic transformation, changing from engineering the country's passive revolution through force to facilitating capital accumulation through establishing hegemony. Within this conceptual framework, I argue that the Chinese party-state rules not only with coercion as the authoritarian thesis argues, but also through the construction of hegemony to uphold predominance of the capitalist class. The Chinese party-state has utilized different state apparatuses of ideological, economic, legal, and political nature to build up, transmit, inculcate, and reproduce capitalist hegemony. The labor law system, a key subject of inquiry in this book, is an example of such apparatuses. Unlike the developmental state perspective that stresses only the economic role of the Chinese state, my theorization also considers socio–economic and juridico-political dimensions of the Chinese state. The coercive and hegemonic mechanisms that the Chinese state uses to mediate capital–labor relations in order to facilitate economic accumulation are of primary concern. Different from the corporatist approach that focuses largely on the corporatist actors, the hegemony approach to the Chinese state analyzes social forces and class struggles that are beyond the corporatist structures in China. I also examine how state–capital–labor relations are reinforced, consolidated, and reproduced through the daily hegemonic practices of class agents, the state, and non-state institutions.

In summary, I advance that, after having steered the passive revolution for almost four decades, the Chinese party-state, as a condensation and materialization of social relations, simultaneously plays a coercive and hegemonic role in mediating labor–capital relations. The Chinese ruling class's long-term ascendency is not simply grounded on the coercive capacity of the party-state; it is also rooted in the state's hegemonic attempt to promote capitalist common sense among the subordinate class in the country. Moreover, hegemony is not a thing, but a historical process of class struggles. It is related to both the economic structures (which lead to economic domination of the capitalist class) and the ethico-political superstructures (which secure the subaltern class's consent to capitalist ideological ascendency), both persuasion (through the formation of national-popular interest and granting economic concessions) and domination (through the use of coercive apparatuses), both ideology (such as capitalist common sense and worldviews) and practice/institutions, and both civil society and political society.

Notes

1. There is no doubt that Gramsci is a Marxian; however, his early works were heavily influenced by Croce, a leading Italian philosopher, and thus show traits of idealism. From 1919 onward, his writings manifest an orthodox Marxist orientation, and he starts to criticize the Crocean ideas in his prison writings. In the latter stages of his life, he illustrates a sophisticated materialist "de-mystification of Hegel" (Femia 1987, 101).
2. This development includes the success of the Russian revolution in 1917, the failure of the factory council movement in Italy in 1920, the economic crisis from 1929 to 1932, the emergency of fascism in Italy during the interwar period and so forth.
3. His early writings were subject to the influence of Sartrean existentialism, but later he was inspired by Gramsci and Althusser in different ways (Poulantzas 2008).
4. His theory also seeks to rebut the pluralist political system approach, which was the focus of inquiries in mainstream sociology and political science during the 1950s and 1960s (Barrow 2003). The political system approach assumes a pluralist society, asserting that the state is not the only actor making political decisions; politicians, businessmen, trade unions, voters and so forth are also involved (Barrow 2003). Poulantzas has

revolted against this trend of undervaluing the state, seeking to revive Marxian critical state theories.

5. Litowitz (2000, 523) writes that "…nor did Gramsci provide an analysis of the various mechanisms by which the existing regime in Italy had become hegemonic" and Stuart Hall states that Poulantzas clearly attempted to give Gramsci's concept of "hegemony" a more theoreticized and systemic "formulation" (Poulantzas 2000, ix).
6. Althusser criticizes Gramsci (and Korsch and Lukacs) for his subjectivist and historicist approach which has reduced knowledge "to its own conditions of existence, thus abandoning altogether Marxism's claim to genuine scientific status" and which has reduced history into "the expression of a subject" (Martin 2008, 7).
7. Poulantzas's state theory is insightful, but it neglects the social dimension of the state. With the exception of *Preliminaries to the Study of Hegemony in the State* (Poulantzas 2008, Chap. 3), which was written during his early academic career, concepts such as civil society and social organizations were largely missed out from his theory.
8. My own emphasis.
9. My own emphasis.

References

Adamson, Walter L. 1980. *Hegemony and Revolution: A Study of Antonio Gramsci's Political and Cultural Theory.* Berkeley: University of California.

Althusser, Louis. 1971. Ideology and Ideological State Apparatuses. http://www.marxists.org/reference/archive/althusser/1970/ideology.htm.

Anderson, Perry. 1976. The Antinomies of Gramsci. *New Left Review* 100 (1976/1977): 18.

Aronowitz, Stanley, and Peter Bratsis. 2003. *Paradigm Lost: State Theory Reconsidered.* Minneapolis, MN: University of Minnesota Press.

Barrow, Clyde W. 2003. The Miliband-Poulantzas Debate: An Intellectual History. In *Paradigm Lost: State Theory Reconsidered*, ed. Stanley Aronowitz and Peter Bratsis. Minneapolis, MN: University of Minnesota Press.

Benney, Mark. 1983. Gramsci on Law, Morality, and Power. *International Journal of the Sociology of Law* 11: 191–208.

Bieler, Andreas, and Adam Morton. 2003. Globalisation, the State and Class Struggle: A Critical Economy Engagement with Open Marxism. *The British Journal of Politics & International Relations* 5 (4): 467–499.

Blecher, Marc. 2002. Hegemony and Workers' Politics in China. *China Quarterly* 170: 283–303.

Brand, Ulrich, Christoph Görg, and Markus Wissen. 2011. Second-Order Condensations of Societal Power Relations: Environmental Politics and the Internationalization of the State from a Neo-Poulantzian Perspective. *Antipode* 43 (1): 149–175.

Buckel, Sonja, and Andreas Fischer Lescano. 2009. Gramsci Reconsidered: Hegemony in Global Law. *Leiden Journal of International Law* 22: 437–454.

Burawoy, Michael. 1979. *Manufacturing Consent: Changes in the Labor Process Under Monopoly Capitalism*. Chicago: University of Chicago Press.

Burawoy, Michael. 2003. For a Sociological Marxism: The Complementary Convergence of Antonio Gramsci and Karl Polanyi. *Politics & Society* 31 (2): 193–261.

Clarke, Simon. 1991. State, Class Struggle, and the Reproduction of Capital. In *The State Debate*, ed. Simon Clarke. London: MacMillan Academic and Professional Ltd.

Culter, A. Claire. 2005. Gramsci, Law and the Culture of Global Capitalism. *Review of International Social and Political Philosophy* 8 (4): 527–542.

Femia, Joseph V. 1987. *Gramsci's Political Thought: Hegemony, Consciousness, and the Revolutionary Process*. Oxford: Clarendon Press.

Friedman, Eli, and Ching Kwan Lee. 2010. Remaking the World of Chinese Labour: A 30-Year Retrospective. *British Journal of Industrial Relations* 48 (3): 507–533.

Frolic, B. Michael. 1997. State-Led Civil Society. In *Civil Society in China*, ed. Timothy Brook and B. Michael Frolic. Armonk, NY: M.E. Sharpe.

Gallas, Alexander, Lars Bretthauer, John Kannankulam, and Ingo Stutzle. 2011. *Reading Poulantzas*. Brecon: The Merlin Press Ltd.

Gramsci, Antonio. 1971. *Selections from the Prison Notebooks*, trans. and ed. Q. Hoare and G.N. Smith. New York: International Publishers.

Gries, Peter Hays. 2004. Popular Nationalism and State Legitimation in China. In *State and Society in 21st-Century China: Crisis, Contention, and Legitimation*, ed. Peter Hays Gries and Stanley Rosen. New York: RoutledgeCurzon.

Gwyn, A. Williams. 1960. The Concept of Egemonia in the Thought of Antonio Gramsci: Some Notes on Interpretation. *Journal of the History of Ideas* 21 (Oct–Dec): 586–599.

Habermas, Jürgen. 1979. Legitimation Problems in the Modern State. In *Communication and the Evolution of Society*, ed. Jürgen Habermas. London: Heinemann Education Books.

Hall, Stuart. 1980. Nicos Poulantzas: State, Power, Socialism. *New Left Review* I (119): 60–68.

Hawley, James P. 1980. Antonio Gramsci's Marxism: Class, State and Work. *Social Problems* 27 (5(June)): 584–600.

Hay, Collin, and Michael Lister. 2006. Introduction: Theories of the State. In *The State: Theories and Issues*, ed. Colin Hay, Michael Lister, and David Marsh.

He, Baogang. 1997. *The Democratic Implications of Civil Society in China*. New York: St. Martin's Press.

Hobsbawm, Eric. 1977. Gramsci and Political Theory. *Marxism Today* 21: 205–213.

Holloway, John, and Sol Picciotto. 1977. Capital, Crisis and the State. *Capital and Class* 2: 76–101.

Hui, Sio-Ieng Elaine, and King Chi Chris Chan. 2012. The "Harmonious Society" as a Hegemonic Project: Labour Conflicts and Changing Labour Policies in China. *Labour, Capital and Society* 44 (2): 153–183.

Hunt, Alan. 1993. *Explorations in Law and Society: Toward a Constitutive Theory of Law*. New York: Routledge.

Jessop, Bob. 1982. *The Capitalist State: Marxist Theories and Methods*. Oxford: Martin Robertson.

Jessop, Bob. 1985. *Nicos Poulantzas: Marxist Theory and Political Strategy*. New York: St. Martin's Press.

Jessop, Bob. 1990. *State Theory: Putting the Capitalist State in Its Place*. Cambridge: Polity Press.

Jessop, Bob. 2008. *State Power: A Strategic-Relational Approach*. Cambridge: Polity Press.

Laclau, Ernesto. 1982. *Politics and Ideology in Marxist Theory: Capitalism, Fascism, Populism*. London: Verso.

Lee, Ching Kwan. 1995. Engendering the Worlds of Labor: Women Workers, Labor Markets, and Production Politics in the South China Economic Miracle. *American Sociological Review* 60 (3): 378–397.

Lenin, Vladimir Il'ich. 1969. The State and Revolution. http://www.marxists.org/archive/lenin/works/1917/staterev/ch01.htm.

Litowitz, Douglas. 2000. Gramsci, Hegemony, and the Law. *Brigham Young University Law Review* 2: 515–551.

Martin, James. 2008. Introduction. In *The Poulantzas Reader: Marxism, Law and the State*, ed. Nicos Poulantzas. London: Verso.

Marx, Karl. 1973. The Eighteenth Brumaire of Louis Bonaparte. In *Survey From Exile: Political Writings*, vol. 2, ed. David Fernbach. London: New Left Review.

Marx, Karl. 1974. The Civil War in France. In *Survey From Exile: Political Writings*, vol. 3, ed. David Fernbach. London: New Left Review.

Marx, Karl, and Frederick Engels. 1978. The Communist Manifesto. In *The Marx-Engels Reader*, ed. Robert Tucker. New York: W.W. Norton.

Merrington, J. 1968. Theory and Practice in Gramsci's Marxism. *Socialist Register* 5: 145–176.

Miliband, Ralph. 1969. *The State in Capitalist Society*. New York: Basic Books.

Mouffe, Chantal. 1979. Hegemony and Ideology in Gramsci. In *Gramsci Marxist Theory*, ed. Chantal Mouffe. London: Routledge and Kegan Paul.

Mouffe, Chantal, and Anne Showstack Sassoon. 1977. Gramsci in France and Italy—A Review of the Literature. *Economy and Society* 6 (1): 31–68.

Potter, Pitman B. 2004. Legal Reform in China: Institutions, Culture, and Selective Adaptation. *Law & Social Inquiry* 29 (2): 465–495.

Poulantzas, Nicos. 1967. Marxist Political Theory in Great Britain. *New Left Review* I (43): 57–74.

Poulantzas, Nicos. 1969. The Problem of the Capitalist State. *New Left Review* I (58): 67–78.

Poulantzas, Nicos. 1972. The Problem of the Capitalist State. In *Ideology in Social Science*, ed. R. Blackburn. London: Fontana.

Poulantzas, Nicos. 1973a. On Social Class. *New Left Review* I (78): 27–54.

Poulantzas, Nicos. 1973b. *Political Power and Social Classes.* London: New Left Review and Sheed and Ward.

Poulantzas, Nicos. 1978. *Classes in Contemporary Capitalism.* London: Verso.

Poulantzas, Nicos. 2000. *State, Power, Socialism.* London: Verso.

Poulantzas, Nicos. 2008. *The Poulantzas Reader: Marxism, Law and the State.* London: Verso.

Pun, Ngai. 1999. Becoming Dagongmei (Working Girls): The Politics of Identity and Difference in Reform China. *China Journal* 42: 1–18.

Pun, Ngai. 2005. *Making in China: Women Factory Workers in a Global Workplace.* Durham: Duke University Press.

Pun, Ngai, and King Chi Chris Chan. 2008. The Subsumption of Class Discourse in China. *boundary 2* 35 (2): 75–91.

Salamini, Leonardo. 1974. Gramsci and Marxist Sociology of Knowledge: An Analysis of Hegemony-Ideology-Knowledge. *Sociological Quarterly* 15 (Summer 1974): 359–380.

Solinger, Dorothy J. 1993. China's Transients and the State: A Form of Civil Society? *Politics & Society* 21: 91–122.

Wallace, Ruth A., and Alison Wolf. 2006. *Contemporary Sociological Theory: Expanding the Classical Tradition.* Upper Saddle River, NJ: Prentice Hall.

Wood, Ellen Meiksins. 1986. *The Retreat from Class: The New "True" Socialism.* London: Verso.

Wright, Erik Olin. 1979. *Class, Crisis and the State.* London: Verso.

Wright, Teresa. 2004. Contesting State Legitimacy in the 1990s: The China Democracy Party and the China Labor Bulletin. In *State and Society in 21st-Century China: Crisis, Contention, and Legitimation*, ed. Peter Hays Gries and Stanley Rosen. New York: RoutledgeCurzon.

CHAPTER 3

The Legal Foundation for Changing State–Capital–Labor Relations

1 Introduction

As introduced in Chap. 1, the cardinal questions under examination in this book are: (1) how the Chinese party-state has built up capitalist hegemony through the labor law system during its hegemonic transformation; (2) under what circumstances workers conform with, contest or transgress legal hegemony; and (3) the fragility and precariousness of legal hegemony in contemporary China. In this chapter, my investigation of the Chinese state's hegemonic transformation focuses on the Chinese labor law system. I will elaborate on the 'legislative intervention' made by the Chinese state during the country's passive revolution that sought to bring radical changes to its economic structures 'in order to accentuate the "plan of production"' (Gramsci 1971, 120). The party-state's legislative intervention, I argue, has contributed to the following vital developments that facilitate capital accumulation: the capitalist class, which was absent in the pre-reform period, has been made while socialist workers and peasants have been turned into the exploited class; labor power is commodified in the newborn labor market that has been built upon an affirmation of private property rights; worker wages is now associated with labor productivity and efficiency; trade unions have been co-opted by the state, and workers are diverted to individualized legal channels to handle grievances. All these state-driven efforts have established a vital and material bedrock for the production of capitalist hegemony in contemporary China.

E.S.I Hui, *Hegemonic Transformation*, Series in Asian Labor and Welfare Policies, DOI 10.1057/978-1-137-50429-6_3

Before proceeding with my main arguments, I will first give an introduction to the Chinese legal system as a background to my analysis. Following its founding in 1949, the PRC enacted its first Constitution in 1954. Shortly afterward, it attempted to build up legal order in the country through establishing legal institutions, producing legal rules, applying laws uniformly, and expanding the legal profession. However, subsequent political strife, including the Anti-Rightist Campaign (1957–1958), the Great Leap Forward (1958–1961), and the Cultural Revolution (1966–1976), rendered this endeavor futile (Potter 1994, 329). In the highly politicized environment, laws and lawyers were viewed as bourgeoisie and counter-revolutionary (Lubman 1999). In the late 1950s, law schools were closed down and lawyers were discharged (Potter 2004); the Ministry of Justice and local Justice Bureaus were abolished in 1959 (Zhu 2004). During the Cultural Revolution, the legal system was further marginalized. Laws were largely the CCP's administrative instrument for exercising political power and implementing social policies (Potter 2004). The state-socialist rule was guided by the CCP's policies, which were loosely translated into 'imprecise, exhortational, tentative' legislations (Lubman 1999, 384). In other words, the legal system was not ascribed any autonomy from the party-state.

Post-Mao China has witnessed greater efforts to rebuild the legal system, including professionalization of judges and legal practitioners (Friedman and Lee 2010), training and regulation of lawyers (Zhu 2004), proliferation of legislation (Ngok 2008), the enactment of the Legislation Law in 2000 which specifies how laws should be legislated (Benney 2013), increasing legal aid to the public, and, most importantly, endorsement of the rule of law. In 1999, the PRC Constitution was amended to declare that '[t]he People's Republic of China governs the country according to law and makes it a socialist country under rule of law'.[1] All these new developments not only demonstrate the rising status of the legal system, but they also reveal the party-state's intention to loosen, however slightly, its grip on the legal system due to political and economic consideration, including to legitimatize its rule with legality (Gallagher 2006), to fulfill the requirements of joining the World Trade Organization (Brandt and Rawski 2008), to acquire consent of the subordinate class and so forth.

Most Chinese laws are based on the legal models of the Soviet Union, Germany, and Europe (Potter 1999). In China, law is a broad concept that incorporates five levels of law (Ngok 2008). At the apex of the legal hierarchy is the PRC Constitution. The first Constitution was enacted in 1954. Then three other Constitutions were promulgated in 1975, 1978, and 1982 respectively. The 1982 Constitution is still currently in effect, but it was amended in 1988, 1993, 1999, and 2004. The second highest legal category is the national law (*falv*), which must be adopted by the National People's Congress and its Standing Committee. The next level consists of administrative regulations (*xingzheng fagui*) effected by the State Council. The second lowest level in the legal hierarchy is made of local regulations (*difangxing fagui*) enacted by the Local People's Congress, while the lowest level is composed of rules (*guizhang*) released by administrative agencies under the State Council or local governments.

The Chinese party-state rarely legislates any national laws without conducting prior experimentation; it usually pilots new legal and social policies before turning them into nationwide laws (Ngok 2008). Laws and rules are deliberately phrased in broad and indeterminate language so as to allow for flexible implementation and interpretation (Lubman 1999). The national Chinese laws need to be supplemented by local legislation, the intent of which is to make the former more concrete and detailed (Zhao 2009). Lubman (1999, 390) has characterized the Chinese legislative system as a 'legal fragmentation' because, first, departments under the State Council have the power to issue and modify binding rules under their jurisdiction with unclear procedures. Second, the state council, local governments, and other relevant administrative agencies are vested not only with the power to make administrative regulations and rules, but also the authority to interpret those same regulations and rules. Courts are only responsible for the application of laws to relevant parties. In other words, most Chinese laws are made by the state bureaucracy rather than legislative bodies; local governments and the State Council exercise extensive power in producing, modifying, and interpreting laws. Cooney (2007, 675, 676) also criticizes the 'disorderly internal structure' of the Chinese legal system.

Concerning the labor law system, industrial relations in China are governed by numerous laws and regulations, such as the 1995 Labour Law, 2001 Trade Union Law, 2004 Provisions on Minimum Wage, 2008 Labour Contract Law, 2008 Law on Labor-dispute Mediation and Arbitration, 2011 Social Insurance Law and so forth. The responsibility of enforcement of labor laws lies with the Ministry of Human Resources and Social Security, labor administration departments, mediation institutions, arbitration commissions, courts and so forth. Labour laws set the minimum standards for issues such as daily and monthly working hours, overtime payment, work injury compensation, occupational health and safety, labor contracts, wages, and social insurance. The Chinese labor laws, on paper, offer workers a wide-range of protections, but in reality, they are often laxly implemented, and violations of workers' legal rights are common (Gallagher 2004; Liebman 2007). Furthermore, the rights of workers to strike, engage in collective bargaining, and organize independently are not enshrined in the national laws. While the 1954 Constitution did not protect the right of workers to strike, they were included in the 1975 Constitution and kept in the 1978 Constitution. However, this right was removed from the 1982 Constitution currently in use. For collective bargaining, there is no unified national law on collective negotiation, and many employers do not conduct collective consultation with worker representatives.[2] Moreover, workers cannot form trade unions that are not subordinate to the ACFTU and CCP; any such attempts are met with suppression.

In the following section, I elaborate on the legal reform carried out in Post-Mao China, which has prompted recomposition of the state–capital–labor relationship in the course of the passive revolution. Section 3 examines the relative autonomy of the Chinese party-state and the legal system resulting from changing political and economic relations. Section 4 summarizes my major arguments.

2 The Labor Law System and Changing Industrial Relations

In state socialism, the party-state possessed direct and full control over production. However, following the introduction of capitalism into the country, the party-state withdrew from the direct organizing of production and left economic activities up to the hand of the market economy. Under these circumstances, the legal system was needed to regulate market institutions, business relations, and capital–labor relations so as to maintain essential conditions for capital accumulation. Jiang Zemin, the third generation of the PRC leaders, once highlighted the importance of establishing a sound legal system:

> Whether it is market regulation or macroeconomic regulation and control by the state, we should constantly sum up our experiences and gradually incorporate them into the law. We cannot possibly foster good order in the socialist market economy in the absence of a sound socialist legal system. (Lubman 1999, 127)

It is widely accepted that the Chinese economic reform has induced the legal reform (Warner 1996; Gallagher 2004; Cooney 2007). In this section, I delve into how the incipient legal system and labor law system expedited China's passive revolution. I focus on five important dimensions: (1) the making of the capitalist class and affirmation of private ownership, (2) the creation of a labor market and the commodification of labor power, (3) the introduction of a market wage system, (4) the individualization of conflict resolution, and (5) the party-state's control of class organizations.

2.1 *The Creation of the Capitalist Class and Affirmation of Private Ownership*

China's passive revolution necessitated the state-driven creation of a private economy and capitalist class, whose existence has become legitimized by the legal system. In contrast to economic reform in some former socialist countries (such as Russia) which first focused on privatizing the state sector, the Chinese government placed a great emphasis on developing the non-state sector throughout the reform (Li 1994). In 1984, the Chinese party-state characterized its economy as a 'socialist commodity economy' (Breslin 2007). In 1987, the CCP's 13th Congress endorsed the private sector as 'a necessary supplement' to the public sector (Clarke et al. 2008, 389). Accordingly, the Constitution was amended in 1988 to permit the private sector to exist and develop alongside the public economy; it also proclaimed that the state safeguards 'the lawful rights and interests of the private sector of the economy, and exercises guidance, supervision and control over the private sector of the economy' (Article 11). In the same year, the State Council issued the Provisional Regulations on Private Enterprises, which legalized partnership firms, sole proprietorships, and limited companies (Clarke et al. 2008). In 1992, the CCP's 14th Congress decided to establish a 'socialist market economy' in China (Lau 1997). In 1993, the CCP Central Committee developed a framework for the socialist market economy (Ngok 2008). In the same year, the Constitution was revised to affirm the socialist market economy. In this way, the 'economic planning on the basis of socialist public owner-ship' (Clarke et al. 2008, 391) or a 'socialist commodity economy' was abandoned for a 'socialist market economy'. However, the 1993 amended Constitution still declared that China was practising 'socialism with Chinese characteristics'. The CCP's 15th Congress in 1997 announced that the private sector was not simply supplementary to the public sector, but had become an important part of the economy (Clarke et al. 2008). Accordingly, the Constitution was amended in 1999 to recognize the non-state sector as constituting 'an important component of the socialist market economy' (Article 16). In 2004, the Constitution was revised again to not only sanction, but also encourage growth of the non-state sector (Clarke et al. 2008). In 2005, the party-state announced that the supplantation of the state-planned economy by the 'socialist market economy' was complete (Breslin 2007).

Due to the party-state's economic policies and legal affirmation of the once non-existent private sector, the capitalist class consisting of various players emerged in the reform era. First, as explained in Chap. 1, having taken advantage of the expansion of global capitalism, post-socialist China attracted immense amounts of transnational capital following the economic crisis of the 1970s. In 1979, the Law on Joint Ventures Using Chinese and Foreign Investment was enacted (Zheng 1987). In 1980, four Special Economic Zones (SEZs) were set up in Shenzhen, Zhuhai, Shantou, and Xiamen as experimental projects to attract FDI and boost exports. In the same year, the Regulations on Special Economic Zones in Guangdong Province were issued to govern the first economic experiments with foreign investment (Lewis and Ottley 1981). A wide range of privileges, such as concessionary taxes, preferential fees for land, and flexible wage schemes, were offered to foreign investors in the SEZs (Ge 1999). In 1984, 14 coastal cities and Hainan Island were opened up. In 1985, cities in the PRD, Yellow River Delta, and Yangtze River Delta were also opened up to foreign investment (So 2013). In 1986, the Provisions of the State Council on the Encouragement of Foreign Investment were issued (Zheng 1987).[3] Since 1988, the party-state has opened up all the coastal area, and eventually, almost all border regions of China followed suit (Ge 1999). As a result of the party-state's legal facilitation, Sino-foreign joint ventures and wholly foreign-owned enterprises have mushroomed in China; the *transnational capitalists* have thus become key figures in the rising capitalist class.

Second, while private entrepreneurship was banned in Maoist China, the economic reform began to permit individual household firms (*getihu*) that could hire no more than eight employees. In 1981, the State Council issued provisions that governed individual household firms in towns and cities. In 1983, it was extended to rural areas (Clarke et al. 2008). The newly created *petty-bourgeoisie* also formed a part of the incipient capitalist class in the country (So 2013).

Third, the economic reform has nurtured many *cadre-turned-capitalists and private domestic capitalists.* In state socialism, numerous rural communes set up collectively owned industrial enterprises, many of which were later turned into township and village enterprises (TVEs) by local cadres that basically acted like economic players in the market (Heston and Sicular 2008). TVEs contributed immensely to rural industrialization during the early reform period. Its development was encouraged by State Council documents issued in 1979 and 1984, and the Law on Township and Village Enterprises in 1996 (Clarke et al. 2008). However, many of them were privatized during the 1990s and landed in the hands of the cadres or their families; they thus have turned into private domestic capitalists. In urban cities, driven by then Premier Zhu Rongji who chanted the slogan 'grasp the big, let go of the small', a large number of SOEs were either corporatized in the form of shareholding companies or sold to private entrepreneurs in the mid-1990s. Through political manipulations, many cadres and their relatives ended up as the largest shareholders or owners of these enterprises (Chen 2003). It is estimated that state assets worth up to 30 trillion yuan were transferred to private enterprises through connections to the government in the course of SOE privatization (Li 2011).

Fourth, SOEs of strategic importance have become key market players. During the 1980s and early 1990s, SOEs were allowed to alter their internal wage structures and wage rates in order to provide incentives to enhance productivity and increase profits (Yueh 2004). In 1997, the CCP's 15th Congress approved the fundamental restructuring of SOEs (Chen 2003). Thereafter, many small and unprofitable SOEs were privatized, while larger, competitive ones were restructured. In this way, the party-state continues to control large SOEs and shape their role in key, strategic sectors, such as telecom, energy, shipping, and banking (Naughton 2008). Although in theory, SOEs are considered 'publicly owned', they keenly pursue capital accumulation like all other capitalists and have become de facto *state-capitalists*.

The infant capitalist class is not only approved of through laws, but also by high-level juridico-political mechanisms. Since the mid-1990s, many owners of private enterprises have become members of local People's Congresses and People's Political Consultative Conferences. Some of them are selected as leaders at the village level (Chen 1999). In 2001, Jiang Zemin, the then President, put forward the principle of 'Three Representatives', which advocates that the CCP should represent, among other things, 'the fundamental interests of the greatest majority of the people' (Holbig 2006, 17). This means the party-state should not only represent the working class, but also the capitalist class, such as entrepreneurs, the self-employed and so forth. The CCP constitution was amended in 2002 to include the thought of 'Three Representatives'. Thereafter, entrepreneurs have been eligible to join the CCP resulting in capitalists constituting the largest proportion of the CCP in comparison to other social classes (Breslin 2007). In 2014, it was reported that close to one-third of the super-rich in the country were CCP members.[4] Furthermore, in the same year, 86 billionaires were members of the National People's Congress; they on average have accumulated wealth of 8.1 billion RMB. In addition, 69 billionaires were members of the People's Political Consultative Conference, who own assets that are valued on average at 11.7 billion RMB.[5] In 2011, net worth of the 70 richest members of the National People's Congress was valued at 565.8 billion RMB ($89.8 billion), which massively surpasses the $7.5 billion net worth owned by all 660 high ranking officials of the USA government.[6] All of this reflects that the party-state has abandoned the working class and peasants as a broader alliance of social classes and that it has built up a 'transformed regime alliance' with the capitalist class in the reform era (Solinger 2006). This is the party-state's trasformismo strategy to coopt the rising capitalist class so as to create 'a new, homogenous, political-economic historical bloc' (Anderson 1976, 19) during the country's passive revolution.

The making of the capitalist class in China has gone hand in hand with the endorsement of private property rights. Following the argument that a legal system protecting private ownership is vital for capital accumulation (Hunt 1993; Marx 1990), I maintain that one of the major contributions of legal reform to China's passive revolution is affirming private ownership and private property rights. Public ownership was practised during the state-socialist era; individual interests were subordinate to collective interests, and the socialist state was seen as the 'guardian of public welfare' (Potter 2000, 9). The pervasiveness of this public ownership system is reflected by laid-off SOE workers who feel nostalgic for socialism and utilize the discourse of public rights in their protests against SOE restructuring (Chen 2003). To foster capitalism in China, the confirmation of private ownership is prerequisite. Marx states that

> Historically and logically, capitalism is tied to the private ownership of the means of production, which allows private appropriation of produced commodities, thus private appropriation of surplus value, and thus private accumulation of capital. It is surely not accidental that the 'rights of private

> property' are thus at the bottom of the whole constitutional and juridical superstructure which centuries of law-making have erected upon the basis of commodity production. (Marx 1990, 57)

If private ownership does not exist, then only exchange of objects with use value takes place within a community. Only when private property rights are clearly established can 'private appropriation of produced commodities', exchange of commodities of different exchange values, and 'appropriation of surplus value' be possible. Put simply, only when private ownership exists can realization of surplus value and capital accumulation be made attainable.

The Chinese legal system is a crucial means for establishing 'a new framework of property rights' in the post-socialist period (Lee 2002, 195). The private property rights of capitalists are recognized by various laws, such as the 1993 Company Law, the 1998 Securities Law (both of which were revised in 2005), the 1999 Contract Law, the 2000 Law on Solely Funded Enterprises, the 2004 amended Constitution, and the 2007 Property Law. Intellectual property is protected by the 1984 Patent Law (revised in 1992), the 1982 Trademark Law (revised in 1993), the 1991 Copyright Law and so forth. In addition to these laws, the property rights of capitalists are also promoted by some local governments who run their own businesses or benefit from investment because their wellbeing is also protected through establishment of private property rights in society (Clarke et al. 2008).

It should be noted that although private ownership is the indispensable foundation for capital accumulation, and laws regulating private property, indeed, safeguard capitalist interests, these laws always take a universal form and protect the private property rights of all people in society (Martin 2008; Hunt 1993). That is why the 1982 Constitution, after amendment in 2004, proclaims that the lawful rights of private property of all citizens, not simply those of the wealthy class, are inviolable. The ideological intention of this universal claim is to depoliticize class relations. As scholars from Critical Legal Studies have pointed out,[7] hierarchies and inequalities in a society are inherited into and reproduced by the legal system, but they are often concealed by 'impersonal' and 'neutral' legal logics, and thus assume an appearance of inevitability and universality (Gordon 1984; Hutchinson and Monahan 1984).

2.2 The Creation of the Labor Market and Commodification of Labor Power

The nascent capitalism introduced by China's passive revolution not only necessitates the affirmation of private property rights and the creation of a capitalist class, but it also requires the formation of a capital market, labor market, and commodity market. All transactions and exchanges taking place in these markets are built upon the implicit, but fundamental, acceptance of private ownership. The capital market is where capitalists raise credit for investment in physical production.[8] The labor market is where workers and capitalists sell and buy labor power. The accumulation of capital hinges on the extraction of surplus value from laborers through capitalist control of production materials and the production processes (Marx 1990). The commodity market facilitates circulation and consumption of commodities so that the surplus value expropriated by capitalists can be realized. From the angle of capital accumulation, the construction of these markets is indispensable for the growth of capitalism in China. In 1993, for the first time, the 3rd Plenary Session of the 14th Central Committee of the CCP called for the development of a labor market and capital market in China, commanding the formulation of a corresponding legislative plan and hastening the law-making process (Ngok 2008).

During the state socialist period, no labor market existed, nor was labor power treated as commodity for sale. The Chinese workers of that period did not acquire jobs via the labor market, as in the capitalist economy, but through a centralized allocation system that distributed employment according to ones' skill and technical level. They enjoyed life-long employment; their wages and welfare were based on seniority rather than determined by the supply and demand logics of a market. In order to create a labor market that commodifies labor power, China's passive revolution has demolished socialist protections (including work units and rural people's communes) so that workers and peasants are forced to subject themselves to capitalist wage-labor relations. Meanwhile, in the 1980s, the labor contract system that facilitates the selling and buying of labor power in the market was introduced into SOEs, as well as to the newly emergent non-state sectors, to replace permanent employment (Zheng 1987). This has resulted in the commodification of labor power and a shift from a system of 'socialist social contract' to that of a 'legal contract' (Friedman and Lee 2010, 508).

In the state sector, the labor contract system was first put forward as an experiment in Shenzhen in 1982. Since 1983, it has been continually extended to other SOEs in most major provinces and cities (Zheng 1987). To nurture the newborn labor market and labor contract system, new laws and regulations have been put into place. In 1986, the State Council promulgated four regulations on contract employment to establish standards for recruitment, dismissal and termination of employees, as well as for settlement of industrial disputes (Zheng 1987).[9] The main purpose of these regulations was to legalize the labor contract system. While most of the already employed state workers continued to enjoy life-long employment, new workers were hired on contracts offering them fewer benefits and job security. Moreover, these regulations allowed SOEs to circumvent the centralized allocation employment system in deciding who to hire, even though the new recruitment process was under local labor bureau's supervision. By the mid-1990s, mandatory recruitment plans were abolished (Yueh 2004), meaning that all recruitment in the state sector is now mediated by the once non-existent labor market.

In the private sector, several laws were enacted to govern labor relations in Sino-foreign joint ventures and foreign-owned enterprises, laying a legal foundation for labor contracts. These include the Regulations on Labour Management in Joint Ventures Using Chinese and Foreign Investment in 1980, Procedures for the Implementation of the Regulations on Labour Management in Joint Ventures Using Chinese and Foreign Investment in 1984 and the Regulations Governing Employment Autonomy, Workers' Wages and Insurance and Welfare Fees in Foreign Investment Enterprises in 1986 (Zheng 1987). All of these laws permitted the use of labor contracts in Sino-foreign joint ventures.

While the 1980s witnessed the party-state's experimental efforts to commodify labor power through smashing the iron rice bowl, ending the job allocation system, throwing workers into an embryonic labor market, and implementing a labor contract system, the 1995 Labour Law delivered the final verdict that consigned life-long employment to the dustbin of history (Josephs 1995). This Law was promulgated in 1994 and became effective in 1995. Before its enactment, various laws were made to guide the contractual employment relations in enterprises of multifarious ownerships (such as SOEs, private firms, joint ventures, wholly foreign-funded companies, etc.). The Labour Law unifies the labor contract system and labor standards across firms of all types of ownership by compiling the already existing regulations and practices into one single law (Warner

1996). The Law legalizes not only open-ended contracts, but also fixed-term labor contracts and contracts for specific tasks, which offer workers fewer protections. In 2008, the Labour Contract Law was enacted. In addition to the three types of contracts covered by the 1995 Labour Law, this new law also allows for precarious part-time employment.

The labor contract system affirmed by these laws transforms Chinese workers into sellers of their labor power, while the capitalists are the buyers. The two parties are mostly considered juridico-political individuals rather than class agents; they encounter each other in the market as exchangers of 'free' and 'equal' commodity, for they are supposedly able to enter into legal contracts out of their own 'free' will. Therefore, at the legal level, workers are viewed as on an equal footing with capitalists, regardless of the former's economic and political subordination (Poulantzas 1973; Harvey 1985). Many critical scholars dismiss this kind of liberty and equality as abstract and formal in nature rather than concrete and substantial (Poulantzas 2000, 2008; Hunt 1976; Klare 1978). This is because in reality, workers, who have no control over the means of production, have no choice but to sell their labor power to earn a living (Hyman 1975). It is not an equal exchange between commodity exchangers either, because the product of workers invariably exceeds, in value, what capitalists pay them. Capitalists offer a price for workers' labor power in the labor market; workers, then, are compelled to sell it under conditions that mostly favor the buyers.

The abstract and formal equality between Chinese workers and capitalists manifests in various newly adopted laws in the reform era. The 1995 Labour Law states that '[c]onclusion and modification of a labor contract shall follow the principles of equality, voluntariness and agreement through consultation...' (Article 17). And the 2008 Labour Contract Law also contains similar provisions. Unlike serfs in feudalism, Chinese workers are not dictated by the state's direct political coercion to render their labor power to capitalists; rather, they are 'free' to choose whether to enter into labor contracts with employers or not. The legal form of labor contracts contributes to the apparent equality between antagonistic classes in China. Another reason that labor contracts appear just and fair stems from their regulation by laws with coercive capacity that is, supposedly, applied evenly. In theory, any parties, regardless of their social and economic status, that violate the contracts have to assume legal responsibilities and face punitive sanctions without discrimination.

In a nutshell, the labor contract system established in the post-Mao period legalizes and crystallizes the inequality and restrictions heaped upon workers in the name of universality, equality, and freedom; all of which is derived from a structural inability to be independent from capitalists to whom they sell their labor power. Put another way, labor contracts, which have replaced life-long employment, are a legal form of promoting and reproducing the commodification of labor power in the labor market. They are abstracted from the real social relations of production, and thus, cannot guarantee substantial egalitarianism.

2.3 *Capitalist Wage Setting*

Maximization of profits is of prime importance to capitalists; therefore, boosting surplus value production and minimizing labor costs (the variable capital in Marxian terms) are key concerns. To achieve this aim, the newly developed labor–capital relations in China and the labor law reforms have bestowed vast power upon employers to minimize wages.

Socialist worker wages were based on seniority and determined by a standard wage system; this was gradually dismantled in the course of China's passive revolution. For the state sectors, in 1985, the Ministry of Labour decided that overall wages allocated to SOEs should be linked to their economic performance (Yueh 2004). In the same year, some state enterprises were allowed to not follow the standard wage scale and establish their own wage determination system (Lau 1997). In 1992, the State Council issued a circular permitting all SOEs to set their internal wage structures, so long as their overall wages did not exceed the total budget. Later, many SOEs adopted the 'position and skills wage system' to replace the standard wage system. Under the new wage system, worker wages consisted of a number of components: position wage, skills wage, seniority wage, efficiency wage, bonuses and so forth (Lau 1997). In 1993, the party-state decided to abolish the standard wage system by 1995–1996; by 1994, 90,000 SOEs had already adopted the new wage system (Lau 1997).

Worker salaries under the old standard wage system were not linked to their positions, skills, or efficiency, but under the new system, they were directly associated with these factors. In other words, the new wage system values efficiency over socialist equality; and

> [w]ages are to be determined with 'efficiency being given priority' by enterprises 'autonomously determining their own wage levels and internal distribution methods in accordance with changes in the supply and demand of employment and relevant government regulations'. (Lau 1997, 51)

For Foreign Invested Enterprises (FIEs), the Regulations on Labor Management in Joint Ventures Using Chinese and Foreign Investment issued by the State Council in 1980 specified that wages in FIEs should amount to 120–150% of real wages of SOE workers in the same region, but some cities had different stipulations (Zheng 1987). In 1986, the Investment Provisions and Personnel Regulations were issued to provide uniform wage standard for FIEs, stating that the board of directors of FIEs could fix worker wages as long as they were equal to or above 120% of the average wages of SOE workers in the same region. Also, it allowed FIEs to not increase wages if they were unprofitable (Zheng 1987). The 1995 Labour Law then unified the wage determination mechanism for both SOEs and FIEs, underscoring that '[t]he employing unit shall, based on the characteristics of its production and business operation as well as economic results, independently determine the form of wage distribution and wage level for its own unit according to law' (Article 47). The Law discards socialist values that guided wage setting; instead, it endorses the principle of wage flexibility and links wage levels to the economic performance of firms. In this way, worker wages have changed from state-fixed to market-determined. The principle of wage flexibility approved by law gives enterprises discretion to determine wage distribution and wage levels, i.e., the variable capital. The lower the variable capital, the greater the amount of surplus value that can be generated. In short, the new legally sanctioned wage system allows for maximization of surplus value and capital accumulation for enterprises.

Wages in China are not entirely determined by the market mechanism because the 1995 Labour Law stipulates a minimum wage (Article 48). Even before the adoption of the Labour Law, the Regulations Concerning Minimum Wages in Enterprises was promulgated in 1993 to govern minimum wages in all types of firms across the country. The Regulations were replaced by the Provisions on Minimum Wage issued by the Ministry of Labor and Social Security in 2004. Two points about the Chinese minimum wage system should be highlighted. First, the Labour Law gives provincial and municipal governments the authority to fix their minimum wage rate. Five factors, including labor productivity and regional economic development, should be taken into consideration in deciding this rate (Article 49).[10] This is a legal affirmation to relate worker wages to their productivity and economic performance. It is, in other words, a legal move to detach wage setting from the socialist concept that the value of labor hinges on the time expended on an object rather than worker economic output. In Marxian language, worker wages are now linked to the quantity of surplus value that they can create.

Second, it is true that the minimum wage system sets a floor wage for Chinese workers in the market economy, but the protection offered by the 1995 Labour Law is actually weakened, not only in comparison to the state-socialist policies, but also when compared to the standards set by the 1980 Regulations on Labor Management in Joint Ventures Using Chinese and Foreign Investment and the 1986 Investment Provisions and Personnel Regulations; both of these stipulate clearly that FIE worker wages should not be lower than 120% of their state counterparts. When assessing the development of wage regulation in China from a broader temporal perspective, it is evident that the 1995 Labour Law did not make progress in wage protection as some researchers believe. Rather, the state abandoned a better practice that emerged in the 1980s and decided to endorse less favorable wage protections. The Chinese legal reform that sanctions linking wages to labor productivity and efficiency helps suppress worker wages to a low level, thus boosting surplus value production for enterprises.

Another characteristic of the new wage system imposed by China's passive revolution is that it provides an individual, rather than collective, legal framework. Although several laws provide for collective consultation, detailed legal regulations on such mechanisms are absent. As there is no single unified law on collective negotiation, many employers deem it not obligatory to conduct collective consultation with employee representatives. When employers/enterprises face pressure from trade unions or governments to carry out collective consultation, many of them merely negotiate out of formality; consultations are usually not serious, or they simply do not take place (Chan 1998; Clarke et al. 2004).[11] Chen (2007) highlights that the Chinese labor laws put more stress on individual rights (such as those related to wages, pensions, contracts, etc.), while the collective rights of workers (such as the right to strike, collectively bargain and organize) have not been provided for in any meaningful way. This unbalanced legal emphasis is, by no means, a coincidence. As some critical legal theories suggest, the juridico-political structures conceal class exploitation and political contradictions by decomposing the working class as a collective force into political 'individual persons' and 'subjects of law' so as to reduce their bargaining power and pre-empt the formation of a self-conscious class (Poulantzas 1973). Being deprived of substantial collective rights, Chinese workers do not have a collective means to bargain for their wages, and thus, most enterprises unilaterally decide their wages. Under these circumstances, worker wages are further suppressed by corporations that seek to keep surplus value high.

In brief, to propel the transition from a socialist wage system to a flexible market wage system, the Chinese party-state has enacted various labor laws to prioritize wage flexibility, labor productivity, and efficiency. In addition, by not giving concrete content to laws related to collective bargaining, the labor law system deprives workers of a legal collective means to negotiate wages with employers; therefore, wages remain an individual concern, rather than a class concern.

2.4 Resolution of Labor–Capital Conflict

To maintain a stable production environment is of tremendous significance for capitalists because instability disrupts capital accumulation. In the event that employers fall short of securing labor compliance and labor–capital conflicts arise, the Chinese party-state, who seemingly withdrew from direct economic relations (but has in fact been forcefully driving the capitalist passive revolution), steps in to help resolve the disputes. In this way, the party-state is able to maintain conditions for production (and thus capital accumulation) and political stability (which can be shaken by labor disputes that explode into larger social conflicts if handled improperly). That is to say, in order to maintain economic stability and political harmony, the newly transformed capital–labor relations in China need the back-up of legally and politically sanctioned mechanisms to settle labor disputes, which include the mediation, arbitration, litigation, and appeal systems.

A labor dispute resolution system was put in place in 1950 shortly after the founding of the PRC, which was guided by the Organization and Operation Rules of Labor Dispute Arbitration Commission issued by the Labour Ministry. This system was deemed unnecessary and abolished in 1955 because the socialist industrial relations were supposedly non-antagonistic (Zhao 2009). Shortly after the inauguration of the passive revolution, the party-state restored the system. In 1987, the Provisional

Regulations on the Handling of Labour Disputes in State Enterprises was issued, stating that SOEs should set up industrial dispute resolution committees, which are comprised of representatives from management, workplace trade unions, and Staff and Worker Congresses (Lau 1997). Later, upon the promulgation of the Regulations Concerning the Handling of Labour Disputes in Enterprises in 1993, the labor dispute settlement system was extended to the non-state sector (Thireau and Hua 2003). Furthermore, the 1995 Labour Law established a unified procedure for handling labor disputes, which includes mediation, arbitration, litigation, and appeal. In 2008, against the background of escalating labor unrest, the Law on Labor-Dispute Mediation and Arbitration was enacted to outline specific details for the four-stage system established by the 1995 Labour Law.

The Chinese labor dispute settlement mechanism, which helps maintain a stable environment for capital accumulation, has a number of characteristics. First, it favors mediation over arbitration and litigation as reflected by the 2008 Law on Labor-Dispute Mediation and Arbitration, which states: '[l]abor disputes shall be resolved on the basis of facts and pursuant to the principles of lawfulness, impartiality and timeliness, *with stress on mediation*, in order to protect the lawful rights and interests of the parties according to law' (Article 3).[12] Moreover, when compared to the 1995 Labour Law, the 2008 Law vests greater power to mediation committees permitting workers to apply for payment orders directly from the court, without going through arbitration if employers fail to execute the mediation agreement concerning matters of wages, medical expenses for work injuries, economic compensation, etc. (Article 16). Furthermore, the 1995 Labour Law suggests that mediation should be conducted by enterprise mediation committees (Articles 79 and 80), but the 2008 Law allows mediation to be carried out by mediation institutions at various administrative levels (Article 10).

The new emphasis conferred on the mediation system by the 2008 Law is not simply an attempt to reduce soaring caseloads of arbitration and court trials, but it is also part of the party-state's effort to promote 'harmonious and stable labor relations'.[13] Mediation is a traditional form of grievance redress that existed even in the Maoist time; People's Mediation Committees were established at the village, community, workplace, and government unit levels to mediate disputes between people. It has been deemed to be a less antagonistic means of solving disputes because no formal legal judgment on who is right or who is wrong is decided, instead, agreements on how disputes would be settled are produced from these mediations. Mediators from mediation institutions do not only appeal to legal regulations when mediating a case, they also make use of pressure and persuasion to drive employers and workers to reach agreements. An overhaul of the mediation system by the 2008 Law seeks to provide greater incentives to workers to resolve disputes through the mediation system either before they enter into binding legal procedures or before their disputes explode into deeper social conflicts.

The second characteristic about the labor dispute settlement process in China is that, similar to the rest of the labor law system, it mostly relies on an individual-based legal framework (Chen 2007). This means workers' grievances are treated as individual matters rather than collective or systematic issues. Despite the fact that the 2008 Law on Labor-Dispute Mediation and Arbitration permits workers to designate one representative in mediation, arbitration, or litigation for group disputes involving more than 10 people (Article 7), the labor dispute resolution system in reality focuses mainly on workers' individual rights and seeks to individualize collective disputes. For example, when labor disputes in SOEs reached a peak due to privatization, the Supreme Court announced in 2003 that civil courts would no longer accept collective labor disputes pertinent to SOE restructuring.[14] Furthermore, it is common for courts to break collective cases down into individual cases (Chen and Tang 2013). In addition, judges resort to divide and conquer tactics to persuade some workers in collective disputes to withdraw their cases, which would weaken the confidence of fellow workers to continue their litigation (Chen and Tang 2013). Considering that the rights of workers to strike (which means their rights to stop selling their labor power to capitalists) was removed from the 1982 Constitution, and their rights to collective bargaining (which means their rights to negotiate a collective price for their labor power) have still not been properly legalized, it is evident that the current labor law system is trying to discourage workers from undertaking collective means to settle labor disputes, enclosing them within individualized spheres. This has happened because collective actions of workers are deemed to provoke and exacerbate labor–capital antagonism, which in turn endangers conditions for production and political stability. In a nutshell, the labor dispute settlement mechanism and the labor law system in China help prevent the formation of worker collectivity and turn the working class into atomized legal subjects.

Third, similar to the previous discussion on private property rights, the Chinese labor dispute resolution system, despite its class bias, assumes an appearance of fairness and impartiality. The relevant Chinese laws proclaim themselves to be upholding 'the principle of legality, justness and promptness',[15] settling disputes in 'an impartial and timely manner'.[16] The biased labor dispute resolution process takes a legal form that disguises them as fair, just, and impartial. As will be elucidated in the coming chapters, this legal framework strengthens legal hegemony in China, but some workers are able to see through the capitalist nature of the labor law system and transgress this legal hegemony.

2.5 *Controlled Class Organizations*

As Poulantzas (1973) points out, one of the goals of the capitalist state's intervention into capital–labor relations is disorganizing the working class (while organizing the capitalist class). While the Chinese labor dispute resolution system seeks to individualize worker grievances with legal tactics, the party-led official trade unions attempt to mediate industrial relations with a quasi collective approach. During the Maoist era, state labor employment relations were deemed harmonious since workers were supposed to have the same economic and political interests as state enterprises. The Chinese trade unions, therefore, did not represent workers vis-à-vis the management as both were indiscriminately regarded as SOE employees. Instead, they acted as transmission belts between the party-state and workers (Clarke 2005). On the one hand, they conveyed top-down instructions from the party-state to workers, mobilising the latter to support the party-state's propaganda and production goals. At the same time, they were designated to organise workers' welfare, transmitting worker interests and concerns upward for consideration by the party-state (Pringle and Clarke 2011). This constituted a state corporatist structure in the state-socialist China (Unger and Chan 1995) which has continued in the reform era.

This socialist corporatist structure has laid a solid foundation for the party-state's absorption of opposition leaders, i.e., trasformismo in Gramsci's term, during China's passive revolution. Understanding the importance of trade unions in counteracting capitalist dominance (Hyman 1975), the Chinese party-state in the reform era continues to co-opt trade unions into its governing structures; this trasformismo tactic is also backed by the labor law system. While the right to independent organizing is denied, the official trade unions are designated by the 1995 Labour Law and the 2001 Trade Union Law to represent the interests of workers vis-à-vis management and protect legal rights of workers. However, as China's passive revolution advances, the party-state's trasformismo strategy to control labor has by and large failed because many workers find official trade unions unable to safeguard their interests, and they have, therefore, taken to the streets (see Chaps. 4–6). In light of their incapability to champion worker interests, some scholars consider the trade unions to be shams (Taylor and Li 2010), transmission belts (Chan 2008; Warner 1996), a layer of government bureaucracy (Friedman 2009), a part of the party apparatus (Lee 2006), or part of the developmentalist machine (Gallagher 2004).

Due to the inadequacy of official trade unions to promote worker interests, labor protests have been surging in China, and they increasingly take collective forms (Chan 2010; Chan and Hui 2012). In addition, their demands during strikes have gradually shifted from rights-based to interest-based (Chan 2011; Chan and Pun 2009). The former indicates that worker demands are based on their legal entitlements (such as minimum wage, standard working hours, social insurance, etc.), and thus, can be met by pursuing legal means. The latter refers to worker requests that go beyond the legal standards (for example, decent wages beyond the legal minimum, trade union reform and so forth), and thus, cannot be satisfied by simply enforcing existing laws. Because of these changes, Chinese workers, more and more, resort to collective action to pursue their demands. In light of this, the party-state, adhering to its trasformismo tactic, has utilized trade unions to circumscribe workers' collectivity through various strategies.

First, since 2000, the ACFTU has carried out unionization campaigns in FIEs, trying to mediate workplace labor disputes, but this has happened without much success. In 2004, a government report found that labor laws were not well respected by FIEs. Following that, the ACFTU blacklisted some FIEs, trying to encourage others to establish trade unions. In March 2006, then President Hu Jintao ordered that 'Do a better job of building Party organizations and trade unions in Foreign-Invested Enterprises' (CLB 2006). Since then, the ACFTU has intensified its efforts to unionize FIEs, paying particular attention to Fortune 500 companies (Chan 2005). By the end of 2008, most Fortune 500 companies in China agreed to set up trade unions.[17] However, many of them were merely 'paper unions' (Taylor and Li 2007).

Second, the ACFTU has deployed new strategies to organize workers. For instance, they use worker collective action to pressure enterprises to set up trade unions and develop new organizational forms of trade unions to organize workers that have been easily excluded under current organizing structures (Taylor and Li 2010).[18] Despite these new endeavours, the party-state's aim of containing labor unrest continues to be a crucial driving force in this effort. The third means to circumscribe workers' collectivity within the party-state's control is through promoting workplace collective consultation. The 2001 Trade Union Law spells out that trade unions shall 'make equal consultations and sign collective contracts with enterprises…' (Article 20). As elaborated previously, collective consultations in China are generally a formality, but labor strikes in recent years have forced 'collective bargaining by riot' upon company managers (Chan and Hui 2014). To forestall collective bargaining by riot, the government currently seeks to promote a party-state-led approach to collective negotiation through official trade unions. The fourth measure taken by trade unions to contain labor unrest is to promote democratic union elections at the plant level, which aims to heighten the representativeness of unions and increase workers' sense of control over trade unions. However, some studies find that these elections are only indirect and quasi-democratic and not necessarily able to pacify aggrieved workers (Hui and Chan 2015).

In brief, if the party-state cannot completely forestall the formation of workers' collectivity, the party-state would prefer to let it grow within a cage of the party-state's design. The quasi-collective strategies of official trade unions try to address the growing interested-based demands of workers and tackle the increasingly collective forms of labor resistance through containing workers' collectivity within the party-state's control apparatuses. However, as will be elucidated in the coming chapters, these quasi-collective strategies are not completely successful, and some workers are trying to break through the cage.

3 The Relative Autonomy of the State and Laws

Thus far, I have elucidated five crucial dimensions of China's passive revolution: the making of the capitalist class along with the endorsement of private property rights, the creation of a labor market augmented by the implementation of a labor contract system, the introduction of capitalist wage setting, individualized resolution of capital–labor conflicts, and control over class organizations for workers. In addition, I have illustrated in what ways the party-state has reformed the legal system and the labor law system in order to engineer this passive revolution that aims to foster the growth of capitalism and shape the nascent labor–capital relations in favor of employers.

In this section, I discuss the wider implication of China's passive revolution for state–capital–labor relations in the country. At the level of production, state–labor relations in socialist workplace were transformed into labor–capital relations in the reform period. No longer acting as workers' employers, the party-state has detached itself from direct production and employment relations, allowing the newborn labor market to regulate relations of production. However, it has not completely withdrawn from capitalist industrial relations and capitalist production; instead, its intervention in the economics now takes an indirect and legal-political form. First, it has created a formal and abstract equality among exchangers of labor power (i.e., labor and capitalists) through the labor contract system and the labor market. Workers are now deemed to be 'free' to enter into labor contracts with employers and 'equal' with capitalists at the legal level. Second, the party-state now appears to be standing apart from capital–labor relations; it acts as a neutral and impartial mediator of these relations through the enforcement of labor laws and official dispute resolution mechanisms. It 'impartially' sets the rules for industrial relations through various labör laws. When labor disputes arise, it provides 'neutral' and 'impartial' legal vehicles through which workers can resolve these disputes. These two newly gained characteristics of the Chinese party-state provide a strong foundation for the establishment of legal hegemony; this will be further elaborated upon in the coming three chapters.

Poulantzas's concept of relative autonomy of the capitalist state (1973, 1978) can help us examine the changing role of the Chinese party-state in connection to state–capital–labor relations. This concept is already explained in Chap. 2, but I will briefly recap it here in light of its significance to my arguments. Poulantzas proposes that capitalist social formations consist of the economic, political, and ideological instances. The political and the ideological, he argues, cannot be reduced to the economic, though the economic level determines them in the last instance. As social formation is shaped by the overdetermined effects of the ensemble of these three levels, Poulantzas further contends that the state is relatively autonomous from capital. Comparing capitalism with feudalism, he comes to the conclusion that the relative separation between the state and the economy is an inherent characteristic of capitalism. Feudalism requires the state to exercise direct political force to extract surplus labor from serfs, who, to a certain degree, had economic possession of the land. Workers under capitalism, who do not own the means of production, appear to be 'free labourers'; the state's intervention into surplus value extraction takes an indirect and legal-political form by creating formal and abstract equality among exchangers of commodities in the market.

China did not enter its capitalist stage from feudalism, but from state socialism. Yet, Poulantzas's insight still has a lot to offer to us. In the state-socialist China, the party-state directly organized production and the economy; it deployed workplace trade unions, party branches and other means, rather than political and legal coercion as in feudalism, to mobilize workers (who supposedly had economic ownership of state enterprises) to produce surplus value. Seen from this light, the Chinese party-state and the economy were intertwined in the state-socialist era. After its transition to capitalism, the overlap of the political and the economic has given way to a relative separation of the two spheres, and the party-state has gained a relative autonomy vis-à-vis the capitalists. The Chinese party-state no longer needs to organize production directly and has disengaged itself from direct employment relations. Instead, it has constructed a labor market wherein workers are turned into 'free' sellers of their labor power. And, it has put relations of production, the process of production, and the organizing of productive forces into the hands of enterprises which are primarily regulated by market forces and various laws. In this way, the Chinese party-state's role in the economic has changed from direct intervention for surplus value extraction into ensuring a formal and abstract equality among sellers and buyers of labor power through the labor law system, as well as into mediating labor–capital conflicts through individualized legal means.

One important point to note is that the Chinese party-state's relative autonomy is not only manifested in the economic realm, but also in the political realm. The party-state has shifted from a self-proclaimed working class state to one that intends to appear impartial and neutral from class interests in the reform period. During state socialism, workers were supposedly the masters of the country. However, following the opinions of the 1981 Resolution on Party History, the 1982 Constitution was made less class antagonistic, spelling out that all 'citizens' are equal before the law because of the 'decline of exploiting classes and the resulting conditions of social equality among members of society' (Potter 1994, 335). Jiang Zemin's advocacy of the Three Representatives further marks the party-state's detachment from the working class and its closer alliance with the capitalists. Politically and legally speaking, the capitalist class in China has been elevated to the same status of workers while maintaining their economic superiority. The Chinese party-state, however, tries to conceal the rising status of the capitalist class and the regime alliance with capitalists by appealing to juridico-political means that give all 'citizens' formal equality, regardless of their differing economic status (Poulantzas 2000, 2008).

Compared to Western liberal capitalist states that appear neutral and autonomous, the Chinese state still occasionally declares itself to be protecting worker interests due to its socialist legacy (though at the same time it claims itself to be representing the interests of all people). Its pro-labor declaration is not merely rhetoric, but also backed by labor legislation and social policies, which have seemingly imposed some constraints on employers. Due to its sometimes pro-labor appearance, some workers have been led to regard the party-state en bloc or the central government as labor friendly; for them, if there were any socio-economic problems, it was only because the party-state as a whole does not possess adequate capability to dictate local governments to enforce its 'good' policies (see Chap. 4). In brief, the state's somewhat pro-labor image has contributed to its relative autonomy from capital.

As a consequence of the aforementioned changes in the economic and political realm, the Chinese party-state has become relatively autonomous from the economic and business when compared to its former role in state-socialism. However, this does not mean that it is neutral or classless in nature. As illustrated, the Chinese party-state has concomitantly initiated economic and legal reform to replace: public ownership with private property rights, the central job allocation system with the labor market, life-long employment with the labor contract system, and the socialist wage system with flexible market wages; it has also forged the emergence of a capitalist class and a state–capital alliance. All of these have promoted the commodification of labor power and facilitated capital accumulation. As will be elucidated in the following chapters, the relative autonomy of the post-Mao party-state has laid a crucial foundation for the reproduction of legal hegemony.

In addition to the relative autonomy of the Chinese party-state, the passive revolution has contributed to the emerging relative autonomy of the legal system vis-à-vis both capital and the state's executive bureaucracy.

In this book, I see laws neither as pure instruments of the state and the capitalist class, nor as fully autonomous from them (as legal liberalism believes[19]). Instead, I hold that the Chinese labor law system has gradually developed its own logic, specificities, and relative autonomy, though it is hardly neutral or classless in essence. In his early essay *Marxist Examination of the Contemporary State* published in 1964, Poulantzas insists that the Marxian approach to laws must contain two important insights. First, it should criticize any theories that accept the 'formal, general and abstract specificity of law' (Poulantzas 2008, 38). Second, it should 'uncover the mediations between the base and this superstructure [laws] *while respecting its current specificity*' (Poulantzas 2008, 38). Poulantzas opposes the reduction of the legal into the economic. He underscores that laws, on the one hand, mediate labor–capital relations in favor of the capitalist class; on the other, they formulate their own specificities and crystallized values, such as (formal and abstract) equality and liberty, that do not necessarily serve the immediate interests of the capitalist class (Poulantzas 2008, 4–5).

Echoing Poulantzas's insights, Burawoy also holds that laws enjoy a relative autonomy from the capitalists because

> [T]he political, legal, and ideological instances are not implicated in the mode of production itself, so we can talk about the political, legal, and ideological as separate spheres of activity. We can even talk about their *relative autonomy. The legal structure...has a coherence and dynamic of its own, and its precepts cannot be arbitrarily changed by external forces.* (Burawoy 1978, 302)[20]

However, Burawoy at the same time underlines the class tendency of laws. The legal masks relations of production, he explicates, by obscuring the distinction between subjects of different economic status and by reconstructing class actors into 'free and equal' citizens (Burawoy 1978, 302).

Pertinent to the relative autonomy of laws vis-a-vis the capitalists, the Chinese labor law system has allowed for legislation and judiciary rulings that sometimes contradict the short-term interests of capitalists as individuals (but not to the long-term interests of capitalists as a class). This has prompted some scholars to conclude that labor laws are a means to repair unbalanced labor relations in China. For instance, Gallagher (2004, 22) argues that the labor contract system newly introduced to China intends to reduce labor exploitation in the private sectors by stipulating the basic rights of workers and the responsibilities of employers. Cooney et al. (2007, 801) conclude that the Labour Contract Law '*makes a contribution to addressing some of the egregious abuses* that occur in China. There is now a much better system of norms, having the status of national law'.[21] Josephs (1995, 559) suggests that the 1995 Labour Law '*lends an importance to worker rights which they did not have previously* and demonstrates a conscious effort of the Chinese government to bring its system of labor law and industrial relations into closer compliance with international standards'.[22]

I do not challenge the argument of these studies that certain labor laws can address grievances of workers as individuals, nor do I suggest that Chinese workers need no legal protection. However, if analyzed through the above-illustrated theoretical lens that simultaneously highlights the relative autonomy of laws and their class inclinations, it is clear that the pro-labor legal contents of laws are simply expressions of the relative autonomy of Chinese laws. As elaborated in section two, legal reform and the labor law system initiated by the passive revolution strengthen capitalism in various crucial dimensions. The Chinese laws are in no way completely autonomous from the capitalists as a class. At most, they protect workers' rights vis-à-vis the capitalists as individuals within the framework of capitalism. The Chinese legal system therefore inevitably hinders workers from challenging and attempting to overcome capitalism.

Pertinent to the relative autonomy of laws vis-a-vis the Chinese state bureaucracy, Potter (2004, 472) is quite dismissive, noting that the relative autonomy of the Chinese legal system is more limited than its European and North American counterparts because, in some circumstances, the Chinese laws remain politically contingent. This comment from the perspective of an international comparison is not incorrect, but a national-temporal comparison of the Chinese legal system will allow us to better understand the significance of the emerging relative autonomy of Chinese laws.

As explicated before, the Maoist state manipulated or marginalized the legal system during state socialism; the laws were used to implement the party-state's policies, rather than being allowed to develop its own specific logic and coherence. During the reform era, it has been permitted to formulate its own legal logic, operations, and mechanisms. The rule of law is now heavily stressed (though its implementation is not without criticism); numerous laws have been made to regulate the criminal and civil domains; the judiciary system has been rebuilt through professionalizing judges and lawyers; laws are made according to specific legal procedures and are open to broader consultation before legislation; mediation, arbitration, and litigation are handled by designated judiciary organs that supposedly conform to legal regulations. All these give the appearance that laws are somehow autonomous from the state bureaucracy; this relative autonomy of the Chinese legal system is another vital foundation for the establishment of legal hegemony in China, as will be expounded on in the coming three chapters.

The rising relative autonomy of laws vis-à-vis the state in China, however, is still fragile. In terms of juridico-political structures, the Chinese legal system is subject to the CCP's strong influences via the CCP Politics and Law Commission (PLC) (*zhengfawei*). The PLC is a powerful party organ established at different administrative levels to oversee legal and political affairs. It supervises and leads all the law enforcement agencies, including the Supreme People's Procuratorate, Supreme People's Court, the Ministry of Justice, the Ministry of Public Security, and the Ministry of State Security (Li 2012; Oksenberg 2001). In the past, the PLC secretary used to be a member of the Standing Committee of the Politburo, which is the apex of power in the CCP. However, after the outbreak of political conflict related to the former PLC secretary, Zhou Yong Kang, who was sentenced to jail for acts of corruption, the new secretary has only been elected into the Central Committee of the Politburo in the 18th CCP National Congress held in 2012 rather than into the Standing Committee. The PLC is highly sensitive and low-profile. My interviewees that are legal scholars, judges, and lawyers all revealed that they do not know much about its operations; some described it as a 'devil' because it is highly influential yet not transparent.[23]

In addition to the PLC, the party-state influences the legal system through other mechanisms. Officially, People's Congresses at the local level have the power to appoint and dismiss judges and court's leadership, but in reality, the local party branches exercise actual power (Clarke et al. 2008). Moreover, the finances of courts are dependent on local governments. As a result of this, decisions of judges and courts have been highly affected by the economic concerns of local governments (Friedman and Lee 2010; Lubman 1999). Additionally, it is difficult to enforce court orders due to local protectionism and weak legal punishment (Liebman 2007).

Considering the above-elaborated development of relations between the legal system and the party-state, I contend that the relative autonomy of the former vis-à-vis the latter is emerging, but it is still fragile. Nonetheless, it has contributed to the formation of legal hegemony, as will be expounded on in the coming chapters.

4 Conclusion

In the early stage of China's passive revolution, there existed no dominant class that possessed mature hegemonic capacity to elicit the popular masses' consent for capitalist development. Therefore, the Chinese party-state had to play a dominant and forceful role in driving the economic reform, which concomitantly induced a legal reform that helped consolidate the infant capitalism in the country. The newly developed legal system and labor law system cover some key dimensions. First, they have helped create and legitimize the rising capitalist class which was non-existent in the Maoist period. It now consists of multifarious components: transnational capitalists, private-domestic capitalists, cadre-turned-capitalists, state-capitalists, and petty-bourgeoisie. To facilitate capital accumulation, the legal system has endorsed private property rights, which were discredited in state socialism but are prerequisite for the growth of capitalism in the reform era. Applying trasformismo strategies, the party-state has co-opted the newly arisen capitalist class into the ruling bloc, forming a transformed regime alliance. As will be discussed in the coming chapters, after carrying out economic reform for over three decades, the ruling class has gradually developed some hegemonic capacity, however minimal, in such ways that the subordinate class has given greater consent to capitalist development.

Second, following the party-state's abandonment of the working class in a social class alliance, the working class that was once hailed as the country's master has been turned into the exploited class. This has been achieved partly with the help of the labor law system. Due to the abolishment of work units, rural communes, the central job allocation system, and life-long employment, workers and peasants are now forced into an incipient labor market that commodifies labor power. Under the legal labor contract system, the selling and buying of labor power is deemed 'fair' and 'equal' because both workers and employers are 'free' to enter into contracts. In addition, the socialist wage system has been substituted by the market wage system, which prioritizes wage flexibility and labor productivity, or, in Marxian terms, the minimization of variable capital and maximization of surplus value.

Third, the party-state is relatively autonomous from the capitalists and the economy in the reform era. As state–labor relations in formerly socialist workplaces have been transformed into labor–capital relations, the party-state has stepped back from direct production. It now behaves as an impartial mediator of industrial relations through the legislation and application of labor laws. However, it is by no means classless in essence. Alongside the economic and legal measures summarized above that expedite capital accumulation, the party-state attempts to maintain a stable environment for production by co-opting potential class organizations (i.e.,trade unions), channeling disgruntled workers into official dispute resolution mechanisms that turn them into atomized legal subjects, and forestalling the formation of workers' collectivity through the quasi-collective approaches of trade unions (such as large-scale unionization, party-state-led collective bargaining, workplace union elections, and new forms of worker organizing).

The legal system and labor law system are important vehicles through which the party-state has fueled the passive revolution. However, they are hardly mere political or economic instruments. They are relatively autonomous from both capitalists and the party-state. During economic reform, the Chinese party-state has allowed for the growth of the legal system. This has led to the development of its own legal logics and rules of operation, which make it not completely susceptible to manipulation by the party-state, especially in comparison to its subordinate role in state socialism. The Chinese legal system and labor law system are also relatively autonomous from capitalists in the sense that they allow for laws and judiciary rulings that deny the short-term interests of capitalists and that mitigate labor exploitation (though only within the framework of capitalism). However, these systems, in fact, are juridico-political endorsements of the abolition of socialist life-long employment, legal affirmations of private property rights and the incipient capitalist economy, the lawful engines for the development of the labor market and commodification of labor power, the legal propellants for the formation of a capitalist class and an exploited class, as well as the judicial pretext that masks unequal relations of production with formal and abstract emphases on equality and freedom of choice. By giving the labor market, the labor contract system, and capital–labor relations a form of equality, fairness, and legality, the labor law system hides its own tendencies and those of the party-state towards the capitalists, masking the economic differences between the conflicting classes and fragmenting the Chinese workers into individualized legal subjects.

By now, it should be clear that China's passive revolution is not simply about the transition from state-socialism to capitalism; it is also about the recomposition of state–capital–labor relations in the country. In the coming three chapters, I illustrate that after implementing economic reform for more than three decades the party-state and capitalist class, i.e., the ruling bloc, have acquired a certain degree of political, moral, and ethical leadership over the working class, and that the recently established labor law system, the labor market, the relative autonomy of the Chinese party-state, and of labor laws have laid down a crucial foundation for the construction of capitalist hegemony in the country.

Notes

1. All English quotations of the Chinese law in this book are taken from the website of the National People's Congress (see http://www.npc.gov.cn/englishnpc/Law/Frameset-index.html), unless otherwise specified.
2. However, there exist some provincial laws on collective negotiation. For examples, the Guangdong Provincial Regulations on Collective Contracts for Enterprises was promulgated in 2014, which states that enterprises cannot fire worker representatives while they are performing their duties of negotiation, but the Regulations also makes it illegal to strike during negotiations—the first such law officially prohibiting strikes.
3. See http://www.lawinfochina.com/display.aspx?lib=law&id=1271&CGid=, accessed on 24th May 2013.
4. See http://news.now.com/home/international/player?newsId=94775, accessed on 26th March 2014.
5. See http://www.ft.com/intl/cms/s/0/ae5c731a-a3bb-11e3-aa85-00144feab7de.html#axzz2x4SRmaz3, both accessed on 26th March 2014.
6. See http://www.bloomberg.com/news/2012-02-26/china-s-billionaire-lawmakers-make-u-s-peers-look-like-paupers.html, accessed on 26th March 2014.
7. Galvanized by the civil rights movement in the USA during the 1950s and 1960s (Tushnet 1991), a group of radical lawyers, law teachers and students organized the first Conference on Critical Legal Studies in 1977 to formulate critiques on the tradition of legal formalism and liberalism. Thereafter, the CLS conference is held annually, and the influence of CLS has become quite remarkable (Gabel and Harris 1982; Hunt 1986; Tushnet 1991).
8. However, as it evolves, it also breeds the creation and circulation of fictitious capital that is based on future realization of surplus value (Marx 1993).
9. These regulations include the Interim Regulations on the Implementation of Labor Contracts in State-Owned Enterprises, Interim Regulations on

the Recruitment of Workers by State-Owned Enterprises, Interim Regulations on Dismissal by State-Owned Enterprises of Employees in Violation of Discipline, and Interim Regulations on Unemployment Insurance For Employees of State-Owned Enterprises.

10. The three other factors are: the minimum living expenses of labourers themselves plus that of the average of all dependents that they support, the average wage level of society as a whole, and the employment rate.
11. For the development of collective bargaining in different periods in China, see Chan and Hui (2014).
12. My own emphasis.
13. See Article 1, Law on Labor-Dispute Mediation and Arbitration.
14. See http://www.clb.org.hk/en/content/chinas-labour-dispute-resolution-system, accessed on 22nd May 2013.
15. Article 78, 1994 Labour Law.
16. Article 1, the Law on Labor-dispute Mediation and Arbitration.
17. Christian Science Monitor, *Unions in China Still Feeble, But Gaining a Foothold*, 29 September 2008.
18. The new organizational forms are United Trade Unions in FIEs, United Unions or Union Committees, and Community Unions (Taylor and Li 2010, 419).
19. Legal liberalism asserts that law should be politically neutral, objective, rational and autonomous (Hunt 1986, 1993), should treat all citizens equally (Klare 1978) and should be able to be used by disadvantaged groups to redress their grievance (Hunt 1993).
20. My own emphasis.
21. My own emphasis.
22. My own emphasis.
23. Interview H3.

References

Anderson, Perry. 1976. The Antinomies of Gramsci. *New Left Review* 100 (1976/1977): 18.

Benney, Jonathan. 2013. *Defending Rights in Contemporary China*. Oxon: Routledge.

Brandt, Loren, and Thomas G. Rawski. 2008. China's Great Economic Transformation. In *China's Great Economic Transformation*, ed. Loren Brandt and Thomas G. Rawski. Cambridge: Cambridge University Press.

Breslin, Shaun. 2007. *China and the Global Political Economy*. New York: Palgrave Macmillan.

Burawoy, Michael. 1978. Toward a Marxist Theory of the Labor Process: Braverman and Beyond. *Politics & Society* 8: 247–312.

Chan, Anita. 1998. Labour Relations in Foreign-Funded Ventures, Chinese Trade Unions, and the Prospects for Collective Bargaining. In *Adjusting to Capitalism: Chinese Workers and the State*, ed. G. O'Leary. Armonk, NY: M. E. Sharpe.

Chan, Anita. 2005. Recent Trends in Chinese Labour Issues-Signs of Change. *China Perspectives* 2009 (20th March).

Chan, Anita. 2008. China's Trade Unions in Corporatist Transition. In *Associations and the Chinese State: Contested Spaces*, ed. Jonathan Unger. New York: M. E. Sharpe Inc.

Chan, Anita. 2011. Strikes in China's Export Industries in Comparative Perspective. *China Journal* 65: 27–52.

Chan, King Chi Chris. 2010. *The Challenge of Labour in China: Strikes and the Changing Labour Regime in Global Factories.* New York: Routledge.

Chan, King-Chi Chris, and Sio-Ieng Elaine Hui. 2012. The Dynamics and Dilemma of Workplace Trade Union Reform in China: The Case of the Honda Workers' Strike. *Journal of Industrial Relations* 54: 653–668.

Chan, King-Chi Chris, and Sio-Ieng Elaine Hui. 2014. The Development of Collective Bargaining in China: From "Collective Bargaining by Riot" to "Party State-led Wage Bargaining. *China Quarterly* 217: 221–242.

Chan, King Chi Chris, and Ngai Pun. 2009. The Making of a New Working Class? A Study of Collective Actions of Migrant Workers in South China. *China Quarterly* 197: 287–303.

Chen, Feng. 1999. An Unfinished Battle in China: The Leftist Criticism of the Reform and the Third Thought Emancipation. *China Quarterly* 158: 447–467.

Chen, Feng. 2003. Industrial Restructuring and Workers' Resistance in China. *Modern China* 29 (2): 237–262.

Chen, Feng. 2007. Individual Rights and Collective Rights: Labor's Predicament in China. *Communist and Post-Communist Studies* 40: 59–79.

Chen, Feng, and Mengxiao Tang. 2013. Labor Conflicts in China: Typologies and Their Implications. *Asian Survey* 53 (3): 559–583.

Clarke, Simon. 2005. Post-socialist Trade Unions: China and Russia. *Industrial Relations Journal 36:1, 2–18* 36 (1): 2–18.

Clarke, Simon, Chang Hee Lee, and Qi Li. 2004. Collective Consultation and Industrial Relations in China. *British Journal of Industrial Relations* 42 (2): 235–254.

Clarke, Donald, Peter Murrell, and Susan Whiting. 2008. The Role of Law in China's Economic Development. In *A Political Economy of China's Economic Transition*, ed. Loren Brandt and Thomas G. Rawski. Cambridge: Cambridge University Press.

CLB (China Labour Bulletin). 2006. *Wal-Mart Unionisation Drive Ordered by Hu Jintao in March—A Total of 17 Union Branches Now Set Up.*China Labour Bulletin.

Cooney, Sean. 2007. China's Labour Law, Compliance and Flaws in Implementing Institutions. *Journal of Industrial Relations* 49: 673–686.

Cooney, Sean, Sarah Biddulph, Kungang Li, and Zhu Ying. 2007. China's New Labour Contract Law: Responding to the Growing Complexity of Labour Relations in the PRC. *University of New South Wales Law Journal* 30 (3): 786–801.

Friedman, Ellen David. 2009. US and Chinese Labour at a Changing Moment in the Global Neoliberal Economy. *Working USA: The Journal of Labor and Society* 12 (2): 219–234.

Friedman, Eli, and Ching Kwan Lee. 2010. Remaking the World of Chinese Labour: A 30-Year Retrospective. *British Journal of Industrial Relations* 48 (3): 507–533.

Gabel, Peter, Harris, Paul. 1982. Building Power and Breaking Images: Critical Legal Theory and the Practice of Law. N. Y. U. Rev. L. & Soc. Change, 11, 369–411.

Gallagher, Mary E. 2004. "Time is Money, Efficiency is Life": The Transformation of Labor Relations in China. *Studies in Comparative International Development* 39 (2): 11–44.

Gallagher, Mary E. 2006. Mobilizing the Law in China: "Informed Disenchantment" and the Development of Legal Consciousness. *Law & Society Review* 40 (4): 783–816.

Ge, W. 1999. Special Economic Zones and the Opening of the Chinese Economy: Some Lessons for Economic Liberalization. *World Development* 27 (7): 1267–1285.

Gordon, Robert W. 1984. Criticial Legal Histories. *Standford Law Review* 36: 57.

Gramsci, Antonio. 1971. *Selections from the Prison Notebooks*, trans. and ed. Q. Hoare and G.N. Smith. New York: International Publishers.

Harvey, David. 1985. The Marxian Theory of the State. *Antipode.*

Heston, Alan, and Terry Sicular. 2008. China and Development Economics. In *China's Great Economic Transformation*, ed. Loren Brandt and Thomas G. Rawski. Cambridge: Cambridge University Press.

Holbig, Heike. 2006. Ideological Reform and Political Legitimacy in China: Challenges in the Post-Jiang Era. In *Program: Legitimacy and Efficiency of Political Systems*, ed. G.I.G.A. Research. Hamburg: German Institute of Global and Area Studies.

Hui, Sio-Ieng Elaine, and King-Chi Chris Chan. 2015. Going Beyond the Union-Centred Approach: A Critical Evaluation of Recent Trade Union Elections in China. *British Journal of Industrial Relations* 53 (3): 601–627.

Hunt, Alan. 1976. Law, State and Class Struggle. *Marxism Today* 2: 178–187.

Hunt, Alan. 1986. The Theory of Critical Legal Studies. *Oxford Journal of Legal Studies* 6 (1): 1–45.

Hunt, Alan. 1993. *Explorations in Law and Society: Toward a Constitutive Theory of Law*. New York: Routledge.

Hutchinson, Allan C., and Patrick J. Monahan. 1984. Law, Politics, and the Critical Legal Scholars: The Unfolding Drama of Americal Legal Thought. *Standford Law Review* 36: 199–245.

Hyman, Richard. 1975. *Industrial Relations: A Marxist Introduction*. London: Macmillan.

Josephs, Hilary K. 1995. Labor Law in a "Socialist Market Economy": The Case of China. *Columbia Journal of Transnational Law* 33: 559–582.

Klare, Karl E. 1978. Judicial Deradicalization of the Wagner Act and the Origins of Modern Legal Consciousness, 1937–1941. *Minnesota Law Review* 62: 265.

Lau, Raymond W.K. 1997. China: Labour Reform and the Challenge Facing the Working Class. *Capital and Class* 21: 45–80.

Lee, Ching Kwan. 2002. From the Specter of Mao to the Spirit of the Law: Labor Insurgency in China. *Theory and Society* 31: 189–228.

Lee, Chang-Hee. 2006. Recent Industrial Relations Developments in China and Viet Nam: The Transformation of Industrial Relations in East Asian Transition Economies. *Journal of Industrial Relations* 48: 415.

Lewis, John Bruce, and Bruce L. Ottley. 1981. China's Developing Labor Law. *Washington Univerity Law Quarterly* 59: 1165–1220.

Li, Jingjie. 1994. The Characteristics of Chinese and Russian Economic Reform. *Journal of Comparative Economics* 18 (3): 309–313.

Li, Minqi. 2011. The Rise of the Working Class and the Future of the Chinese Revolution. *Monthly Review* 63 (2): 38.

Li, Cheng. 2012. The End of the CCP's Resilient Authoritarianism? A Tripartite Assessment of Shifting Power in China. *China Quarterly* (211): 595–623.

Liebman, Benjamin. 2007. China's Court: Restricted Reform. *China Quarterly* 191: 620–638.

Lubman, Stanley. 1999. Bird in a Cage: Chinese Law Reform After Twenty Years. *Northwestern Journal of International Law & Business* 20: 383–424.

Martin, James. 2008. Introduction. In *The Poulantzas Reader: Marxism, Law and the State*, ed. Nicos Poulantzas. London: Verso.

Marx, Karl. 1990. *Capital: Volume 1: A Critique of Political Economy*. London: Penguin Classics.

Marx, Karl. 1993. *Capital: A Critique of Political Economy*, vol. 3. London: Penguin Classics.

Naughton, Barry. 2008. *A Political Economy of China's Economic Transition*, ed. Loren Brandt and Thomas G. Rawski. Cambridge: Cambridge University Press.

Ngok, Kinglun. 2008. The Changes of Chinese Labor Policy and Labor Legislation in the Context of Market Transition. *International Labor and Working-Class History* 73: 45–64.

Oksenberg, Michel. 2001. China's Political System: Challenges of the Twenty-First Century. *China Journal* 45: 21–35.

Potter, Pitman B. 1994. Riding the Tiger: Legitimacy and Legal Culture in Post-Mao China. *China Quarterly* 138: 325–358.

Potter, Pitman B. 1999. The Chinese Legal System: Continuing Commitment to the Primacy of State Power. *China Quarterly* 159: 673–683.

Potter, Pitman B. 2000. Globalisation and Local Legal Culture Dilemmas of China's Use of Liberal Ideals of Private Property Rights. *Asian Law* 2: 1–33.

Potter, Pitman B. 2004. Legal Reform in China: Institutions, Culture, and Selective Adaptation. *Law & Social Inquiry* 29 (2): 465–495.

Poulantzas, Nicos. 1973. *Political Power and Social Classes.* London: New Left Review and Sheed and Ward.

Poulantzas, Nicos. 1978. *Classes in Contemporary Capitalism.* London: Verso.

Poulantzas, Nicos. 2000. *State, Power, Socialism.* London: Verso.

Poulantzas, Nicos. 2008. *The Poulantzas Reader: Marxism, Law and the State.* London: Verso.

Pringle, Tim, and Simon Clarke. 2011. *The Challenge of Transition: Trade Unions in Russia, China and Vietnam.* New York: Palgrave Macmillan.

So, Alvin Y. 2013. *Class and Class Conflict in Post-socialist China.* Singapore: World Scientific.

Solinger, Dorothy J. 2006. The Creation of a New Underclass in China and Its Implications. *Environment and Urbanization* 18 (2): 177–193.

Taylor, Bill, and Qi Li. 2007. Is the ACFTU a Union and Does it Matter? *Journal of Industrial Relations* 49: 701–715.

Taylor, Bill, and Qi Li. 2010. China's Creative Approach to 'Union' Organizing. *Labor History* 51 (3): 411–428.

Thireau, Isabelle, and Linshan Hua. 2003. The Moral Universe of Aggrieved Chinese Workers: Workers' Appeals to Arbitration Committees and Letters and Visits Offices. *China Journal* 50: 83–103.

Tushnet, Mark. 1991. Critical Legal Studies: A Political History. *Yale Law Journal* 100 (5 (March)): 1515–1544.

Unger, Jonathan, and Anita Chan. 1995. China, Corporatism and the East Asian Model. *The Australian Journal of Chinese Affairs* 33: 29–53.

Warner, Malcolm. 1996. Chinese Enterprise Reform, Human Resources and the 1994 Lahour Law. *The International Journal of Human Resource Management* 7 (4): 779–796.

Yueh, Linda Y. 2004. Wage Reforms in China During the 1990s. *Asian Economic Journal* 18 (2): 149–164.

Zhao, Yun. 2009. China's New Labour Dispute Resolution Law: A Catalyst for the Establishment of Harmonious Labor Relationship? *Comparative Labor Law & Policy Journal* 30: 409–430.

Zheng, Henry R. 1987. An Introduction to the Labor Law of the People's Republic of China. *Harvard International Law Journal* 28 (2): 385–432.

Zhu, Sanzhu. 2004. Reforming State Institutions: Privatizing the Lawyers' System. In *Governance in China*, ed. Jude Howell. Maryland, MD: Rowman & Littlefield Publishers, Inc.

CHAPTER 4

Workers' Active Consent

1 Introduction

In the last chapter, I elaborated on the party-state's legal interventions which have fueled China's passive revolution. Turning China into a capitalist country was initially a state-directed project.[1] It was neither led by any dominant social forces, nor supported by the popular masses. Instead, it was mostly built upon the authoritarian practices and strong political power of the party-state. Having carried out the economic reform for more than three decades, the state's effort to foster capitalism and capitalist social relations of production has resulted in the formation of a capitalist class and an exploited class. While workers are no longer treated as a key component of the ruling class as in the state-socialist era, the party-state and the fledgling capitalist class have started to form a ruling bloc. This development has a three-fold implication.

First, instead of remaining state-imposed, the capitalist reform in China is gaining a social base and being embraced by a rising social force, the capitalist class. In other words, the passive revolution is no longer purely passive; it has become actively pursued from below. Second, those who have been turned into the exploited class through the mechanisms elaborated on in Chap. 3, especially migrant workers, increasingly contest elements of this newborn capitalist economy, as manifested by the proliferation of labor protests (Lee 2007; Chan 2010). Third, the rising capitalist class has joined hands with the party-state to promote the capitalist economy, forming a ruling bloc that has gradually acquired political,

E.S.I Hui, *Hegemonic Transformation*, Series in Asian Labor and Welfare Policies, DOI 10.1057/978-1-137-50429-6_4

moral, and ethical leadership over the working class, as will be explicated in this chapter. In this way, the Chinese party-state has been undergoing a hegemonic transformation—a process of changing its role from vigorously engineering the passive revolution from above to helping obtain the bottom-up consent of workers for capitalist development.

As Gramsci (1971, 195) underscores, the state often uses laws to 'assimilate' the masses into the dominant class and to 'educate' them to conform to conditions that are 'useful to the ruling group's line of development'. In this chapter and the following three chapters, I explore the emerging hegemonic capacity of the party-state by focusing on the labor law system. These chapters investigate four key questions: (1) *through what mechanisms the labor law system has mediated hegemonic relations among the state, capital, and labor*; (2) *to what extent Chinese workers have been subjected to legal hegemony*; (3) *under what situations workers will conform with, negotiate, or transgress hegemonic boundaries*; and (4) *what the factors contributing to the fragility and instability of legal hegemony in China are.*

I contend, in this book, that Chinese workers have accepted or rejected the capitalist leadership mediated through the labor law system to differing extents—some workers have conferred active consent to legal hegemony, some have only given passive consent, while some have completely rejected it. In the following section, I put forward a typology of worker susceptibility towards legal hegemony so as to provide an analytical tool for examining the hegemonic impact of the labor law system. In addition, through anatomizing stories of workers with different labor dispute experiences, Sect. 3 focuses on workers who have granted active consent to hegemony mediated by the labor law system (while Chaps. 5 and 6 will illuminate workers who have rendered passive or no consent to legal hegemony respectively). Section 4 pinpoints the mechanisms through which the labor law system mediates hegemonic relations between the state, capital, and labor, and summarizes the major arguments of this chapter.

2 The Typology of Legal Hegemony

Having systematically analyzed my fieldwork data and interviews with workers, I create a typology of legal hegemony, propounding that Chinese workers manifest five different types of attitude—affirmative, indifferent, ambivalent, critical, and radical—towards legal hegemony (see Table 1). Workers are classified into these five modes according to three criteria. The

Table 1 A self-constructed typology of worker susceptibility towards legal hegemony

	Active consent	*Passive consent*			*Complete rejection*
	Affirmative workers	*Indifferent workers*	*Ambivalent workers*	*Critical workers*	*Radical workers*
1) Relevancy of laws to workers • Level of legal knowledge • Motivation to learn about labor laws	A fair understanding of labor laws	No basic idea of labor laws. Unmotivated to learn laws	A fair understanding of labor laws	A fair understanding of labor laws	A fair understanding of labor laws
2) Degree of trust or distrust towards labor laws • To what extent they accept or reject official legal discourses and legal practices	Endorsement	No special opinions; resignation	Partial acceptance and partial discredit	Discredit	Rejection
3) Degree of susceptibility to legal hegemony • Have they identified any legal defects? • How do they account for defects?	If legal loopholes exist at all, they are caused by individuals	No special opinions; resignation	Legal loopholes are caused by individuals. Criticisms are framed with the ruling class's logics and target implementational issues	Legal loopholes are caused by individuals. Criticisms are framed with the ruling class's logics and target implementational issues	Legal defects are results of systemic socio–economic asymmetry. Active contestation of the ruling class's worldviews reproduced through the labor law system

first criterion is *the level of their knowledge of labor laws and their motivation to gain such knowledge.* This reflects if, and to what degree, workers regard labor laws as relevant to them. As will be explained, if workers have high motivation to learn about labor laws or have fair legal knowledge, they are more easily (though not necessarily) subject to legal hegemony. If they have low motivation to learn about labor laws and have poor legal knowledge, the labor law system tends to exert limited hegemonic impact on them.

The second criterion is *the degree to which workers accept or reject the labor law system, which consists of the party-state-constructed legal discourses* and *legal practices.* This reflects how much they trust or distrust the labor law system. Concerning the official legal discourses, the rule of law (*fazhi*) is one of the predominant discourses promulgated by the party-state. As elaborated on in Chap. 3, the legal system was marginalized during the Maoist period, but it has been given greater weight in the reform era. The 1982 Constitution was the first step in changing the party-state's mode of governance from basing it on the CCP's socialist policies to one based upon laws (Lubman 1999). In 1985, the NPC Standing Committee adopted a resolution that highlighted the importance of placing 'the law in the hands of the masses of people so that they will know what the law is, abide by the law, acquire a sense of legality and learn to use the law as a weapon against all acts committed in violation of the Constitution and the law' (Gallagher 2006, 793). In 1999, the PRC Constitution was amended to pronounce that China is a socialist country under the rule of law. The rule of law in China is demonstrated by the establishment of new legal institutions, a greater emphasis on procedures and rules, professionalization of legal practitioners, increasing legislation, and the reducing importance of traditional grievance resolution mechanisms (Gallagher 2006; Friedman and Lee 2010).

Prior research suggests that the Chinese party-state has promoted the rule of law to the public through law dissemination campaigns (*pufa yundong*) in institutions such as schools and workplaces (Exner 1995; Gallagher 2007), as well as with the help of the ACWF and CCYL (Exner 1995). The media also plays a crucial role in diffusing legal knowledge by covering legal news and information (Gallagher 2006). My research findings echo these studies. Some of my worker-informants first learned about the rule of law in their schools, others from online media, newspapers, and TV programs. In addition to this, some of them have become aware of the rule of law through the course of labor disputes.

The rule of law in China has been heavily criticized. Lubman (1999) highlights the discrepancy between the state's claim of upholding the rule of law and the CCP's absolute dominance over the legal system in reality, which suggests that the party-state is unwilling to establish a meaningful rule of law. Peerenboom (2002) shows greater optimism, arguing that economic reform has necessitated the party-state's increasing reliance on the legal system, which lays the foundation for the rule of law in China. Gallagher (2004) argues that the rule of law is a state-led project which offers a certain degree of political liberalization, but without compromising the CCP's political power (2006). Potter holds that China practises 'rule through law' rather than 'rule of law' because the Chinese laws do not aim to protect the rights of individuals or constrain the party-state; they are merely 'a mechanism by which political power is exercised and protected' (Potter 1999, 674). Similarly, Lee distinguishes between the rule of law and the rule by law, contending that China is only enacting the latter as its legal system is 'committed to the primacy of state power' (Lee 2002, 195).

Another important legal discourse related to labor–capital relations is rights-defense according to law, or legal rights defense (*yifa weiquan*). The 5th five-year plan for legal promulgation and education made by the Ministry of Justice and the Propaganda Department of the CCP considered making education and guidance of the popular masses to carry out legal rights defense one of the major goals, emphasizing that laws should be actively enforced within enterprises and that the government and party cadres should 'actively guide workers to learn laws and use laws…*heighten workers' awareness of legal rights defense*, of fulfilling their legal duties and of bearing their responsibilities'.[2] In 2013, when the 6th five-year plan of the Ministry of Justice began, the Ministry's goal was to bring laws to rural areas through, among other things, guiding the rural masses to carry out legal rights defense and fulfilling their legal duties.[3] However, the notion of rights defense is highly ambiguous in China (Benney 2013). It was first developed and disseminated by the party-state to direct grievances of workers and people through legal channels, but by 2001, it was appropriated and redefined by various social actors, such as rights-lawyers, workers, social groups, human rights advocates and so forth, to advance their resistance. Thereafter, the government has used the term legal rights defense less often, but it has not abandoned it completely. The party-state has never openly condemned this idea or any rights defense activities carried out within the legal realm (Benney 2013). The term is still widely used by the media, public, and some government officials.

Alongside promulgating legal discourses such as the rule of law and rights-defense in accordance with laws, the Chinese party-state has strengthened legal practices in connection to the labor law system in order to better handle volatile labor relations. These legal practices include legislating labor laws which set the minimum standards for labor issues, introducing party-state-led collective negotiation, setting up a mediation, arbitration, and litigation system (see Chap. 3), sending judges to protest spots to mediate industrial conflicts (He and Yang 2010), and so forth. As will be elucidated, if workers show a high degree of acceptance of legal discourses and legal practices, this indicates that they trust the labor law system and are susceptible to legal hegemony. On the contrary, if they demonstrate a high degree of skepticism, this implies that they distrust the labor law system and are less vulnerable to legal hegemony.

The third criterion according to which workers are classified in the typology is whether they have identified any defects in the labor law system; if yes, how they account for these defects. If workers attribute these defects to the faults of individual officials, local governments, and employers, they are considered more susceptible to legal hegemony. If they attribute these defects to systemic causes pertinent to the legal system, the state, and the market economy, they are considered less susceptible to legal hegemony. As pointed out by many scholars, workers' attribution of their suffering to structural causes is an indicator of a certain level of class consciousness (Portes 1971; Dahrendorf 1965). Therefore, the third criterion I formulate here indicates the *degree to which workers are susceptible* to the values and ideologies the labor law system reproduces.

In brief, the first criterion about the level of legal knowledge of workers and their motivation to gain such knowledge reflects the 'relevancy of laws' to workers. The second criterion on legal discourses and legal practice indicates their 'degree of trust/distrust' towards the labor law system. The third criterion on how they account for legal defects reveals their 'degree of susceptibility' to the values embodied in the labor law system. These three criteria combined will shed light on the varying degrees of impact imposed by legal hegemony on workers.

Distinguishing between the concepts of '*active consent*' and '*passive consent*' rendered by workers to capitalist leadership (Femia 1975, 32–34), I argue that the affirmative workers have granted active consent to legal hegemony whereas the indifferent, ambivalent, and critical workers have only rendered passive consent; the radical workers have rejected it altogether. Active consent indicates that workers have internalized capitalist worldviews, and their consent 'takes the form of active commitment, based on a deeply held belief that the superior position of the ruling group is legitimate' and that the capitalist class represents the interests of larger society (Femia 1987, 32). Passive consent signifies that workers have only partially assimilated into capitalist values, or that they feel the status quo is inequitable, but there is not viable alternative. Workers have developed passive consent 'not so much because the masses profoundly regard the social order as an expression of their aspirations as because they lack the conceptual tools' to conceive of viable alternatives (Femia 1987, 33).

Under my self-constructed typology, the affirmative group of workers displays active consent to legal hegemony. They feel the relevancy of labor laws to them, and have endorsed the party-state-constructed legal discourses and legal practices in such ways that they have internalized the values associated with state–capital–labor relations reproduced by laws. For this kind of worker, if legal loopholes exist at all, they are only caused by personal misbehavior rather than by manipulations of the ruling class.

The indifferent group of workers has rendered passive consent to legal hegemony as they are full of resignation and submissiveness. They face unfair treatment at work, but feel that labor laws are irrelevant to them; they do not have any basic awareness of labor laws and are unmotivated to gain that legal knowledge. Due to this sense of irrelevancy and apathy, they do not care to trust or distrust the labor law system. Neither are they concerned about the causes behind legal flaws. They simply submit themselves to the socio-political and economic status quo.

The critical group of workers discredits the legal discourses and legal practices, but this does not imply that they are not susceptible to legal hegemony. Their criticism of the labor law system is framed within the logics advocated by the state and market economy; they attribute the shortcomings of the system to individual acts and do not fundamentally question the state and the capitalist class. The ambivalent group of workers is those who hover between the affirmative and critical types. They partly endorse the official legal discourses and legal practices, yet they partly discredit them. They see the positive sides of the labor law system, but they are at the same time aware of legal loopholes which they attribute to the improper behavior of individuals rather than systemic bias. Although both the critical and ambivalent workers have not fully internalized the capitalist values, and they both have criticisms against the socio-economic and legal systems, they have partially assimilated to capitalist logics. In other words, they have conferred passive consent to capitalist hegemony that has been mediated through the labor law system.

The radical group of workers grants no consent, not even passive consent, to legal hegemony. They reject the party-state-constructed legal discourses and legal practices, thereby rejecting the dominant class's worldviews that are reproduced through the labor law system. For them, legal shortcomings are not simply the results of personal misdeeds (as the critical and ambivalent workers believe), but that of the structural social and economic asymmetry, such as unequal social relations, and the party-state's bias towards the wealthy classes.

This self-constructed typology benefits the study of legal hegemony in two ways. First, as explicated in Chap. 2, hegemony is a historical process of class struggles from which a balance of the forces between antagonistic classes is derived. Hegemony cannot be regarded as something that either exists or does not exist, or as something that the ruling class either fully possesses or does not possess. Instead of conceiving of hegemony as a zero-sum phenomenon, this typology permits us to conceptualize the differing degrees of hegemonic effect transmitted through the labor law system and the varying extents of worker susceptibility towards legal hegemony. Second, while previous studies on hegemony in China focus on how the ruling class reproduces dominance (Blecher 2002, 2004), this typology points to the possibility of transforming workers' susceptibility to legal hegemony. Ideas and values are 'neither consistent over time nor necessarily coherent' (Femia 1975, 34). Workers categorized into different modes under the typology are not stationary; their positions may shift from one mode to another over time as a result of changing life experiences and class consciousness. This possibility of transformation hints at the instability of legal hegemony and highlights the fact that it remains a product of continuous class struggles between classes in conflict.

Having formulated a critical typology of legal hegemony, in the following section, I examine the affirmative workers who have conferred active consent to legal hegemony.

3 Affirmative Workers

3.1 Workers Without Labor Dispute Experiences

Comparatively speaking, the worker-interviewees that never ran into labor disputes viewed labor laws in a more positive light, and they were quite receptive to legal hegemony. Many of them manifested an affirmative position towards labor laws and the values the laws embody.

Zhi Hui, a 23-year-old male from Hunan, is a second-generation migrant worker.[4] He completed vocational secondary school and is better educated than his parent's generation. He has been hired by a large-scale factory in Guangzhou, which supplies spare parts to Toyota, one of the biggest Japanese automobile manufacturing companies. The automobile industry is a vital pillar for the Chinese economy and has been strongly supported by the government. In 2009, China surpassed the USA to become the world's largest auto market (Hui 2011). The automobile industry demands workers that are equipped with a certain skill level, and it has recently become quite strike-prone, as exemplified by the 2010 Honda workers' strike (Chan and Hui 2012). Due to its economic significance and enterprise concern for maintaining a stable skillful workforce, employment conditions in the automobile industry are more attractive than in other industries. Zhi Hui's basic monthly salary is around 2600 yuan, double that of the Guangzhou minimum wage (which is 1300 yuan at the time of research).[5] Similar to most car factories, every year the factory distributes a lump-sum bonus to workers; in 2012, he received a bonus equivalent to 4.5 times of his basic monthly salary. Unlike workers from the shoe, garment or electronics industries, he is not required to work much overtime and can enjoy two days off every week as prescribed by the Labour Law. According to the fieldwork investigation, car factories in Guangzhou have been more willing to raise wages subsequent to the Honda strike. Many of them have started to conduct annual collective wage negotiation with their enterprise trade unions.

Zhi Hui has worked in this factory for 5 years and does not have many complaints about his job. He has a fair understanding of labor laws. For instance, while some workers are still unaware of their legal entitlement concerning overtime payment, he correctly explains that workers are entitled to 1.5 times their regular wages when working overtime on weekdays, 2 times when working on rest days, and 3 times when working on statutory holidays. He states, 'We know how to calculate overtime compensation. We keep a record of our overtime work.' On the topic of whether labor laws and the Chinese state have offered proper protections to workers, the following conversation with Zhi Hui ensued.

Researcher:	Do labour laws provide sufficient protection to workers?
Zhi Hui:	Various laws exist, but I don't have a deep understanding of them. I think the laws are fair and treat people equally, and they safeguard our legitimate interests [*hefa liyi*]. I think we can trust the laws. When we took political classes in vocational secondary school, the teachers told us that there were labour laws.
Researcher:	What did the teachers say about labour laws?
Zhi Hui:	They said the laws are just and fair, and serve the people.
Researcher:	Do you believe that?
Zhi Hui:	Yes, I do.
Researcher:	Then has the government provided sufficient protection to workers?
Zhi Hui:	How should I say this....I don't know much...um...it's ok [*hai keyi*].
Researcher:	You think it's ok?
Zhi Hui:	I've come across news report on greedy and corrupt government officials, but my friends say we shouldn't focus narrowly on one point. They say the government's big, and we shouldn't let individual officials stain our impression of the whole government, and we shouldn't conclude that the government's bad simply because of individual corrupt officials.
Researcher:	Do you agree with your friends?
Zhi Hui:	Yes, I think if the government knew about any corruption, it wouldn't tolerate it.

Zhi Hui holds a positive view of labor laws. This is probably not only because of indoctrination from his teachers, but, more importantly, is because his work experiences do not clash with official legal discourses and the image of the law implanted in him. As explicated, his factory does not simply follow legal regulations; it also offers wages and benefits that significantly exceed legal requirements. No major episode in his working life contradicts the official representation of the labor law system; therefore, he tends to accept state-constructed legal discourses.

Concerning the party-state, Zhi Hui is cognizant of government corruption and shows a slight disdain for it. He understands corruption as a result of the misbehavior of individual cadres rather than as that of systemic problems within the political system. His opinion can be explained by the decentralized politics in China. As Lee (2007) points out, local governments are responsible for economic accumulation whereas the central government is more concerned with political legitimacy. The consequences of this division are that, local governments have established close ties to business, which often use bribery of material advantage in exchange for government patronage. Conversely, in the face of grave public dissatisfaction, the central government has taken stringent measures to stamp out corruption. When compared to Jiang Zemin, the Hu-Wen government has taken corruption and bribery more seriously. The new president Xi Jinping has stepped up efforts further to combat both 'corrupt flies and tigers' (*laohu cangying yiqi da*) within the political regime. Many official circulars have been issued to ban government practices that may create opportunities for corruption.[6] It is estimated that 19 provincial cadres were suspended in 2013 due to suspected corruption.[7] The most scandalous cases were related to Liu Zhijun, the former railway minister, Bo Xilai and Zhou Yongkang, former members of the CCP Politburo, Xu Caihou, the retired deputy commander of the People's Liberation Army. For Zhi Hui and some of the informants, the central government's endeavor to fight against corruption is evidence that the government, as a whole, does not collude with business, and that the greed of individual cadres is where corruption and bribery mainly stem from.

Qiang Lai's background is quite different from Zhi Hui's.[8] He is about 40 years old and briefly lived through the socialist state period. He only has a primary school education. He moved from Sichuan to work in the cities in 1988; about 10 years ago, he was hired by a domestically owned electronics factory in Shenzhen. His basic salary equals Shenzhen's legal minimum wage (1500 yuan), which is much lower than Zhi Hui's (2600 yuan). He has a positive opinion of labor laws, remarking that 'it is better to have labor laws than be without them'. He made this comment most likely because he lived through the period when the 1995 Labour Law had not yet been legislated (he first came to work in the cities in 1988). He recalls that during the 1980s, laws were not much emphasized, and the rule of law was weakly upheld, but now they are better implemented. When he first worked in Chongqing during the 1980s, he did not possess much legal knowledge; it was only in the 1990s that he started to take initiative to learn about labor laws because 'society has changed, people should follow'. After clarification, I realized that what he means by 'changed' is that more and more labor disputes are now resolved through legal channels; he, therefore, deems it necessary to gain some legal knowledge.

Regarding whether labor laws protect workers, Qiang Lai replies that workers wish to earn better salaries, but employers want to pay less; it is therefore difficult to reach a balance. He adds:

> Laws cannot maintain a perfect balance, only a relative balance. Only when laws exist can there be standards for social practices; otherwise, there would be no [social] standards…I think labour laws are partial towards workers more than towards employers, as is the government. For example, the government and labour laws require employers to sign employment contracts with workers and buy social insurance for them.

On the topic of rights-defense according to laws, Qiang Lai comments that it is a good idea because there are laws to protect him; when he runs into labor disputes, he can resolve them through legal channels. In addition, he shows appreciation for the rule of law, which for him signifies that the NPC makes laws to regulate society, and that people have to comply with them after promulgation. The rule of law, according to him, is adequately implemented in China; evidence lies in the improvement of public safety over the years. Both Zhi Hui and Qiang Lai endorse the labor law system, albeit for different reasons. Zhi Hui's affirmation is due to external impositions of the party-state-constructed legal discourses, which fit squarely within his lived experiences as a post-90s worker hired by a law-abiding factory. Qiang Lai's approval stems from a comparison between his present experience and his former exposure during the early reform period when labor laws and the rule of law were not yet promoted.

Qiang Lai's principal concern is low wages; his 1500 yuan monthly salary hardly allows him to accumulate any savings. Talking about China's economic development and opening up, the following dialogue occured.

Researcher: In your opinion, what changes have been brought about by the economic reform?

Qiang Lai: Following China's opening up, we can now go to work and earn money in the cities. The supply of electronic appliances was limited in the pre-reform days, but now we have better material lives. Before the reform, we were contained within small towns and couldn't travel across provinces, but now we can move around easily to get a job.

Researcher: What do you think about the wealth gap in China?

Qiang Lai: It's huge.

Researcher: What are the causes?

Qiang Lai: Those who were born in the 1980s received more education than those who were born in the 1970s; they, therefore, earn more. Regional difference is another reason; the coastal areas are better developed than the inland areas. This is related to the government's policies, which were to first conduct economic reform in the coastal areas. It started to promote western development (*xibu kaifa*) only after 2000.

Researcher: Have you heard the slogan 'let some people get rich first'?

Qiang Lai: Yes, it was proposed by Deng Xiaoping.

Researcher: What do you think about it? Is it a good policy?

Qiang Lai: It's good if implemented well; it's bad if poorly carried out.

Researcher: Could you explain more?

Qiang Lai: If those who get rich first help other people get rich, then it's a good policy. If they get rich but don't help others, then it's bad policy.

Researcher: Which scenario is happening in China?

Qiang Lai: I think it's the former case [i.e., it's good policy]. After some people get wealthy, they become employers and hire us. This has boosted the Chinese economy.

Qiang Lai provides two explanations for the serious wealth gap in China, as reflected by the proximity to 0.5 on the Gini coefficient scale.[9] The first explanation is tied to the personal attributes of workers—some people earn less because they are less educated. This reflects the liberal market ideology of individualism, self-sufficiency, and self-reliance that has emerged in the reform period, replacing collectivism and the socialist state ethos (Won 2004). This new ideology offers workers, like Qiang Lai, individual explanations to socially created problems—workers are poor because they lack the qualities that would make them self-sufficient and self-reliant rather than because of the capitalist mode of production. The liberal ideology disseminates the idea that some people received more education, and therefore, they have acquired the qualities that enable them to sell their labor power for higher prices.

His second explanation is the state's uneven developmental strategies. He is right that the social inequality in China is rooted to state policies. The party-state took advantage of the expansion of global capitalism to turn the country into a global manufacturing hub. It has ensured an abundant supply of labor by abolishing work units and communes, and by loosening the household registration system (hukou) to allow peasants to work in the cities (Solinger 1999). It also suppresses labor costs by keeping the legal minimum wage much lower than average wages in cities,[10] by turning a blind eye to company legal violations, and by banning independent worker organizations which would strengthen workers' collective bargaining power vis-à-vis employers (see Chap. 3). In addition, it has put abundant resources into the socio-economic advancement of southeastern China, but neglected the development of western and inland areas until recently (McNally 2004). Plainly speaking, the party-state's uneven developmental strategies have turned some social groups into the wealthy class at the expense of the majority. Qiang Lai is dissatisfied with his low wages and the widening wealth-gap in China; he understands well that they are the results of the state's biased policies. However, paradoxically, he believes that these policies are, overall, beneficial to workers because they are now given the opportunity to work and earn money, and they can also take part in some material enjoyment, which they were denied before the reform.

Qiang Lai shows strong approval of capitalist economic development, though he does not benefit much from it in terms of wages. He regards his personal interests and the Chinese economy as closely tied to the success of a particular social class, which has been able to create job opportunities for workers ['After some people get rich, they become employers and hire us. This has boosted the Chinese economy']. Other interviewees share a similar view. One of them notes, 'It would help the employment situation if the government supports businesses. If companies earn more, we, as their employees, will take pride in them. If the government helps the enterprises, it will benefit us, too, because it will be easier for us to get a job'.[11] This 'common sense', or 'spontaneous feeling' (Gramsci 1971, 198) about economic development is widely held by my informants, although it does not serve their interests. Qiang Lai and some workers endorse the party-state's policy of 'let some people get rich first', which resembles the liberal 'trickle-down' theory whereby the government's support of businesses and the rich will subsequently benefit other members of society because the capitalist class will have driven the economy as a whole. Viewed from a Gramscian perspective, Qiang Lai has conferred active consent to the capitalist leadership and interprets his living experience from the dominant class's worldviews—a neo-liberal framework that sees capitalists as creating jobs for workers and economic prosperity for the country, rather than a perspective that views employers as exploitative. This reflects that to a certain degree, the capitalist class in China has gained a trans-class appeal, and its interests are being universalized as the interests of both the working class and the country.

Acquiescing to capitalist hegemony does not imply that Qiang Lai is oblivious to the negative impacts imposed by the market economy, such as the widening wealth gap and social inequality. However, these side effects are somehow offset by the labor law system, which he considers able to do him justice. Qiang Lai thinks that the government prejudices towards workers more than towards employers because labor laws require employers to sign labor contracts with workers and buy social insurance for them. Moreover, he believes he can entrust workplace disputes to the legal system, should they arise in future. Qiang Lai's viewpoints demonstrate that labor laws have buffered the market economy and the state from fundamental criticism. First, labor laws make Qiang Lai feel as if the current socio-economic system is not completely unfair or biased, and that the exploitation he encounters is not systemic; if his employer were to commit any wrongdoings, he would be able to seek redress through the labor law system. In other words, Qiang Lai deems the labor law system to be able to curb misdeeds in the economic sphere, rather than seeing it as an apparatus that facilitates economic accumulation through sanctioning capitalist exploitation (as explained in Chap. 3). Second, for Qiang Lai, the 'protection' given by labor law is proof that the state cares about workers. He, therefore, does not attribute his personal poverty to the party-state's bias towards the wealthy class. And he does not blame the party-state as a whole for the plight of workers.

It is important to note that legal hegemony is not equivalent to a false consciousness imposed on workers (Jessop 1982). In order to acquire worker acquiescence to capitalist leadership and forestall them from revolting against the capitalist system, the ruling bloc has to grant concessions on secondary issues to them. In China, these concessions have partly taken the form of legal protections that are compatible with the capitalist juridico-political structures (see Chap. 3). The reform of the labor mediation, arbitration, and litigation systems, the promulgation of the Labour Law and the Labour Contract Law, etc. are legal concessions fought for by the working class. They contradict the short-term interests of individual capitalists, but through the above-elaborated buffering effects on state–capital–labor relations, at the same time, they help strengthen the leadership of the capitalist class in the long run.

The buffering effects of the labor law system are observable in many of my informants. In her early 20s, Xiao Mei came from Shanxi to work in a domestically owned electronics factory in Shenzhen in 2007.[12] After a few years of effort, she became a team leader of a production line. She has a reasonable understanding of labor laws; in our interview, she keenly explained to me the implementation of the 2011 Social Insurance Laws in Shenzhen. She complains that inflation is too high, and her salary can hardly keep up.[13] Working as much overtime as she can, every month she earns about 3000 yuan, from which over 800 yuan are spent on rent and about another 1500 yuan on food, water, electricity, and other daily necessities. Since her little brother is studying at home, she also needs to send money back to her parents. Therefore, there is not much left for her savings.

Researcher: Do you think workers are sharing the fruits of the economic growth?

Xiao Mei: We can't catch up in many aspects…we haven't benefited much from the rapid development. Although our wages have gone up, prices increase faster.

Researcher: Has economic development brought about any positive impact?

Xiao Mei: It probably has. At least our country has grown stronger. This is not really related to us, but when our country is strong, other countries will respect it in regards to issues like the Diaoyu Islands.

Researcher: What are the benefits for workers if our country is strong?

Xiao Mei: For us….we can't get any substantial benefit in economic terms, I think probably not much. It [China being a strong nation] doesn't affect us much. However, it'll be good for us if our nation is stable. If it were stable, we wouldn't have much to worry about.

Researcher: So you want our country to grow stronger, right?

Xiao Mei: Yes. Who wants their own nation to be worse off than others'? I suppose everybody thinks like this.

Researcher: Have you heard about the slogan 'let some people get rich first'?

Xiao Mei: This means letting a group of people become wealthy first, and they'll then help others get rich…this is what our textbooks in school say.

Researcher: What do you think about this?

Xiao Mei: I think it's what ought to be done. *If there are no employers, how can people like us get jobs, right? Only when they're rich and successful can they hire us.*

Researcher: Don't you think some employers earn a lot but still don't pay workers decent wages?

Xiao Mei: I haven't thought about this much. Even when I think about it, there's no way to change it, right? *It's ok as long as employers pay our wages according to the Labour Law.* I've already worked in this factory for 5 years and there haven't been any labour disputes. Basically this factory is ok.

Despite her complaint that inflation grew faster than her wages, she still expresses approval towards the meager wages offered by employers. For her, if employers do not violate the Labour Law, then paying workers low wages is not unjust. Such a belief in the legitimacy and authority of labor laws is commonly held by workers who have never been involved in labor disputes. One female worker remarks, 'I go to work according to schedule; it is fair and just, so long as my employer does not underpay me.'[14] Another male worker notes that 'labor laws must have been passed for good reason. They were made by professionals; they, thus, must have taken into consideration national and social needs'.[15] Another male interviewee comments that 'laws are products of many peoples' efforts and are made by the nation, therefore, they have their legitimacy'.[16] Social and legal structures are the aggregate consequences of the actions of people in the past; yet the elaboration and continuation of these structures over time makes them appear as external objects to social actors (Archer 1982). Labour laws are one such object for some workers; they seldom go so far as to challenge whether the legal contents are just, or to question the unequal power relations dictating the law-making process. For these workers, laws are credible and authoritative yardsticks for judging employers—if employers act lawfully, then there is no ground to blame them for the plight of workers.

Moreover, although Xiao Mei feels that workers do not share the fruit of economic progress, she nonetheless endorses the state's developmental policy of 'let some people get rich first', which favors certain social classes over another. She does not attribute workers' exclusion from economic prosperity to the state's support to the capitalist class. Similar to Qiang Lai, she interprets her work experiences from a neo-liberal lens, which conceives of capitalists as creating jobs and driving the economy rather than exploiting workers. Xiao Mei does not question the unbalanced economic development, which has led to meager wages of workers, not only because of her employer's lawful acts, but also because of nationalist sentiments. She deems economic growth as not so much related to herself individually as to the nation. Although she recognizes that she has not benefited from China being strong, she considers it important for China to be powerful so that it can possess political and economic leverage over other countries. The Diaoyu Island dispute she mentioned refers to a long-running dispute between China and Japan over a group of outlying islands in the East China Sea, which are believed to contain rich natural resources. Over the years, the two countries have, from time to time, incurred serious political strife over the islands. In 2012, after the Japanese government nationalized the Diaoyu Islands, the relationship between the two countries turned sour. In China, numerous protests against the Japanese government broke out in August and September that year. The news reported that some Japanese brand cars parked by the roadside were damaged by demonstrators,[17] and a Japanese diplomat in Beijing was stopped in his car by demonstrators who removed the Japanese flag from his car.[18]

Xiao Mei's national sentiment, as expressed in her comment on the Diaoyu Islands, is also witnessed in other informants. A female worker remarks, 'I have not gained any personal benefits from the economic development, but it is good for the country.' [19] As a matter of fact, one important ideological construction of the Chinese party-state is nationalism and anti-western sentiments. No longer organizing the people according to class, the party-state now seeks to maintain its legitimacy partly by appealing to national identity (Zhao 1998; Breslin 2007). Chinese nationalism has fostered people's sense of pride in the country's economic success, as well as creates an impression that some Western countries are attempting to suppress China's development; for this reason, the party-state needs to defend national interests (Breslin 2007). This nationalistic and anti-western ideology has helped mobilize people from all classes, including victims of high-speed growth like Xiao Mei, to support the party-state and economic development. In China, hegemony is not only about approving the market economy; it is simultaneously blended with state-led nationalism, which has added a national-popular appearance to the capitalist leadership.

3.2 Workers with Individual Labor Dispute Experiences

In comparison to workers who encountered no industrial disputes previously, workers who have experienced industrial disputes (individual and collective alike) have nurtured a better understanding of labor laws and legal procedures for dispute resolution. Some of them even assist fellow workers in need with active cases in the capacity of volunteers, agent ad litem (*gongmin daili*), or NGO staff.

Qing Fa is 28 years old and has completed vocational school.[20] In 2011 he worked in an electronics factory in Shenzhen, but his employer decided not to hire him after the probationary period for unspecified reasons. Moreover, asserting that Qing Fa performed his duties poorly, his boss only paid him half of the monthly wages for a month of work. Qing Fa lodged a complaint with the labor bureau, but action was only taken after he had gone to the office four times. The labor bureau officer called his boss to enquire about the case, after which a mediation meeting was held between Qing Fa and his boss. At the end, his employer paid him back the other half of his monthly salaries.

Qing Fa holds a high opinion of the labor law system, most likely because he managed to retrieve his half-month wages through labor mediation. He states:

> In my case, labour mediation helps a lot. *The labour bureau officers have the capability to implement the laws, but sometime they just don't do it.* Actually, *they have improved a lot*; many government officials are now scared of people's complaints because these may affect their careers. Some government officials may appear indifferent; but *if you are persistent and determined enough to go through the process, they will have to handle your case properly.* On the contrary, if you go to the labour bureau just once or twice, they won't handle your case seriously. *The key to rights-defense is persistence and determination.* If you don't strive for your own interests, they won't help you.

Qing Fa rightly points out the problem of weak legal implementation, which has been highlighted by many studies (Gallagher 2004; Wang et al. 2009; Lubman 1999). When I asked him if poor legal enforcement was caused by the government's bias towards employers, Qing Fa firmly said no. He reiterates, 'as long as you are determined to defend your rights, they will help you, and you will get what you deserve. But this process may be quite long and complicated because they need time to verify and discuss your case.' When explaining why some workers cannot successfully defend their interests, he puts the blame on their inadequate persistence and determination rather than on the loose implementation of labor laws or the government's ineffective monitoring of enterprises ['The key to rights-defense is persistence and determination. If you don't strive for your own interests, they won't help you']. In other words, he attributes workers' suffering to their own psychological and behavioral shortcomings rather than deeming it a failure of the labor law system.

Despite Qing Fa's affirmation towards the labor law system, he does notice its weaknesses. When I asked him if China was a society based on the rule of law, he responded:

> *Government departments have the capacity to enforce laws, but in many cases, they do not do their jobs.* At the moment, *we have laws, but they are ill-implemented.* If you complain to a government department, the officers will say that they are busy, and they always delay handling your case. If you urge them, they will tell you that they don't just serve you, and that they have to take care of many other matters. They are very polite, but they just don't help you resolve the disputes.

Qing Fa attributes the failure of the labor law system in protecting workers to the irresponsibility of government officers rather than to the party-state's systemic bias towards capitalists.

In his mid-forties, Ah Wen has been working in the cities since 1985.[21] Belonging to the first generation of migrant workers who witnessed China's opening up, he opines that Chinese society has become better after the economic reform because 'at least peasants from villages can come to work in the cities', and they now 'have greater access to education'. At the same time, however, he notes that workers do not benefit from China's economic development—'although our wages have gone up, prices have become very high. It's very hard to raise a family'.

Ah Wen's finger was cut by a machine in an accident when he worked in a metal factory in Dongguan. According to the Regulation on Work-Related Injury Insurance, employers have a legal responsibility to apply to the Social Security Department for a determination of work-related injury (*gongshang rending*) within 30 days of the occurrence of the incident. Should employers fail to comply with this, worker-victims can apply for the determination themselves within a year. Assuming that the employers concerned had contributed to the Work-Related Injury Insurance for their workers according to law (which may not often be the case), the Insurance should pay for medical expenses and food subsidies for victims during the period of medical treatment (*yi liaoqi*). In addition, the employers have to pay victims their average monthly salaries until they have recuperated and are able to return to work. After the victims recover, or when their health situation stabilizes, an assessment of work capability (*laodong nengli jianding*) to determine the level of permanent harm that has been inflicted by the work injury to the victims' work performance capabilities must be conducted. The employers have to pay a lump sum compensation in accordance with the assessments.

On the surface, the legal procedures related to the handling of work injuries seem straightforward and protective of workers. However, in reality, many injured workers encounter obstacles when asserting their legal rights. In the case of Ah Wen, his factory initially agreed that the accident was work-related and the Social Security Department had already determined so. Nonetheless, after Ah Wen conducted the assessment of work capabilities, his employer started to dispute that the accident was work connected. His boss argued that Ah Wen did not immediately report the accident or go to the hospital right after the accident broke out, but only did so on the following day; it was, therefore, possible that he did not hurt himself at work. His employer applied to the Dongguang city government for administrative reconsideration (*xingzheng fuyi*) of the case, which adhered to the initial decision that his injury was work-related.[22] His boss then filed an appeal to the court against the decision of the Social Security Department; the court case was yet to be heard at the time of our interview.

Ah Wen believes that the labor law system is fair and can protect workers. Similar to Qiang Lai, having lived through a period when most labor laws were not yet enacted probably makes him feel the positive impact of labor laws on workers. He opines that 'the laws made by the central government are very just and fair', but their implementation at the local level is unsatisfactory. He takes the Labour Contract Law as an example, pointing out that although it requires employers to sign labor contracts with workers, many of them, including his employer, do not do so; many government officials simply turned a blind eye to the situation. In other words, for him, the labor law system is protective of workers, but the personal misdeeds of employers and government officials have contributed to its lax enforcement.

Ah Wen demonstrates a trust in labor laws and gives them his active consent.

Researcher:	What do you think about your boss? Are you angry with him?
Ah Wen:	Being angry or not makes no difference. *I act according to laws.* If he loses the court case, he has to compensate me. Even if I'm angry, it's useless. *Things need to be decided through the legal platform.*
Researcher:	Were you scared when talking to your employer and the labour bureau officers?
Ah Wen:	There is nothing to be scared of. No matter how high-ranking they are, they're just human beings; I am a human being, too. *We're equal before the law.* What should I be scared of? *It's fine as long as I don't violate any laws.*
Researcher:	If your employer wins the court case, what will you do?
Ah Wen:	I will appeal to the intermediary court.
Researcher:	Will you consider taking extra-legal actions?
Ah Wen:	*I will only consider legal means.*
Researcher:	Why?
Ah Wen:	*If the judge rules that my boss is wrong, then he must be wrong. But if the judge decides that this is not a work injury, I probably don't have any legal grounds; then I'll accept it.*

The above dialogue illustrates that labor laws simultaneously embolden and debilitate Ah Wen's rights-defense. First, they lend confidence to him. Acting through legal channels assures him that he has done the 'right thing' and that he possesses the right to do the 'right thing' ['It is fine as long as I do not violate any laws']. Moreover, laws make him feel that his boss and government officials are not superior, but are 'human beings' like him ['We are equal before the laws']. In this regard, the Chinese labor laws wield a positive impact, however limited, on workers, providing a weapon for their resistance and boosting their courage to assert their rights (within legal boundaries). This observation echoes the reminder by some scholars that laws, despite their capitalist nature, are not completely detrimental (Poulantzas 2000), and that the working class can utilize them proactively to safeguard their interests (Thompson 1977), as will be elaborated more in the next two chapters.

On the other hand, labor laws debilitate Ah Wen's activism by shaping his values and constricting his actions within legal channels. For him, labor laws and courts rulings are authoritative yardsticks of what are right and what are not—if the judge rules that his boss loses the case, then his boss must be wrong; otherwise, his claims are not well grounded. This demonstrates how the labor law system has justified his employer's actions, even though the boss is considered unscrupulous from a critical point of view; the legal justifications confound Ah Wen from discerning that labor laws are skewed towards the dominant class. Moreover, labor laws have become a guide for Ah Wen's actions. Should he lose the court case related to his work injury, he would only 'consider the legal means' as a follow-up; actions beyond the legal platform are out of the question for him. Other interviewees of mine also express the same kind of legal conformity. One stresses, 'If I lose my case, I won't take extra-legal actions. It's helpless. I think we should only use legal means to resolve disputes.'[23]

Concerning the dispute with his employer, Ah Wen once sought legal advice from a labor NGO. He never approached trade unions for aid as he 'doesn't know much about them' and thought 'they wouldn't help'. Some of my interviewees share this feeling, and therefore, resort to NGOs for assistance. One interviewee remarks, 'I never went to consult trade unions because they are only a formality; they can't do or say much for workers. Although their money comes from workers, they are under the leadership of the government.'[24] Another worker shares, 'The staff and participants in labor NGOs are friendlier; there is no distance between us. Rights-defense is easy on paper, but it is very challenging in reality. The NGO staff have helped me a lot.'[25]

Ah Rong, in his mid-forties, first came from his hometown in Yunnan to work in the cities in 2000.[26] For him, the economic reform has positively influenced workers' lives because it has attracted numerous foreign companies to invest in China, which in turn improves people's living standards and job opportunities. Since 2005, he has been working in an electronics factory in Shenzhen. Unfortunately, he hurt his back in 2011 when moving heavy boxes in the workplace. His employer denies responsibility for his work injury. Therefore, he appealed to the Labour Bureau, Social Security Bureau, and eventually to the court to resolve the dispute, which was still ongoing at the time of our interview. This was not the first industrial dispute he had run into. In 2005, when he worked in another factory, his boss did not pay him legal overtime compensation. He complained to the Labour Bureau and the Social Security Department a number of times. Initially, they did not give him any proper feedback; he thus kept calling them. Later, he went to talk to the official in charge, after which she called the factory manager and pressured him to rectify the problem. At the end, his boss gave him back the due compensation.

Although Ah Rong faced huge obstacles when championing his rights, he views the labor law system in a positive light.

Ah Rong: *Labour laws are quite fair* and can protect workers, who are a marginalized social group (*ruoshi qunti*). Employers are in superior positions; when they like, they give you more, but when they don't, they give you nothing. Luckily, *the labor laws made by the central government contain compulsory regulations* that employers must follow. Many regulations are clearly written into laws; *the problem is that they can't be fully implemented.*

Researcher: What do you think about the labour bureaus? Do they protect workers or enterprises?

Ah Rong: I think the *labour bureaus at the street-level are slanted towards employers, who have brought them tremendous advantages.* Many enterprises regularly present gifts to Labour Bureau officers. My factory even organised a free trip to Taiwan for them. The Labour Bureaus and the street-level governments want to keep businesses in their districts so that they can save up some wealth. Comparing the contributions made by workers to that by enterprises, which one's greater in the eyes of the street-level governments? For the district government, who's deemed to have created economic growth?

Researcher: What do you think about the Social Security Department?

Ah Rong: I think it's better. Judging from how it's handled my work-injury case, I can tell it's fairer. Overall, *government departments above the district level are fairer and more neutral* because they don't have a tight economic relation with enterprises in the community; their interests are, therefore, not closely linked to enterprises. They'll examine your case from a more objective position.

Ah Rong distinguishes between government officers/departments above the district level and those at the district level or below, suggesting that the more distant (in terms of hierarchical positions) the government officers are from enterprises at the community level, the more neutral they are; the closer they are to enterprises, the more biased they are towards the latter, and thus, less willing to enforce labor laws. His observations echo the findings of some studies. Naughton (2008) notes that local officials have forged close alliances with local businesses. Lee maintains that local government officials have benefited individually and collectively from taxes and management fees collected from enterprises; this has given rise to the 'permissive regime of labour regulation' (Lee 2002, 201).

Ah Rong is right to point out the variations within the Chinese government regarding their bureaucratic practices and relationships with firms. However, the belief that higher-level government departments and the central state are more autonomous from businesses, and that they seek to constrain enterprises with labor laws, is disputable. As Friedman and Lee underscore, violations of labor rights 'cannot be attributed to the activity of a few "bad apples", but rather, are a fundamental feature of the model of development that the Chinese state has pursued over the past 30 years' (2010, 513). The labor law system creates the perception that the central state is relatively autonomous from the capitalists. Ah Rong considers labor laws fair and protective of workers because the central government has made them mandatory ['the labor laws made by the central government contain compulsory regulations that employers must follow']. Although he is aware of the implementation problems of the labor law system, he attributes them to the close ties between district-level governments and businesses in the community rather than to the inbred tendency of the whole government towards capitalist accumulation. The labor law system has shifted his criticism from the central government's development strategies and the deep-seated state–capital collusion to the misdeeds of individual government officers or local governments.

After the outbreak of his labor disputes, Ah Rong actively equips himself with legal knowledge through reading books on labor laws. Like Ah Wen, he also sought assistance from a labor NGO staff, who visited him and other work injury victims in the hospital. Subsequent to his release from the hospital, he frequently visited the NGO, attending their classes on labor laws, forums on social affairs, and various educational activities. Additionally, as he has become more knowledgeable about labor laws that are connected to work injury, he often joins the NGO's outreach activities in industrial areas to provide legal consultation to workers in need. Ah Rong holds high opinions of labor NGOs:

> Labor NGOs help workers exercise their rights which are enshrined by labor laws; they teach us laws and tell us about our rights. Various government departments provide legal services, but those offered by the district-level governments are skewed towards employers. They don't treat our concerns seriously, always shifting their responsibilities or delaying actions.

The experience of labor disputes and positive encounters with labor NGOs do not only heighten Ah Rong's awareness of labor rights, but also imbue in him a feeling of class identification and empathy. Wherever he goes now, and whenever he sees workers taking actions to defend their rights, he stops and observes them. When opportunities arise, he talks to them, finding out their problems and giving them information on rights-defense. This is because he 'know[s] how they feel' and 'workers are walking the same path (*tonglu ren*)'. Ah Rong's rights-defense was triggered by his employer's challenge to his economic interests. The negative experiences with government officials, the NGO's support of his rights assertion, and the encounter with other workers in the NGO made him realize that the conflict with his boss was not a particular or discrete instance, and that there exist wider antagonisms between workers as a social group and employers. Due to his understanding of the shared positions and interests of workers, he has taken initiative to help other workers.

3.3 Workers with Collective Labor Dispute Experiences

Liu Chi is in his early thirties and has completed college-level education.[27] He has worked for 4 years as a quality-control engineer in a factory that supplies a Japanese automobile brand in Guangzhou. In 2010, the Honda workers in Foshan struck for 17 days to demand an 800 yuan monthly wage increase and the democratic reform of their workplace trade union; this sparked a wave of extra-trade union strikes in the automobile industry and other industries in the PRD (Chan and Hui 2012; Hui 2011). According to Chen Weiguang, the president of the Guangzhou Federation of Trade Unions at the time, several tens of thousands of workers from over 60 factories in Guangzhou walked out over wage issues in the 2 months following the Honda strike.[28] Liu Chi was hired by one of these striking factories, which employed about 1200 workers. Workers in this factory went on strike for one and a half days to demand a 500 yuan monthly wage increase and better benefits. The Labour Bureau officials and management came to talk to the strikers, pressuring them to resume working. After some negotiations between the strike representatives and management, the company raised worker monthly wages by 300 yuan.

Some workers informed Liu Chi about the walkout and mobilized him to join it. Strongly agreeing with the strike demands, he followed other workers by halting work. It was his first strike experience. He comments that the momentum of this strike came from the rank-and-file workers and technical workers, whose wages were inadequately low; 'a few hundred yuan wage increase is crucial to us, though it means nothing to the managerial-level staff, who earn high salaries'. When asked if he was worried about retaliation from management for walking out, he responded: 'I was not afraid at that time because so many workers joined the strike. The factory would not fire all of us because if it did so nobody would be producing for it.' A combination of factors drove Liu Chi to participate in the strike. First, his (and other workers') meagre wages provided a material incentive for his walkout. Second, subjected to peer influence, he felt emboldened by the collectivity of and solidarity among the strikers. While labor laws emboldened Ah Wen (Sect. 3.2) to pursue his interests, Liu Chi demonstrated that workers' collectivity could also spur worker resistance. Third, Liu Chi understood well that labor power hinged on their productive capacity, and hence, did not fear retaliation or losing his job for walking out.

Upon the district-level trade union's request, the workplace trade union in Liu Chi's factory was set up in 2008. Not much different from typical Chinese trade unions, it focused mostly on provision of welfare to workers, such as organizing recreational activities and gift-giving to workers at the time of festivals. However, its failure to address workers' concerns, such as poor wages and welfare, provoked workers to bypass the workplace union and walk out. As pointed out, similar strike stories were witnessed in other automobile factories in the PRD following the Honda strike. In light of this, the Guangdong Federation of Trade Unions subsequently took greater initiative to promote workplace union elections and collective wage negotiation in the automobile industry to stabilize volatile labor relations. As a result, 'democratic' and 'direct' trade union elections and wage bargaining became more common in automobile factories.[29] The higher level trade unions now provide more training and assistance concerning wage bargaining to trade union officials in some automobile factories.[30]

Additionally, in 2011 the Federation of Trade Unions for the Spare Auto Parts Industry was set up in the Guangzhou Economic and Technological Development Zone to advance unionization and wage negotiation in the industry.[31] In the wake of this development, Liu Chi ran for the workplace trade union election in 2011 and was elected as the union official. He remarks, 'After the strike, I think I can help improve worker well-being through talking to the boss via the platform of a trade union; therefore, I decided to run for the election.' The strike experience made him realize the opposing interests between workers and management, motivating him to take steps to further workers' common interests.

Subsequent to the strike, Liu Chi notes, the company became less autocratic and would consult the trade union before making important decisions. In the past, the management never conducted wage negotiations with the trade union, but now it is done once every year. He, as a trade union official, participated in the wage negotiations in 2012. In his opinion, labor laws, especially those related to collective consultation, are fair and just; they are of 'great use' to workers because they lay down the direction and procedures for wage negotiation so that the company cannot unilaterally decide workers' pay raises as it did previously. His positive assessment of labor laws is grounded on a comparison between the period when his factory conducted no wage negotiations and that wherein it follows legal guidelines to negotiate wages with the trade union. In this sense, Liu Chi is similar to some affirmative workers in this chapter, whose endorsement of the labor law system is based on the feeling that they are now better protected by labor laws than during the period wherein no or few labor laws existed.

When I asked Liu Chi how his trade union pressured the company to agree to higher wage increases during negotiations, he replied:

> We can negotiate for as long of a period as we want; the longer the negotiation lasts, the greater the pressure facing the company. The workers' salaries increase every year in July and they have already built up an expectation around this. *If the company does not do so, workers get restless and easily take radical actions such as strikes; this would seriously affect production* or even that of other supplying factories.

Liu Chi is cognizant of workers' workplace bargaining power derived from their strategic position in the car industry (Silver 2003; Wright 2000). In the PRD, many industrial zones are established for car making, wherein supplying factories specialized in producing automobile components cluster together to expedite Post-Fordist just-in-time production. When strikes break out in one of these factories that constitutes the production chain, workers in other supplying factories quickly learn the news because their production would soon be affected by the striking factory.[32] This echoes what Silver propounds about '...workers who are enmeshed in tightly integrated production processes, where a localized work stoppage in a key node can cause disruptions on a much wider scale than the stoppage itself' (Silver 2003: 13). The fieldwork reveals that many automotive workers are aware of their workplace bargaining power. One of them says, 'If management does not agree to our wage proposals, we will go on strike. This will bring a great loss to the company, and may also affect nearby car factories'.[33]

When asked what constitutes a fair wage, Liu Chi stresses:

> The legal minimum wage is not enough for worker survival. *A fair pay rise should take into consideration inflation, food prices, companies' profits, and so forth.* Factories should adequately distribute their profits to workers as wages. However, *when there isn't much profit, workers shouldn't be too aggressive and opening their mouths wide like hungry lions* (*shizi kai dakou*). Our boss is a capitalist, who regardless, needs to extract surplus value from workers and maximize profits; he has no reason for making a deficit in order to raise worker wages.

Unlike Xiao Mei (sect. 3.1) who considers her employer fair for paying her legal minimum wage, Liu Chi does not deem legal minimum wage just. Instead, he reckons that workers' wages should be set in relation to the price level and enterprise profits. At the same time, however, he shows an understanding, if not approval, of the core capitalist practices: appropriation of surplus value and maximization of profits, believing that workers' wage increases should be linked to company profits (i.e., the realization of surplus value) rather than workers' input or the value produced by workers. The higher-level trade union officials stress to him that workers are a part of the company, and thus, should think for the company and not request 'unreasonable' wage increases. Liu Chi's opinions reveal that although higher-level trade unions and government have promoted wage bargaining more actively, which grants workers salaries higher than the legal minimum standards, they at the same time seek to 'manufacture consent' (Burawoy

1979) among workers towards a 'reasonable' level of wage increase, which is argued to be linked to company profits.

Cai Lin is in her early thirties and has finished junior high school in her hometown in Guanxi.[34] She works in a Japanese electronics factory in Shenzhen. Compared to the automobile industry, wages and employment conditions in the electronics industry are worse off. Most electronics factories in the PRD pay workers salaries that are equal to or even lower than the legal minimum wage (Smith et al. 2006), but automotive worker salaries are usually higher than the legal requirement, and collective wage negotiations have become more commonly witnessed in automobile factories after the 2010 strike wave. Electronics workers are usually not well educated (some of whom have not even completed primary school) and less skillful than car worker (many of whom are graduates from vocational secondary schools). As explicated previously, automobile workers possess strong workplace bargaining power, but their counterparts in electronics factories do not. It is because they produce cheap, low-end products, and thus, their skills are highly replaceable. Moreover, the labor regime in electronics factories tends to be despotic (Lee 1995); arbitrary and disciplinary managerial practices are commonly witnessed (Xue 2008). In contrast, following the promotion of 'direct' elections and collective wage negotiation in the automotive industry in the PRD, as explained earlier, the labor regime in car factories has shown signs of transforming into the hegemonic regime (Burawoy 1979; Chan and Hui 2016).

In Cai Lin's factory, workers have to work overtime everyday, and they only enjoy two rest days per month, rather than four days as stipulated by the Labour Law. Workers have to apply for permission from their supervisors before going to the washroom. They are allowed to excuse themselves for at most once every 2 hours and for no more than 5 minutes each time; otherwise, they are fined. Moreover, workers can be fined 20–50 yuan for talking to each other, using cell phones, not tidying up their hair and so forth while working. Cai Lin comments, 'I have learnt nothing from working in this factory. Everyday, I spend 10 hours in a work space of one meter square; my work is meaningless.'

Cai Lin's monthly wages totaled 480 yuan when she first joined this factory in 2004. When the government increases the minimum wage rate, her salary is adjusted upwards to the new level. She remarks that the minimum wage can only feed workers with enough food, but not nutritious food; it only keeps them from dying. Cai Lin is correct in her

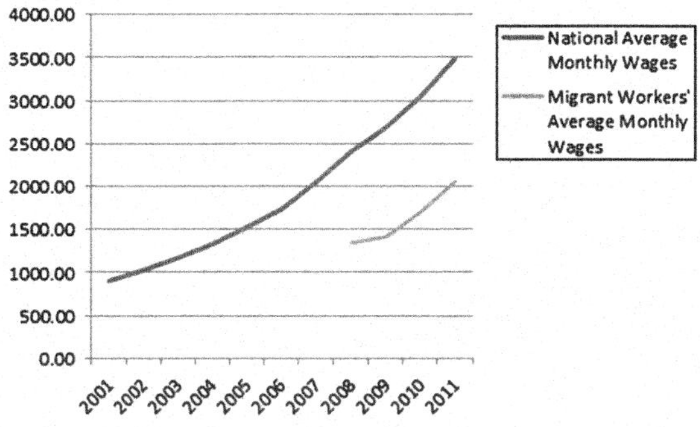

Graph 1 Comparison between migrant worker average monthly wages and the national average. *Source* China Labour Bulletin 2013 (Compiled with data from National Bureau of Statistics, China Statistical Yearbook 2012) http://www.clb.org.hk/en/content/wages-china

observation. Although the 2004 Provisions on Minimum Wage suggests that the minimum wage should be set around 40–60% of the average monthly wage in the corresponding city, the levels in many cities are still below this benchmark.[35] Moreover, the average monthly wages of migrant workers are far below the national average; in 2011, the former was about 75% less than the latter (see Graph 1). In addition, workers' pay raises are often partly, if not largely, cancelled out by the high inflation rate of food products; in 2008 and 2011, inflation was only slightly lower than the average wage increase of workers (see Graph 2).

Despite the complaint that her wage cannot afford her a decent living, Cai Lin does not show great dissatisfaction because it is 'in line with legal standards, and the boss does follow regulations for the minimum wage'. It is of little use, she opines, to bring the issues of wages and benefits to the company's attention because it already follows labor laws. In other words, labor laws have stopped her from proactively questioning the minimum wage system, which indeed helps keep worker wages at a low level. However, when workers act collectively, it becomes easier for them to overcome legal boundaries. In 2010, Cai Lin's factory decided to reduce the time for each production process from 44 to 39 seconds in order to boost labor productivity; this made the workers furious. Furthermore, workers were discontented with their meager wages (1200 yuan at the time) and poor benefits. They, therefore, staged a wild-cat strike for less

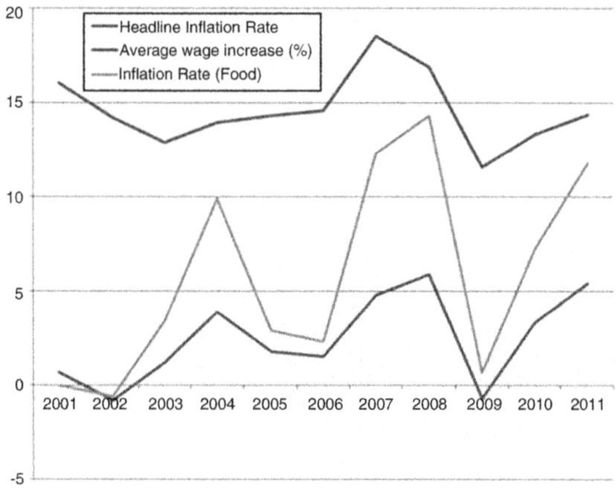

Graph 2 Worker average wage increase and inflation rates. *Source* China Labour Bulletin 2013 (Compiled with data from China Statistical Yearbook 2012) http://www.clb.org.hk/en/content/wages-china

than a day; some workers blocked the factory entrance to bar the car of the Japanese CEO from leaving. With mediation led by local Labor Bureau officials, management agreed to restore production time to 44 seconds, increase workers' basic monthly salaries by 8.3%, and raise housing and living allowances.

Cai Lin followed others in the walk out because 'everybody stopped working and it was for a good cause'. Like Liu Chi, Cai Lin felt emboldened when acting collectively with other workers. For her, the seeds of discontent with capitalist production had already been sown; when workers acted in unison, she was emboldened to and did overcome legal hegemony, which directed workers to resolve labor conflicts through individualized legal channels. She notes that in addition to applying pressure to employers, strikes could also arouse the Labor Bureau's concern for industrial conflicts so that they would also push employers to improve wages and other employment conditions. At the time of the strike, she did not fear retaliation or other adverse consequences:

> I was not worried at all. In the worst case, *I might not be able to get my salary or get fired. But this is not really a big issue.*

In China, turnover rates in factories are high because, first, the disorganized despotic labor regime (Lee 1999) developed in the labor intensive and export-oriented manufacturing industries usually offers employment terms that just meet minimum legal standards, or, in some of the worse cases, below legal standards; therefore, they cannot keep workers, who can easily find a similar job in the market, for long. Second, labor shortage in the PRD has increased workers' marketplace bargaining power (Silver 2003; Chan 2010). Waves of labor shortages have emerged in the country since late 2003 (Chan 2010). They were caused by, first, higher labor demand created by rising inflow of FDI after China's admission to the WTO in 2001. Second, since 2004, the central government and some provincial governments have adopted policies that led to the increase of farming income[36]; as a result, some migrant workers, especially older ones, have been incentivized to return to their home villages (Chan 2010). Third, increasing industrial development in inland areas has discouraged some migrant workers from seeking jobs in the coastal areas. Fourth, the one child policy, which has been implemented for decades, has led to a significant reduction of the labor force (Kuruvilla et al. 2011). As a consequence of these factors, the overall supply of labor in the market has diminished, and many workers try to improve their income through frequent job-hopping. As the span of time in which workers will remain in a factory is usually short, maybe ranging from a year to a few at most, going on strike does not cost them much; at most, it costs them a job with second-rate employment conditions. One NGO staff person remarks, 'What strikers fear least is being fired. If a factory fires workers, it has to give them compensation. But if workers quit by themselves, the factories do not need to compensate them for anything. Therefore, if workers are discontented with a factory, it is all for the better that the factory fires them.'[37]

Initially Cai Lin knew nothing about labor laws, of which her school and the factory did not inform her. She came to learn more about labor laws in a labor NGO in Shenzhen. Now, she often tells other workers about laws and refers them to this NGO if they have problems. Cai Lin opines that labor laws are of great help to workers for they spell out what rights workers hold, such as entitlements to minimum wages, social insurance, and overtime compensation. She notes:

> In the past, there were no regulations on wages, and we just earned a little. But now, enterprises must follow the laws and pay us the minimum wage. Our situation is much better now, though some employers still underpay workers.

Like Qiang Lai (sect. 3.1), Cai Lin's positive evaluation of labor laws are grounded on a comparison between the period (during the 1990s) wherein only a few legal protections for workers existed but were usually poorly implemented, and the period (during 2000s) wherein more labor laws have been put into place and relatively better enforced. This type of comparison is more frequently demonstrable in older migrant workers (usually born in the 70s or early 80s), who have work experience in both periods. In contrast, the younger generation, who are usually born after the mid-80s or 90s and have not worked in the period when the labor law system was in its infancy, do not hint at this comparison as often.

Despite her positive opinion of labor laws, Cai Lin remarks that 'the degree of protections offered by labor laws depends on law-enforcement entities; if they do not implement the laws, then the laws are useless'. Taking minimum wages as an example, she points out that some factories do not pay workers the minimum wage, but the Labor Bureaus take no action. Like many workers, she reckons that the legal deficits lay at the implementation level and are caused by the failings of law enforcers. Moreover, she believes that the degree of protection rendered by labor laws also hinge on workers themselves, 'if they are not persistent in pursuing their own rights, nobody can help them'. A similar comment is made by Qing Fa (sect. 3.2). This reflects that some workers tend to attribute the failure of workers' rights-defense to inadequate personal qualities, i.e., insufficient persistence and determination rather than a failure of the labor law system.

4 Summary Discussion: Double Legal Hegemony

In this chapter, I put forward a typology to illustrate Chinese worker susceptibility to legal hegemony during the party-state's hegemonic transformation from engineering the country's passive revolution to establishing capitalist ethico-political leadership. Workers are classified into affirmative, indifferent, ambivalent, critical, and radical modes according to three criteria: (a) their level of legal knowledge and motivation to acquire legal information, (b) the degree of their acceptance or rejection of the labor law system, including official legal discourses and legal practices, and (c) justification of legal defects, including whether they result from personal misconduct or structural asymmetry. The affirmative workers, as elucidated in this chapter, grant their active consent to legal hegemony, positively accepting the values and ideas disseminated through the labor law system. The indifferent, ambivalent, and critical workers, as will be illustrated in Chap. 5, have conferred passive consent to legal hegemony, either showing resignation to the status quo, or criticizing the socio-political, legal, and economic system within the capitalist-legal framework. The radical workers, as will be elaborated on in Chap. 6, have rendered no consent to legal hegemony, actively challenging the worldviews reproduced by the labor law system.

Thus far, I have expounded on how the affirmative workers perceive labor laws, and their relations with the state and market economy. All the informants in this chapter endorse economic reform and development in China, believing that it has brought them material enjoyment and job opportunities, though at the same time, they complain about high inflation, low wages, and uneven social development. Some regard their well-being as closely connected to the success of the wealthy class because the latter has become rich and is able to hire them. Some even approve of the capitalist appropriation of surplus value and maximization of profits. In the following, I summarize the mechanisms through which the labor law system exercises *double hegemonic effects on state–capital–labor relations, thereby simultaneously buffering the capitalist economy and party-state from systemic challenges from workers.*[38]

4.1 Labor Laws Buffer the Capitalist Economy

The labor law system has buttressed the capitalist economy against fundamental challenges from affirmative workers to the capitalist operational logics through two mechanisms: a *normalizing mechanism* and *countervailing mechanism.*

First, some affirmative workers (such as Xiao Mei, Ah Wen and Cai Lin) see labor laws as having taken on their own life, rather than as shaped by the ruling bloc. For them, laws are reified, authoritative and legitimate barometers for measuring employers' actions—if employers conform to labor laws, then they have not committed any wrongdoing, and thus, should not be reproved for paying workers meager wages. This *normalizing mechanism* hinders workers from discerning that labor laws are skewed towards the dominant class, and makes laws seem incontrovertible. This mechanism is so strongly in operation that some workers deem actions beyond legal channels as out of the question.

Burawoy (1979) argues that collective bargaining and the hegemonic labor regime in factories in the USA obscure the process of surplus value extraction in the workplace. Post-Mao China, however, is different from the Western context within which Burawoy conducted his study. While collective bargaining is poorly implemented in China (Chan and Hui 2014), and the Chinese labor regime is largely despotic rather than hegemonic (Lee 1995, 1999) (especially in low-end industries), the Chinese labor law system is playing a more crucial role in veiling surplus value appropriation by normalizing wage-labor relations built upon unequal exchange between capitalists and workers, and upon 'market-oriented, voluntaristic and individualistic' labor contracts (Friedman and Lee 2010, 509). The labor law system permits surplus value extraction from labor and regulates employer only under this precondition. It strengthens and reproduces capitalist hegemony by normalizing wage-labor relations, values, and practices that are conducive to capitalist accumulation. Due to the authoritative and reified appeal of labor laws, some workers readily measure their employers through the lens of these biased laws, thereby accepting the worldviews that they reproduce.

In addition to its normalizing mechanism, the labor law system buttresses the market economy with a *countervailing mechanism*. Although many workers have encountered unfair treatment at work, the labor law system, to a certain extent, provides them a channel for redressing grievances; this has convinced some workers that the socio-economic system is not completely inequitable (for example Qiang Lai). Due to this countervailing mechanism, some informants (such as Cai Lin, Qiang Lai, Qing Fa) attribute workers' plight to individually inadequate personal qualities, such as poor education and lack of persistence in rights-assertion rather than to the market economy. Put simply, the labor law system counteracts some adverse impacts imposed by capitalism on workers. The affirmative workers express appreciation for the labor law system, through which they believe they can resolve disputes with their employers. For them, labor laws are a tool to curb misbehavior within the economic arena rather than a juridico-political apparatus for normalizing wage-labor relations and sustaining capital accumulation, as explained in Chap. 3. They regard the labor law system as standing apart from the economic, rather than being (partly) subsumed under the economic.

Poulantzas's concept of relative autonomy of laws (see Chap. 3) can help us comprehend the apparent separation between laws and the economic, as well as the countervailing mechanism of the Chinese labor law system. The protections offered by labor laws, however limited, are real legal constraints imposed on businesses and are antithetical to the short-term interests of individual capitalists. This is why many enterprises and business associations fiercely opposed the legislation of the Labour Contract Law and other labor regulations (Gallagher and Dong 2011). The affirmative workers, therefore, have come to believe that labor laws are able to rein back employers' misdeeds in the economic sphere, while in reality labor laws are only relatively autonomous from the capitalist class because the juridico-political structures in reform China have been laid down to propel capital accumulation and perpetuate the long-term dominance of the capitalist class (see Chap. 3).

4.2 *Labor Laws Buffer the Party-State*

The labor law system does not only deflect workers' criticism away from the capitalist economy; it also buttresses the party-state from the criticism of reproducing capitalist class superiority. In Western society, parliamentary democracy and the division of governmental power help secure the consent of the subordinate class to government (Hobsbawm 1977; Merrington 1968). While parliamentary democracy is absent in China, the labor law system has, to a large extent, performed this function. The fact that labor laws have endowed a certain degree of protection to workers, such as minimum wage, overtime compensation, rest days, social insurance, labor contracts, and so forth have convinced some workers (such as Qiang Lai) that the party-state is on the side of workers and not favoring business interests. With this *concealing mechanism*, the labor law system has somehow covered up the party-state's bias towards the capitalist class, bestowing upon it an outlook of autonomy from capitalists. This mechanism induces some workers (such as Qiang Lai, Cai Lin, Qian Fa) to attribute workers' plight to individually inadequate psychological or personal qualities, rather than to the party-state or the failing labor law system. In brief, the availability of legal vehicles has masked some workers from recognizing the state's support to the capitalist economy.

The pro-labor perception of the party-state held by some affirmative workers and the concealing mechanism of the labor law system have to be understood in reference to Chinese state socialist history. Although socialist ideology has significantly declined in reform China, the impression that the party-state safeguards worker interests lingers. As mentioned in Chap. 3, the Chinese state still occasionally declares itself to be protecting workers' well-being; and the actual promulgation of some legal protections for workers has resonated with the lingering socialist image of the state, inducing some workers to believe that the state, as a whole, stands apart from business. In other words, in some workers' eyes, the labor law system is proof that the Chinese party-state is autonomous from the capitalists, while in reality this is only a relative autonomy of the Chinese state, as its attempt to restrain businesses with labor laws has, indeed, contributed to the long-term domination of the capitalist class through eliciting worker acquiescence to its leadership.

Moreover, the labor law system buffers the party-state through the *transmuting mechanism*. The decentralized politics in post-Mao China has also created the pro-labor perception of the central party-state, transmuting worker discontent from targeting the party-state as a whole to honing in on local governments or individual officials. Having delegated the mission of economic accumulation to local governments, the central government is more concerned with political legitimacy, and thus, appears to be impartial with regard to capital–labor relations, if not labor-friendly. In terms of rhetoric, it always holds high the banner of the rule of law. For example, almost every year the State Council work-report highlights that the party-state has adopted the rule of law and rules the country according to laws. The rule of law is one of the twelve core socialist values promoted by the Xi-Li government.[39] The Decision of the Central Committee of the Communist Party of China on Some Major Issues Concerning Comprehensively Deepening the Reform adopted in 2013, an important CCP document guiding the next stage of China's economic reform, has vowed to continue upholding the rule of law.[40]

In terms of laws and policies, the Hu-Wen government promulgated the Labour Contract Law, the Law on Labor-Dispute Mediation and Arbitration, and the Social Insurance Law, which are conceived to be protection for workers. Under the Xi-Li government, one of the emphases made by the 18th CCP Congress was raising average income and deepening reform for an income redistribution mechanism.[41] Also, in 2013, the State Council released the Opinion on Deepening the Reform of Income

Distribution Mechanisms to all local governments and agencies.[42] All of these, among other things, have created the impression that the central government is not inclined towards capitalists. Due to the perceived autonomy of the central party-state from businesses, and its apparent attempt to constrain the latter with laws, many workers regard government corruption and its bias towards enterprises as a result of immoral acts of individual cadres or problems of idiosyncratic local governments, rather than originating from systemic collusions between the party-state and the wealthy class. This transmuting mechanism has shifted the target of workers' criticism from the economic and political system to individuals, or from the party-state as a whole to local governments (see Ah Rong, Cai Lin, Zhi Hui, Ah Wen, Qing Fa). It should be noted that the transmuting mechanism of the labor law system echoes and capitalizes on the cultural perception of the Chinese state as a protector of the people and as a benign ruler (Wong 2011). As Lee (2007, 28) underscores, workers hold 'a hierarchical political imagination—the central state is the source of omnipotent power and paternal authority from which flows protection for workers'. And Perry (2008, 45) highlights that many protests in China seek to remove unpopular government officials from lower levels rather than challenging the CCP's authority or its ruling ideology.

4.3 *Interplay Between Worker Subjective Experiences and the Hegemonic Effects of Laws*

It should be highlighted that worker susceptibility to legal hegemony is not solely a result of the above-explained constitutive mechanisms embedded in the labor law system. It is also shaped by the lives and work exposure of workers as well as other subjective experiences. First, workers who have positive work experiences (usually in more advanced industries that offer employment conditions above legal standards) and have never encountered labor disputes are more easily subject to legal hegemony. It is because the official legal discourses have not contradicted their work experience. Also, no concrete work exposure has ever triggered their reflection on the official representation of the labor law system.

Second, workers who have lived through the period wherein no or few labor laws existed tend to appreciate the labor law system. It is because they were exposed to poorly regulated working conditions, and thus, strongly feel the improvements brought about by the labor laws. For them, an imperfect labor law system is better than having no laws at all. As underscored in Chap. 2, capitalist hegemony is built upon concessions to the subordinate class. The affirmative workers confer their consent to legally mediated hegemony because of the legal concessions given to them, which in turn brings them a minimal degree of economic concessions. Prior to enactment of the labor laws, workers' wages and benefits were purely determined by market forces. Although the labor laws cannot fully eradicate the race-to-the-bottom practices in the labor market, they set the minimum standards pertinent to wages, working hours, overtime payment and so forth, with which employers need to comply.

Third, for workers who have encountered individual labor disputes, their exposure in the process of legal mobilization has shaped their vulnerability to legal hegemony. Those workers who manage to win, or partially win, a dispute tend to deem the labor law system fair and just. Their active consent given to the labor law system is, indeed, closely related to their successful legal rights-defense; without these positive legal experiences, many of them would have become critical or radical in relation to the system, as will be illustrated in the coming two chapters. Graph 3

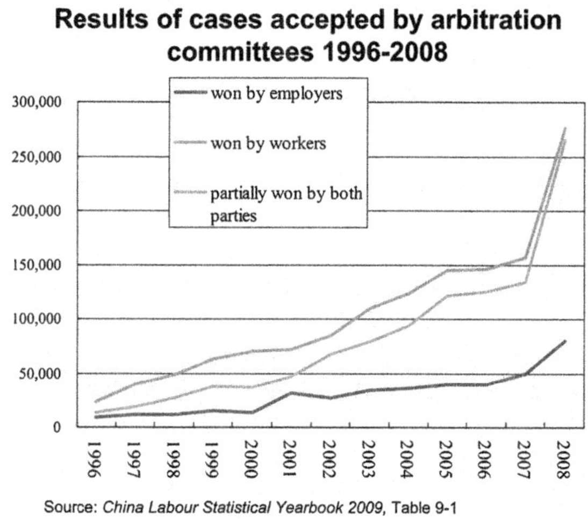

Graph 3 Analysis of cases accepted by arbitration committees, 1996–2008. *Source* http://www.clb.org.hk/en/files/share/File/statistics/disputes/Results_of_cases_accepted_by_arbitration_committees_1996-2008.pdf, accessed on 1st July 2014

displays the results of arbitration cases from 1996 to 2008; the number of cases won by workers and partially won by both employers and workers exceedingly outnumber those won by employers. Friedman and Lee (2010) find that about 50–80% of worker grievances can be addressed through arbitration. Chen and Tang underscore that there is a high success rate for worker cases in courts (2013). To reiterate, legal hegemony is not simply a matter of ideological influence; it is grounded upon concrete legal concessions granted to individual workers. For the labor law system to exercise hegemonic effects, it must, to a certain extent, be able to address worker grievances favorably.

Fourth, for workers who have experienced collective labor disputes, it is often workers' collectivity and solidarity rather than labor laws (as in the case of some workers who underwent individual disputes) that emboldens them to take action to defend their interests. They somehow transcended, at least during the course of their collective actions, the normalizing mechanism of legal hegemony to question the minimum standards set by labor laws, such as minimum wages. However, they still hold an affirmative attitude towards the labor law system because subsequent to the disruptive conjuncture, i.e., strikes or other collective actions, the companies or the state utilize labor laws to pacify them. For example, in Liu Chi's case, his factory organized 'democratic' trade union elections and collective wage negotiations in accordance with various labor laws after the waves of labor strikes in 2010. His consent to legal hegemony is based on a comparison between the period wherein his factory unilaterally fixed workers' wages and the period wherein it conducts wage negotiations with worker representatives and 'democratic' elections according to laws.

In brief, I have captured the interplay between the hegemonic mechanisms of the labor law system and the subjective experiences of workers in shaping the latter's vulnerability towards legal hegemony. However, as highlighted at the beginning of this chapter, not all workers are susceptible to legal hegemony; the indifferent, ambivalent, critical, and radical workers have rendered passive or no consent to it. This implies that legal hegemony in China is neither sturdy nor stable and contains fragile elements; some workers are able to transgress legal hegemony, as will be elucidated in the coming two chapters.

Notes

1. This, however, does not mean that the party-state is a unitary actor or without any internal conflicts. In fact, some studies point out that the factions within CCP held different attitudes towards the economic reform, resulting in internal power conflicts and fluctuating state policies during the 1980s. For example, Deng Xiaoping strongly pushed for the reform while Chen Yun and Li Xiangnian were not enthusiastic. Since the mid 1990s, however, the party-state has become less fragmented and economic reform has become a more accepted goal within the CCP (Naughton 2008).
2. http://www.moh.gov.cn/mohzcfgs/s6525/200804/18397.shtml, accessed on 3rd April 2013. My own emphasis.
3. http://www.xchen.com.cn/jihua/sifagongzuojihua/624539.html, accessed on 3rd April 2013.
4. Interview Q7.
5. Still, Zhi Hui's salaries are much lower than the 5313 yuan monthly average wage of Guangzhou.
6. See for example, http://hk.apple.nextmedia.com/financeestate/art/20140213/18624150, accessed on 28th March 2014.
7. http://news.now.com/home/international/player?newsId=90473, accessed on 28th March 2014.
8. Interview Q6.
9. http://www-wds.worldbank.org/external/default/WDSContentServer/IW3P/IB/2013/06/13/000158349_20130613150441/Rendered/PDF/WPS6482.pdf, accessed on 28th March 2014.
10. See graph 1 in sect. 3.3.
11. Interview Q9.
12. Interview Q10.
13. See graph 2 in sect. 3.3.
14. Interview Q9.
15. Interview Q3
16. Interview Q1.
17. http://news.now.com/home/international/player?newsId=43102, accessed on 2nd July 2014.
18. http://hk.apple.nextmedia.com/international/art/20120828/18001946, accessed on 1st July 2014.
19. Interview Q2
20. Interview Q14.
21. Interview Q12.
22. Article 2, the Law on Administrative Reconsideration stipulates that citizens can "apply to administrative organs for administrative reconsideration

when they consider that certain specific administrative acts infringe upon their lawful rights or interests".

23. Interview Q15.
24. Interview Q18.
25. Interview Q14.
26. Interview Q18.
27. Interview Q19.
28. http://column.global-labour-university.org/2011/01/trade-unions-and-worker-struggles-in.html, accessed on 12th December 2011.
29. Some studies, however, show that these elections are not completely direct or democratic (Hui and Chan 2015).
30. Interview Q21, S11, R18, S9, S10, G1.
31. http://gonghui.luogang.gov.cn/gz33cmsweb/CMShtml/xwzx/xwzw_gzdt/2011-8/1/09_25_33_961.html, accessed on 30th March 2014.
32. Interview S15 and S11.
33. Interview S14.
34. Interview Q20.
35. For example, the minimum wage rate in Shanghai in 2012 was only 31% of the city's average wage while in Beijing and Chongqing in 2011, they were, respectively, 25% and 26% of the city's average wage. For detail, see http://www.clb.org.hk/en/content/wages-china, accessed on 10th July 2014.
36. For example, policies that abolished the agricultural tax and provided agricultural subsidies to farmers.
37. Interview S4.
38. The term "double hegemony" is inspired by Scherrer (2001), who argues that US hegemony exerted in the world market is interlinked with hegemony of the corporate internationalists within the country.
39. http://news.xinhuanet.com/english/china/2014-02/25/c_126190257.htm, accessed on 2nd April 2014.
40. http://www.china.org.cn/chinese/2014-01/17/content_31226494_9.htm, accessed on 1st April 2014.
41. http://www.qstheory.cn/jj/jjggyfz/201311/t20131111_289477.htm, accessed on 1st April 2014.
42. http://finance.sina.com.cn/china/20130205/201514511683.shtml, accessed on 1st April 2014.

References

Archer, Margaret. 1982. Morphogenesis Versus Structuration: On Combining Structure and Action. *British Journal of Sociology* 33 (4): 455–483.

Benney, Jonathan. 2013. *Defending Rights in Contemporary China*. Oxon: Routledge.

Blecher, Marc. 2002. Hegemony and Workers' Politics in China. *China Quarterly* 170: 283–303.

Blecher, Marc. 2004. The Working Class and Governance. In *Governance in China*, ed. Jude Howell. Lanham, MD: Rowman & Littlefield Publishers, Inc.

Breslin, Shaun. 2007. *China and the Global Political Economy*. New York: Palgrave Macmillan.

Burawoy, Michael. 1979. *Manufacturing Consent: Changes in the Labor Process Under Monopoly Capitalism*. Chicago: University of Chicago Press.

Chan, King Chi Chris. 2010. *The Challenge of Labour in China: Strikes and the Changing Labour Regime in Global Factories*. New York: Routledge.

Chan, King-Chi Chris, and Sio-Ieng Elaine Hui. 2012. The Dynamics and Dilemma of Workplace Trade Union Reform in China: The Case of the Honda Workers' Strike. *Journal of Industrial Relations* 54: 653–668.

Chan, King-Chi Chris, and Sio-Ieng Elaine Hui. 2014. The Development of Collective Bargaining in China: From "Collective Bargaining by Riot" to "Party State-Led Wage Bargaining". *China Quarterly* 217: 221–242.

Chan, King-Chi Chris, and Sio-Ieng Elaine Hui. 2016. Direct Elections of Workplace Trade Unions in China: Implications for the Changing Labour Regime. In *China at Work: A Labour Process Perspective on the Transformation of Work and Employment in China*, ed. M.W. Liu, and C. Smith, 255–280. Basingstoke: Palgrave.

Chen, Feng, and Mengxiao Tang. 2013. Labor Conflicts in China: Typologies and Their Implications. *Asian Survey* 53 (3): 559–583.

Dahrendorf, Ralf. 1965. *Class and Class Conflict in Industrial Society*. CA: Stanford University Press.

Exner, Mechthild. 1995. The Convergence of Ideology and the Law: The Functions of the Legal Education Campaign in Building a Chinese Legal System. *Issues and Studies* 31 (8): 68–102.

Femia, Joseph V. 1975. Hegemony and Consciousness in the Thought of Antonio Gramsci. *Political Studies* 23 (1): 29–48.

Femia, Joseph V. 1987. *Gramsci's Political Thought: Hegemony, Consciousness, and the Revolutionary Process*. Oxford: Clarendon Press.

Friedman, Eli, and Ching Kwan Lee. 2010. Remaking the World of Chinese Labour: A 30-Year Retrospective. *British Journal of Industrial Relations* 48 (3): 507–533.

Gallagher, Mary E. 2004. Time is Money, Efficiency is Life: The Transformation of Labor Relations in China. *Studies in Comparative International Development* 39 (2): 11–44.

Gallagher, Mary E. 2006. Mobilizing the law in China: "informed disenchantment" and the development of legal consciousness. *Law & Society Review* 40 (4): 783–816.

Gallagher, Mary E. 2007. Hope for Protection and Hopeless Choices: Labour Legal Aid in the PRC. In *Grassroots Political Reform in Contemporary China*, ed. Elizabeth J. Perry, and Merle Goldman. London: Harvard University Press.

Gallagher, Mary E., and Baohua Dong. 2011. Legislating Harmony: Labor Law Reform in Contemporary China. In *From Iron Rice Bowl to Informalization Markets, Workers, and the State in a Changing China*, ed. Sarosh Kuruvilla, Ching Kwan Lee, and Mary E. Gallagher. Ithaca, NY: ILR Press.

Gramsci, Antonio. 1971. *Selections from the Prison Notebooks*, trans. and ed. Q. Hoare, and G.N. Smith. New York: International Publishers.

He, Xin, and Su Yang. 2010. Street as Courtroom: State Accommodation of Labor Protest in South China. *Law and Society Review* 44 (1): 157–184.

Hobsbawm, Eric. 1977. Gramsci and Political Theory. *MARXISM TODAY*, July.

Hui, Sio-Ieng Elaine. 2011. Understanding Labour Activism in the Chinese Automotive Industry—The Case of Honda Workers' Strike. In *China's Labor Question*, ed. Christoph Scherrer. Mering: Rainer Hampp Verlag.

Hui, Sio-Ieng Elaine, and King-Chi Chris Chan. 2015. Going beyond the Union-Centred Approach: A Critical Evaluation of Recent Trade Union Elections in China. *British Journal of Industrial Relations.*

Jessop, Bob. 1982. *The Capitalist State: Marxist Theories and Methods.* Oxford: Martin Robertson.

Kuruvilla, S., C.K. Lee, and M.E. Gallagher. 2011. *From Iron Rice Bowl to Informalization: Markets, Workers, and the State in a Changing China*. Ithaca, NY: ILR Press.

Lee, Ching Kwan. 1995. Engendering the Worlds of Labor: Women Workers, Labor Markets, and Production Politics in the South China Economic Miracle. *American Sociological Review* 60 (3): 378–397.

Lee, Ching Kwan. 1999. From Organized Dependence to Disorganized Despotism: Changing Labour Regimes in Chinese Factories. *China Quarterly* 157: 44–71.

Lee, Ching Kwan. 2002. From the Specter of Mao to the Spirit of the Law: Labor Insurgency in China. *Theory and Society* 31: 189–228.

Lee, Ching Kwan. 2007. *Against the Law: Labor Protests in China's Rustbelt and Sunbelt.* Berkeley: University of California Press.

Lubman, Stanley. 1999. Bird in a Cage: Chinese Law Reform after Twenty Years. *Northwestern Journal of International Law & Business* 20: 383–424.

McNally, Christoph A. 2004. Sichuan: Driving Capitalist Development Westward. *The China Quarterly* 178: 426–447.

Merrington, J. 1968. Theory and Practice in Gramsci's Marxism. *Socialist Register* 145–176.

Naughton, Barry. 2008. *A Political Economy of China's Economic Transition*, ed. Loren Brandt, and Thomas G. Rawski. Cambridge: Cambridge University Press.

Peerenboom, Randall P. 2002. *China's Long March Toward Rule of Law*. New York: Cambridge University Press.

Perry, Elizabeth J. 2008. Chinese Conceptions of "Rights": From Mencius to Mao —and Now. *Perspectives on Politics* 6 (1): 37–50.

Portes, Alejandro. 1971. On the Interpretation of Class Consciousness. *American Journal of Sociology* 77 (2): 228–244.

Potter, Pitman B. 1999. The Chinese Legal System: Continuing Commitment to the Primacy of State Power. *China Quarterly* 159: 673–683.

Poulantzas, Nicos. 2000. *State, Power, Socialism*. London: Verso.

Scherrer, Christoph. 2001. Double Hegemony'? State and Class in American Foreign Economic Policymaking. *Amerikastudien/American Studies* 46 (4): 573–591.

Silver, Beverly. 2003. *Forces of Labor: Workers' Movements and Globalisation Since 1870*. Cambridge: Cambridge University Press.

Smith, Ted, David Allan Sonnenfeld, and David N. Pellow. 2006. *Challenging the Chip: Labor Rights and Environmental Justice in the Global Electronics Industry*. Philadelphia: Temple University Press.

Solinger, Dorothy J. 1999. *Contesting Citizenship in Urban China. Peasant Migrants, the State, and the Logic of the Market*. Berkeley: University of California Press.

Thompson, E.P. 1977. *Whigs and Hunters: The Origin of the Black Act*. Harmondsworth: Penguin.

Wang, Haiyan, Richard P. Appelbaum, Degiuli Francesca, and Nelson Lichtenstein. 2009. China's New Labour Contract Law: Is China Moving Towards Increased Power for Workers? *Third World Quarterly* 30 (3): 485–501.

Won, Jaeyoun. 2004. Withering Away of the Iron Rice Bowl? The Reemployment Project of Post-Socialist China. *Studies in Comparative International Development* 39 (2): 71–93.

Wong, Linda. 2011. Chinese Migrant Workers: Rights Attainment Deficits, Rights Consciousness and Personal Strategies. *China Quarterly* 208: 870–892.

Wright, Erik Olin. 2000. Working-Class Power, the Capitalist-Class Interests, and Class Compromise. *American Journal of Sociology* 104 (4): 957–1002.

Xue, Hong. 2008. Local Strategies of Labor Control: A Case Study of Three Electronics Factories in China. *International Labor and Working-Class History* 73: 85–103.

Zhao, Suisheng. 1998. A State-Led Nationalism: The Patriotic Education Campaign in Post-Tiananmen China. *Communist and Post-Communist Studies* 31 (3): 287–302.

CHAPTER 5

Workers' Passive Consent

1 Introduction

In the previous chapter, I have constructed a typology of Chinese migrant worker susceptibility towards legal hegemony and elucidated four mechanisms through which the labor law system exercises a double hegemonic effect to buttress both the party-state and capitalist economy. In addition, I have elaborated on in what ways affirmative workers grant their active consent to legal hegemony and readily embrace capitalist values. In this chapter, I focus on the indifferent, ambivalent, and critical workers, all of which render passive consent to legal hegemony, either being partially assimilated to capitalist worldviews or exhibiting signs of submissiveness.

2 Indifferent Workers

Indifferent workers are those who found labor laws irrelevant to them, caring little about legal regulations or whether their employers violate labor laws or not. They are usually unmotivated to gain legal knowledge; all of them have not encountered any disputes. They neither actively endorse capitalist values, nor do they demonstrate any criticism towards the legal, political, and economic systems. They instead, reveal a strong sense of passivity and apathy, believing that the socio-political and economic status quo cannot be changed.

E.S.I Hui, *Hegemonic Transformation*, Series in Asian Labor and Welfare Policies, DOI 10.1057/978-1-137-50429-6_5

Ah Qing is a 36-year old female worker.[1] Coming from Hunan province, she now works in a Taiwanese-invested shoe factory, one of the declining industries in Shenzhen. In Shenzhen and some parts of the coastal area, factory relocation has become commonplace due to the Guangdong provincial government's plans for an industrial upgrade.[2] According to a retired provincial trade unionist, the Shenzhen government intends to relocate 15 thousands firms from the city within 5 years in order to make space for the development of high-value industries.[3] Since the economic reforms in 1978, Shenzhen and the PRD have been manufacturing hubs for labor intensive, low-end, export-oriented industries, but now, the Guangdong government is attempting to direct these industries to the second tier cities in the province or to other inland provinces so as to transform the first-tier city economy into one concentrated on high-value production, and the financial and service industries. To achieve this goal, the government has reduced tax breaks and land privileges to low-end factories, disallowed factories that did not meet legal environmental standards to stay in cities and so forth.[4] As a result, many factories in Shenzhen are facing relocation, which has consequently triggered a growing number of strikes to demand compensation and back pay of benefits.[5]

Working in a shrinking industry, Ah Qing does not earn much. Her monthly basic salary is the same as Shenzhen's legal minimum wage, which is 1500 yuan at the time of the interview. She has to work much overtime in order to gain a monthly gross income of around 3000 yuan, which is still far lower than the average wages in Shenzhen in 2012 (4918 yuan). I met Ah Qing when joining a labor NGO outreach activities in an industrial area. She pays no attention to labor laws as she deems it unnecessary, 'My salary is ok. It's higher than what I earned back home. I would just quit my job if there are any problems with the factory.' During our conversation, I found out that Ah Qing's employer has not paid her the overtime premium according to labor laws; the overtime compensation she receives is simply the same as the straight piece-rate wages, rather than 1.5–3 times the piece-rate as required by the 1995 Labour Law. Ah Qing is unaware of this legal regulation, which is common knowledge among many, if not most, workers. Her initial response to my legal advice was objection, insisting that she was not entitled to 1.5–3 times overtime compensation as she was a piece-rate worker, not a hourly-rate worker. I then gave her a booklet produced by the NGO, which explained the labor laws on overtime work. I encouraged her to take a look at it or to consult the labor bureau, hinting that she could file a complaint for it. Later she became uncertain with her original view and revealed greater interest in what labor laws stipulate, but she still reiterated several times that she would just quit her job and return to the rural village if the factory work became problematic.

Building upon Hirschman's insights (1970), Freeman suggests that workers have the option of 'exit' and 'voice' if there are gaps between the actual and expected outcomes concerning their jobs (Freeman 1976; Allen 1984). It is obvious that Ah Qing tends to choose 'exit' if 'silence' is no longer an optimal strategy for her. She does not care about labor laws and her manager's illegal action because she considers her monthly gross salary acceptable when compared to the meager income she earned in her hometown. She thinks that she can escape from unpleasant situations at work by exercising her 'freedom' to exit the factory. As explicated in Chap. 3, the legal system has turned workers from class agents into juridico-political individuals whom are thought to be on an equal footing with employers. Affected by this constitutive effect of the labor contract system, Ah Qing believes that she is 'free' to end the labor contract with her boss whenever she likes.

Ah Qing's indifference to labor laws can be explained by age-, gender-, and education-related factors, all of which have created a feeling of impotence for her and a sense of alienation from urban lives. She is a typical first-generation female migrant worker (see Pun and Lu 2010), born in the 70s and deemed old for factory jobs when compared to post-80s and post-90s workers[6]; she only has primary schooling while second-generation migrant workers have usually graduated from junior secondary schools or vocational schools; she bears heavy familial responsibilities as she has five dependents, including three children at home, whereas second-generation migrant workers are usually unmarried and free from this kind of burden; she views her employment and life in the city as transitory and considers her home village to be where she will stay in the long term while young migrant workers aspire to urban lives. Due to her weak marketplace power (Silver 2003) and detachment from cities, Ah Qing regards the undesirable and illegal work environment she faces as tolerable and transitory. Therefore, she is unmotivated to change it. She also deems laws, which could be a means of pursuing a change, to be irrelevant to her.

A Ying shows similar apathy towards labor laws.[7] I came to know her when I paid a visit to workers in their dormitories in Shenzhen. We talked for an hour in her room shared with three other workers. Ah Ying is 34 years old and has completed primary school. Her husband and her

2-year-old daughter live in her hometown in Hunan. She started to work in urban cities in 2004, but on and off, she has gone back home and helped her father with farming. She now has a job in an electronics factory that produces watch components for a famous Japanese brand. As mentioned in Chap. 4, electronics production is one of the key export-oriented industries in China, yet its employment conditions are quite terrible. Wages below the legal standards, long working hours, no rest days, and despotic management are all commonly practiced in electronics factories (Xue 2008). This has, therefore, provoked many labor strikes in the past decade. Trying to stabilize the working force, some big or strike-prone firms offer workers better pay and benefits. This is why Ah Ying, working in a large-scale electronics factory, earns 1700 yuan a month, which is 200 yuan higher than the Shenzhen minimum wage.

While talking to me, Ah Ying was stitching a piece of embroidery at the same time. She proudly explained to me that she would use it to decorate her home in Hunan. Like Ah Qing, she has no plan to settle down in the cities; she mentions to me a few times that she may quit her job and return home before the Lunar New Year. When I asked for her opinions on labor laws, she responds, 'I don't know much about laws. I have never encountered any labor disputes; labor laws are not useful to me. I don't know whether they are good or not.' She adds, 'What can I do if there are problems with the factory? I think I could simply leave the factory.' Talking about the economy and the party-state, she reveals a sense of passivity, noting, 'Economic development is not so much related to me and the government is far away from me. I cannot do anything even if I am discontented, right? If I am unhappy with my life in the city, I better go back home'.

On the surface, 'exit' seems to be Ah Ying and Ah Qing's personal preferences. However, their choices are indeed made under the constraints imposed by socio-economic structures. Migrant workers are facing iniquitous social treatment; it is only after 2002 that the party-state recognizes them as a part of the working class, and thus, deserving some protection and basic civil rights (Wong 2011). The household registration system and other labor and social policies have contributed to the spatial separation of production in urban cities and reproduction in rural areas (Pun and Lu 2010). Migrant workers like Ah Qing and Ah Ying are encouraged to sell their labor power in cities under poorly regulated conditions, but they are denied proper social benefits that urban citizens enjoy. The party-state has attempted to reform the household registration system and provide better social welfare protection to migrant workers, as reflected by the 2003 Suggestion for Advancing the Reform of the Hukou Administration System in Small Cities and Towns issued by the State Council, the 2006 Certain Opinions of the State Council on Solving the Problems of Peasant Workers, the 2014 Opinion on Further Reform of the Household Registration System issued by the Political Bureau of the CCP[8]; but migrant workers still receive unequal social treatment concerning medical care, housing, their children's education, and so forth. Discriminatory social and welfare policies plus poor wages mean that migrant workers and their family cannot live decently in cities; but at home, prices are more affordable and they still own a piece of land from which they can derive subsistence. The labor and social policies have forced Ah Qing and Ah Ying to consider their life in cities as transitory. Therefore appalling working conditions and/or illegal practices of employers do not seem to be a serious concern for them as long as their employers pay them the promised wages on time. For indifferent workers, labor laws are irrelevant to them; they have neither actively embraced the values reproduced by the labor law system, nor have they formulated any doubts over it. However, they are passively assimilated into some of the ideas of the dominant class, such as contractual equality. They exhibit a sense of submissiveness and apathy towards the socio-political and economic status quo, believing that it cannot be altered or challenged. In other words, they render passive consent to legal hegemony.

3 Critical Workers

The critical workers have also conferred passive consent to legal hegemony, but in different ways from the indifferent workers. Although many of them reveal an air of resignation to the status quo, they do not deem the labor law system irrelevant to them and demonstrate a certain level of criticism of it. However, their disapprovals are framed along the lines of the dominant ideologies as they have not yet developed an alternative worldview that allows them to formulate discontent 'manifest in the activity uniting them "in the practical transformation of reality"' (Femia 1975, 33).

3.1 Workers Without Labor Disputes Experiences

Zhang Lin is a production worker in an electronics factory.[9] After finishing the vocational secondary school three and a half years ago, she left her home in Henan to work in Shenzhen. She is 21 years old and earns less than 3000 yuan per month. The first factory where she worked did not pay her overtime compensation according to labor laws, but she did not bring up the issue with her managers or the Labour Bureau.

Researcher: Did you demand the managers to pay you the legal overtime premium?
Zhang Lin: Talk to them? Many people in that factory have worked like this for years. Would it make any changes for a newcomer like me to rebel?
Researcher: So you did not bring this issue up to the boss?
Zhang Lin: Society is like that. *If you think it's fine to work in this factory, stay here; otherwise, just leave.* What bargaining power do I have? *When the enterprise offers you a contract, you can sign it or turn it down if you don't like the terms.* How can I talk to them about it now (after signing the contract)?
Researcher: Do labour laws protect workers or employers?
Zhang Lin: Laws…*I think they are of little use to us.*
Researcher: Why?
Zhang Lin: Although there exist certain legal stipulations, *employers can make use of their guanxi [connections with government officials] to avoid the laws.* They own the factories; what they say must be followed. If you think the working conditions are unacceptable, you can leave the factory.
Me: Is it better to have labour laws or not?
Zhang Lin: Of course it is better to have labour laws. They certainly offer us some degree of protection, but *they are not comprehensive enough.*

Shaped by the labor contract system, Zhang Lin believes that workers are 'free' to enter into labor contracts with employers and 'free' to end the contracts ['If you think it is fine to work in this factory, stay here; otherwise, just leave it…When the enterprise offers you a contract, you can sign it, or turn it down if you don't like the terms']. In the end, she exercised her abstract and formal 'freedom' to quit this problematic factory after having worked there for 6 months. As explained in Chap. 4, workers' life and work experiences shape their attitude towards the labor law system. Due to that unfair experience where her employer took advantage of her illegally, Zhang Lin has developed a critical attitude towards labor laws, which she regards as offering limited protection to workers. In contrast, Zhi Hui (Chap. 4, Sect. 3.1) takes labor laws as just and fair because he has not suffered from any illegal treatment afflicted by his employer.

Zhang Lin attributes the weak legal protection for workers to *guanxi* politics in China, i.e., the politics associated with the interwoven personal connections among government officials and corporations. As explicated in Chap. 4, local governments are responsible for economic accumulation, and thus, have cultivated close relations with enterprises and the rich (Pearson 1997). The businesses bring investment and economic growth to the locality, while local governments offer them formal privileges, such as tax breaks, cheap land and informal benefits, including lax implementation of labor laws. Some local governments have even turned themselves into 'entrepreneurial states' as they are directly involved in running businesses (Blecher and Shue 1996). The strong connections between local governments and businesses often result in corruption (Wedeman 2005). A human resources manager from a domestic firm in Shenzhen notes to me that 'cadres and businesses always shelter each other when one of them get into trouble…they always do things in the black box. In the least developed areas in China, it is easier to cover things up…'.[10] This remark reflects what some scholars call 'network capitalism' (McNally 2008), or the 'guanxi capitalism' (Yang 2002; McNally 2011) in China. Zhang Lin regards the shortcomings of the labor law system as being rooted in the intricate connection between local governments and businesses.

Chen Fei is a 23-year old male production worker.[11] From 2008 to 2011, he worked in a large state-owned electronics factory in Zhuhai. His team leader would deduct 50 yuan from the wages of workers that did not agree to work overtime, and workers had to have lunch while working on the assembly line. Some of his colleagues brought these issues to the attention of a higher-level manager. Later in a meeting, the team leader threatened them not to make any trouble and warned them to 'watch out'. Chen Fei's colleagues then complained about these issues to the Labor Bureau, which, did not respond. Chen Fei was frustrated by the experience of his colleagues, feeling that lodging complaints was useless and that labor laws could barely safeguard worker interests. He, therefore, bore in silence the team leader's illegal treatment for 3 years. In 2012, when he was informed of a job opportunity in a foreign-owned factory in Guangzhou, it took him less than a few minutes to decide to travel immediately from Zhuhai to Guangzhou for an interview. He passed the interview and has been working in that factory since then.

Chen Fei comments that the Chinese labor laws are good enough on paper, but the problem lies in their weak implementation. He says that many government officials do not enforce the laws strictly and are acting with 'one eye closed, one eye open' towards the legal violations of factories; therefore, 'laws have been turned into a blank sheet of paper'. His remark echoes the findings of current studies on the lax implementation of labor laws (Gallagher 2004, 23; Wang et al. 2009, 486; Lubman 1999). When asked about the reasons for poor legal enforcement, he replied, 'Guanxi plays an important role in China, and everything is about guanxi.' Our further conversation on this topic revealed the following:

Researcher: Have you heard about *yifa weiquan* [legal rights defense]?

Chen Fei: Um…*weiquan* [rights-defense]…like in my previous factory, what was the result of workers' rights-defense? The Labor Bureau didn't respond to us or take any action. We don't have confidence in them.

Researcher: How does one solve this problem? What should the government do?

Chen Fei: How can I put this …China is corrupted from outside to inside, and it's hard to change it. China is big; it'll take a long time to change it. I'm not sure if we will witness the change before our death.

Researcher: Is it a problem of the government being biased towards employers or that of individual irresponsible government officials?

Chen Fei: Probably individuals, many individuals. At the grassroots level, the relations between government cadres and businesses are well established; and so are they at the higher levels, too. Anyways, many individuals contribute to this problem.

Compared to the affirmative informants who have encountered no labor disputes in Chap. 4, Chen Fei is more critical towards the labor law system and the state. The affirmative interviewees (such as Xiao Mei and Qiang Lai) take labor laws as fair and just, but Chen Fei points to discrepancies between the laws on paper versus the laws in reality. Some affirmative informants display positive sentiments towards the state (such as Xiao Mei), but Chen Fei casts serious doubts over government officials. However, it should be highlighted that although Chen Fei does not trust the labor law system, his disapproval is formulated within the boundaries set by legal hegemony. His criticism of labor laws hovers at the level of implementation rather than pinpointing the unbalanced power relations embedded into the laws and the law-making process. His skepticism towards the state remains at the level of individual government officials rather than targeting the state, as a whole, in supporting the wealthy class. For him, labor laws on paper are protective of workers; it is only the fault of individual government cadres that cause workers to suffer from weak legal implementation. The existence of the theoretically protective labor laws buffers the state, as a whole, against the criticism of leaning towards the privileged class (i.e., the concealing mechanism of labor laws); and, hence, individual cadres at the local level serve as scapegoats for the systemic failure of the juridico-political system in safeguarding workers (i.e., the transmuting mechanism). In brief, the party state en bloc or the central government is somehow legitimized in the eyes of Chen Fei due to the hegemonic effects of the labor law system.

3.2 Workers with Individual Labor Dispute Experiences

In his mid-forties now, Shu Ren first came from Henan to work in the cities in 1989.[12] He is now working at a Taiwanese furniture factory in Dongguan. When we were talking about economic development, Shu Ren highlighted the huge wealth gap in China, 'The rich and the poor work the same number of hours and put in the same amount of labor, but their incomes are not comparable.'[13] Also, he criticizes the household registration system, which in his opinion has restrained migrant workers from obtaining the same social welfare that urban citizens get, for exacerbating social disparity.

In 2008, Shu Ren's left eyeball was hurt in an occupational accident. When he was hospitalized, another work injury victim gave him a labor NGO-produced booklet on labor laws connected to occupational health and safety. He considered this booklet 'a treasure' for it contained useful information on how work-accident victims can pursue their legal rights. Later, he called the NGO's hotline enquiring about questions such as whether his employer was responsible for paying him wages during his recuperation, if yes, how much it should be, etc. Following this, he met the NGO staff and found out even more about his legal rights.

Shu Ren always watches TV news and a TV program called 'walking together with laws' (*yufa tongxing*); he already had a rough idea of what labor laws were prior to his work injury. However, when he needed to apply the labor laws to his own case, he was uncertain about what he should do exactly; he thus, sought help from the NGO. After being released from the hospital, he attended the classes on labor laws organized by the NGO and became an active participant; he has, thus, become more legally knowledgeable. Similar to Ah Rong and Ah Wen in Chap. 4 (Sect. 3.2), Shu Ren has an affirmative appraisal of the NGO due to its intense support to him. Despite the fact that local trade unions were alleged to provide greater legal assistance, consultation, and representation to workers (Chen 2004), he was unaware of the existence of enterprise-level or higher-level trade unions at the time; therefore, he did not approach them for help. However, having learned more about them subsequently, he reflects that 'trade unions don't exercise any real power; they are like decorations'.

When Shu Ren was still undergoing medical treatment, his employer urged him to conduct an assessment of work capability so that he could return to work as soon as possible (see Chap. 4 for the legal procedures for handling work accidents). His employer threatened to discontinue his monthly salary should he refuse to do the assessment. Being well-equipped with legal knowledge, Shu Ren talked to his employer. He recounted the situation as the following:

> I told my boss, 'My eye still hurts. According to labor laws, I'm still undergoing medical treatment. Why are you urging me to conduct the assessment? You said you would stop my salary if I don't do the assessment. But *our national laws stipulate clearly that work injury victims are entitled to salaries equivalent to their average monthly pay as well as other benefits during the period of medical treatment. I have to remind you that I can sue you for not paying me my due salary*' My employer responded, saying that he didn't know about these laws. I said, 'No problem. I can show you some information. You can decide what to do after reading them.' *Everything that I said to him at the time had legal grounds. If what I said were inconsistent with the laws, he could simply ignore me, right?* After reading the information I gave him, he didn't reply to me or discontinue my salary.

Shu Ren demonstrates a high degree of confidence when confronting his employer, who used to be in a superior position in the workplace ['I have to remind you that I can sue you for not paying me my due salary']. Labor laws have emboldened him to overcome the uneven power relations between himself as wage-labor and his manager so that he could reason with him as an equal. Although the legal system and the labor law system have turned workers from class agents into juridico-political subjects, blurring capitalist domination over workers, the same systems have bestowed workers with a feeling of equality in relation to their bosses. Undeniably, it is only an abstract and formal equality, but in some circumstances, it gives workers courage to confront their employers.

Another illegal practice of Shu Ren's employer is connected to the work-related injury insurance. According to the Regulation on Work-Related Injury Insurance, employers must contribute to the Insurance on the basis of the gross income of workers, which covers basic salary, overtime pay, and other monetary benefits. However, Shu Ren's boss only paid the Insurance according to his basic salary which amounted to 760 yuan (whereas his actual average monthly salary was around 900 yuan). Due to his boss's underpayment, the work-related injury insurance gave him a lump-sum of disability allowance on the basis of 760 yuan rather than 900 yuan. As a consequence, the allowance he received was around 2000 yuan less than what he was entitled to. Shu Ren brought this issue up to his employer, but he did not properly respond to him. He then complained to the Social Security Department. The officer there asked him to apply for arbitration from the Labor Bureau, but he insisted that the Social Security Department should rectify the matter for him. Later a high-ranking officer intervened; Shu Ren showed him a leaflet produced by the Social Security Department on work injury insurance, saying to him:

> The Social Insurance Laws are made by our government, not by me. The responsibility of the Social Security Department in regards to social insurance is clearly written here, right? *Please enact the legal regulations; it's not good to shift your responsibility.* Your subordinate asked me to apply for labor arbitration, but it's unnecessary. Here is the Social Security Department, but you fail to protect me (on issues related to the work injury insurance). *What I am demanding is what has been stipulated by laws.* I am not cheating you. I would rather not have to face such a situation. If you could cure my eye, I would prefer that over getting a single cent from you. I wish I could have a healthy body rather than having to get any money from you.

This high ranking officer did not give Shu Ren any immediate reply. Shu Ren then went to talk to his employer again, who unexpectedly agreed to pay back the insurance he owned. Shu Ren guesses that the Social Security Department had probably given his boss pressure. This incident attests to the emboldening effect of labor laws on Shu Ren once again. He does not only display a high level of familiarity with labor laws, but also strong confidence and audacity in front of government officials ['Please enact the legal regulations; it's not good to shift your responsibility', 'What I am demanding are what have been prescribed by laws']. He has skillfully and vigorously applied his legal knowledge to champion his rights.

This labor dispute has made Shu Ren critical of the labor law system. He was dismissive of the legal discourses on the rule of law and rights-defense according to laws.

Researcher: Have labour laws offered enough protection to workers?

Shu Ren: I think the government doesn't care. It doesn't know how much value workers have created. It only sees the value created by firms and doesn't know that the value created by businesses are, in fact, produced by workers. *If workers don't work, enterprises wouldn't be able to produce any value.*

Researcher: Are you referring to the central government or local governments?

Shu Ren: I think *the central government doesn't have any problems; it has legislated many labor laws to protect workers. The problem lies with the local governments* who protect businesses too much.

Researcher: Can you elaborate more?

Shu Ren: When workers complain about their employers providing illegal working conditions, the most that the Labor Bureaus do is call the factories asking about what happened; it seldom conducts on-site investigations or punishes factories. In many cases, *worker complaints end up nowhere (bu liaoliao zhi)*. The Labor Bureaus seldom go to check if factories have signed labor contracts with workers, if their labor contracts conform to labor regulations, etc. *This so called rule of law and legal rights-defense are deceiving.*

In contrast to the affirmative workers, Shu Ren is skeptical of the official legal discourses and renders no active consent to the labor law system ['The so called rule of law and legal rights-defense are deceiving']. He attributes the failing labor law system to local government officials who lean towards enterprises and turn a blind eye to worker grievances ['it seldom conducts on-site investigations or punishes the factories. In many cases, *worker complaints would end up nowhere*']. For him, the central government has made numerous labor laws, and thus, has accomplished its duties; it is the local governments that value businesses over workers and contribute to infringement of labor rights ['the central government doesn't have many problems; it has made many labor laws to protect workers. It's the problem of local governments']. The transmuting mechanism of the labor law system shifts the target of his criticism from the central government, which has, indeed, strongly driven the capitalist economic reform, to local government officials, who are the ones that do not perform their duties satisfactorily.

Another fact to note is the normalizing effect of laws on Shu Ren's perception of worker resistance. Although he does not disapprove of worker strikes or other collective actions, he tries to justify them by referencing laws. He imparts:

> *Workers carry out strikes and other forms of disturbances only to express their reasonable demands, which are supposed to be legally protected.* Their demands are in line with legal regulations. Occasionally, something disruptive may happen, but we can't help it. The government departments fail to do their jobs (*bu daowei*)—workers complain to them, but they do not take any actions. *When workers are left with no other means to solve their problems, they are forced to take extreme actions.* All workers want harmony and fairness; nobody wants to fight or argue with others.

Taking the law as the cornerstone, Shu Ren holds that the demands of workers are legally grounded, and thus, their extra-legal actions are justified. In his opinion, labor strikes do not affect social stability. If they engage in disruptive actions that transgress laws, it is only because their legally reasonable demands have been denied ['The government departments fail to do their job...When workers are left with no other means to solve their problems, they are forced to take extreme actions']. For him, workers prefer 'harmony' and try to act within the legal arena, but they are 'forced' to take extra-legal actions.

Fu Shan is in her mid-twenties and has completed vocational secondary school.[14] She has not stayed the whole time in cities; on and off, she returns to her home village in Guizhou as her children are being raised there. As a migrant worker, she is denied proper social welfare in cities; therefore, she is compelled to work in urban factories to earn money but fulfill her reproductive responsibilities in the rural village. Currently, she has been hired by a Japanese electronics factory in Shenzhen.

In 2010, she happened upon a recruitment counter set up by a dispatch company on the street (which is a frequent occurrence in industrial areas). After she decided to go for the job, the recruitment personnel of the dispatch company took her to the factory to sign an employment contract; then, she started to work there. Labour dispatch has become commonplace in FIEs, SOEs, or even government departments in China. It has been estimated that there were 37 million dispatch workers in China in 2012.[15] The factories for which dispatch workers generate surplus value do not establish any employment relations with the workers, but they still exercise strict control over the latter. Dispatch workers sign labor contracts with dispatch companies who obtain service payments from factories, retain a substantial proportion of the payment and then pay the remaining to dispatch workers as wages. Under this mode of employment, dispatch companies can send dispatch workers to work in any factory to which they assign dispatch workers. Firms prefer using dispatch workers over direct employment because it reduces their costs and increases operational flexibility (Xu 2009). It has been reported that in some big SOE, one-third to two-thirds of the staff are dispatch workers (Xu 2009). One of my interviewees estimates that dispatch workers made up three-fifths of the total workforce in the FIE factory he worked for.[16] Despite new legal regulations on labor dispatch,[17] this form of precarious work continues to result in labor abuse, such as unequal pay for equal work, and thus, triggering labor protests.[18]

At the time, Fu Shan knew nothing about the labor dispatch system; the dispatch company explained nothing to her. She thought she had signed a contract with the factory, rather than with the dispatch company. After working in the factory for a month, she found out her wages were below the city's minimum standard, and she also did not receive any overtime compensation. Fu Shan then talked to the factory's manager, who revealed that the dispatch company was her actual employer and that the factory already gave the company her wages, thus fulfilling its obligations. Fu Shan had no idea how to reach the boss of the dispatch company as she was never given any contact information. She went to report the case to the police, but officers said labor disputes were not within its jurisdiction. She severely criticizes the government for giving inadequate attention to labor disputes; even though workers are underpaid by employers and incur monetary losses, the latter are not dealt with as seriously as other law breakers simply because 'they have not hurt you physically or robbed your money like bandits'. However, for her 'the degree of harm imposed by employers on workers is the same as that by bandits'. At the time, when she encountered this labor dispute, non-payment of wages was considered a civil dispute. However, in 2011, the Criminal Law was amended to make it a criminal offence. In 2012, 120 employers were sentenced for wages in arrears.[19] This is a small number in comparison to the 9.24 million, 4.13 million, 3.39 million, and 2.02 million migrant workers suffering from wages in arrears in the years from 2008 to 2011 respectively.[20]

Fu Shan then filed a complaint to the local Labor Bureau. At first, an officer asked her to talk to the factory. Upon her second visit to the bureau, however, another officer said she had to talk to the dispatch company as she had established the employment relation with the dispatch company, not the factory. In her two visits to the Labor Bureau, none of the officers took the initiative to investigate her case. Fu Shan comments:

> To make it plain, *labor laws do not protect workers, only the rich.* How can we trust the Chinese labor laws? When nothing happens, the Labor Bureau claims that it protects workers and their interests; but when you have an issue, it says it can't handle your case because it is a third party, and it simply asks you to talk directly to the factory.

The labor law system is supposed to safeguard worker interests, opines Fu Shan, but the labor bureau she encountered is not on the side of workers. She has not opted for labor mediation or arbitration because it would take a long time. According to my lawyer-informants, labor arbitration in Shenzhen usually takes 4–6 months, though the Labor Dispute Mediation and Arbitration Law (Article 43) stipulates that it must be concluded within 2 months[21]; arbitration and litigation together often last for as long as a year.[22] Moreover, in 2013 an official TV channel estimated that workers need to spend at least 820 yuan for various charges when going through the whole process of mediation, arbitration, and litigation. If one takes the time costs into consideration, legal rights-defense costs workers at least 1571–2254 yuan,[23] which roughly equals 1 month of pay. In light of the complicated legal procedures and the related costs, many workers, like Fu Shan, simply give up defending their rights.

Fu Shan did not seek help from lawyers, as hiring one would be expensive in comparison to the amount of money the dispatch company owed her. She never thought of approaching trade unions either, as she did not know what they were at the time. Her teacher in vocational secondary school advised her to contact the ACWF, but she did not do so, believing that it would not be helpful. Neither did she solicit aid from any labor NGOs as she did not know any. Other workers hired by the dispatch company, indeed, encountered the same problem. Fu Shan stresses that it would help if all of them were to unite together to put pressure on the company; but they quit, one by one, rather than stand up in unity against the company. Fu Shan reflects:

> Other workers left the company. We were not so close to each other. *But if we united together, I think the boss would have given us back our money.* We should have all gone to talk to him. If he did not give us any response, we would have then gone together to the Labor Bureau. They would help us since we would have had so many people. *Solidarity means power* (*tuanjie jiushi liliang*).

Fu Shan realizes that workers as individuals can do little in defense of their rights, even if their claims are legally grounded, and that they have vaster power if united together. This illustrates her awareness that workers share common interests vis-à-vis the capitalists and that their resistance can become more powerful when they act collectively.

Despite her disapproval of the labor law system and law enforcement agencies, the normalizing effect of legal hegemony is evident in Fu Shan. She opines:

> Plainly speaking, workers are selling their labor power (*chumai laodong li*). *As long as what I gain matches the amount of labor power I put in, it is okay. As long as my boss pays me wages and overtime compensation according to labor laws, it is okay.*

She also comments that

> *If I become a boss one day, I would definitely pay workers according to labour laws.* If I were to earn more, I might be able to give them more. But it is impossible for me to give them all of my money. I couldn't give them 0.5

> million if I only got 1 million. I have to buy all the machinery and production tools in order to create the wealth; workers are just hired by me, right? *I would only pay workers what their labor power was worth*; if it was worth 10 yuan, I couldn't pay them 100 yuan, right?

No matter whether Fu Shan is a worker or a boss, she considers employers fair and above reproach if they pay workers in accordance with labor laws, which for her are a barometer to measure capital–labor relations. The labor law system has normalized surplus value extraction and other capitalist practices. As long as employers observe legal standards, Fu Shan does not consider them exploitative.

Fu Shan believes Chinese economic development has had both positive and negative impact on workers. On the one hand, peasant-workers can now 'get a job and earn money with their own labor', whereas prior to economic reform, they 'farmed everyday but earned very little; what they cultivated could only feed themselves for a while'. On the other, she says it is unfair that workers work diligently but earn poor wages when compared to their bosses, who do not labor much. Despite her ambivalence on economic development, she expresses approbation of the policy of 'let some people get rich first'. In her opinion, China cannot afford to adopt developmental strategies that seek to make all people wealthy at the same time; the geographical differences between villages and cities, hilly areas and non-hilly areas determine that 'letting some people get rich first' is a better policy for China.

In her early twenties, Xin Xin began to work in the cities in 2005 after graduating from junior high school in Henan.[24] She was diagnosed with leukemia after working in an electronics factory in Shenzhen for 4 years. She believes her illness is caused by the frequent use of benzene and other chemicals at work. Her factory once arranged a health inspection for workers; with the exception of her, all workers were given their health reports. She, therefore, suspects that the factory tried to hide something from her.

She applied for a diagnosis of occupational disease from the Shenzhen Prevention and Treatment Center for Occupational Disease according to the 2011 Law on the Prevention and Control of Occupational Diseases. It was, however, determined that her leukemia was not caused by her job. Later, she applied for a verification of occupational disease from the municipal public health administration department, but again, her illness was diagnosed as non-occupationally related. She then applied for verification from the provincial-level public health administration department, which came to the final conclusion that her leukemia was not occupationally related.

Xin Xin admits that the evidence she submitted for the first diagnosis was not well-prepared because she was unfamiliar with the procedure and barely knew what do to. However, she finds the two verifications conducted by the public health departments problematic. The officers from the city-level public health department arranged factory investigations that conflicted with her medical treatments. As a result, she was not able to participate in the investigations which were guided only by the factory managers. Besides, according to Xin Xin, the two verifications relied mostly on the reports submitted by the factory. I had no means to verify whether Xin Xin's leukemia was, indeed, occupationally caused. However, it is possible, in China, for public health departments to help cover up employer wrongdoings. In 2009, a worker named Zhang Haichao was denied a diagnosis of pneumoconiosis, an occupational disease, by the Prevention and Treatment Center for Occupational Disease in Zhengzhou, which was attempting to shelter Zhang's employer. In order to prove that he had pneumoconiosis, he insisted on surgically open his lungs to examine the lung issues (*kaixiong yanfei*).[25] After numerous protests against the government, at the end he was diagnosed as having job-related pneumoconiosis.

Xin Xin is critical of the labor law system, discrediting it for not monitoring factories rigorously. She comments:

> *Many labour laws are ill-implemented*; otherwise I would not have suffered so much. I was perfectly healthy before working in this factory, but I got leukemia after working there. Why do I have to go through so many complicated legal procedures to prove that my leukemia is occupational-related? *Why does the government not monitor the factory*?

In her opinion, the government is on the side of employers because the latter have created immense wealth for the country and given a vast amount in taxes to the government, whereas workers only contribute meagerly to government income. She notes:

> *The capitalists have fostered the mushrooming of corrupt officials at the local level.* They earn profits through exploiting workers, and thus, need the shelter

> of government officials. *They bribe officials through different means*; therefore, the officials keep one eye open and one eye shut to their illegal activities.

Xin Xin opines that economic reform mostly benefits the rich, enterprises, and the government; workers create wealth for them but cannot profit similarly from the economic growth. Despite blatant government corruption, she believes that there are some good officials executing the central government's policies and laws for the benefit of the people. For her, the central government is better than local governments, and it is not as corrupt as the latter. However, 'the emperor is far away and the mountains are high' (*shangao huangdi yuan*), and thus central government orders often look different once they reach the lower-levels of government. The transmuting mechanism of the labor law system deflects Xin Xin's criticism away from targeting the central government and the party-state, as a whole, and lands onto local government officials.

Due to her own experience, Xin Xin is skeptical and disappointed about the discourse on legal rights defense, criticizing that the road for rights-defense is 'craggy'. In spite of this, she is not utterly disillusioned, noting that there are successful cases in which workers win what they deserve, and that 'we won't know the outcomes of our rights-assertions unless we strive to the end'. This shows that she preserves a minimal degree of hope in legal rights-defense.

Prior to the labor dispute, Xin Xin knew nothing about labor laws and took no initiative to learn about them. This dispute has transformed her from being in an indifferent mode into taking on the critical mode. During the course of her dispute, a labor NGO offered her great aid, informing her of labor laws and affording her psychological support. She also sought help from her enterprise trade union, which organized a fundraiser among factory workers and gave her a 26,000 yuan donation. However, it provided no assistance to her application for the diagnosis of occupational disease. The manager once threatened that if she did not give up her claims, the trade union would stop raising money for her. She was not intimidated at all and decided to continue her rights-defense. She points out that the workplace trade union is led by managers, and thus, it is impossible to serve worker interests.

Xin Xin feels grateful towards the labor NGO and is determined to learn more about labor rights and help other workers through this NGO. She hopes to 'inform more workers of their rights so that they can go influence a lot more workers'. Like Ah Rong in Chap. 4 (Sect. 3.2), she has developed class empathy for and class connection with other workers. She realizes that many workers are facing unfair treatment inflicted by employers and she is ready to devote her energy to help advance their rights.

3.3 *Workers with Collective Labor Disputes Experiences*

Originally from Meizhou, You Yang has worked in the cities for over 10 years.[26] He used to be a skilled worker in a small moulding factory in Shenzhen, which had to be relocated to another city against the policies of industrial upgrade in Shenzhen and Guangdong. According to the Labour Contract Law (Articles 46 and 47), employers need to compensate workers in cases of termination (which amount to their monthly wages times the number of years of service). Yet it is unclear if employers need to pay any compensation in situations of factory relocation, which for many workers is equivalent to forced cessation of employment relations. To evade compensating the workers, You Yang's boss tried to make the senior workers resign by altering their job duties and reducing their salaries. You Yang and some workers who had worked in the factory for five to 10 plus years were assigned new positions that were lower than their original ones. For instance, some skilled workers were asked to perform custodial duties, and their salaries were decreased to the level of ordinary workers. Despite these tricks, the boss was not considered to be acting illegally because the labor contracts stated that the factory could change the positions of workers once every year.

You Yang's boss did not officially announce the factory's relocation, but the news still reached the workers. In the face of these ploys by the boss, You Yang and other workers started to strategize their response. They consulted a labor NGO, which advised them to gain leverage over the boss through exposing his illegal labor practices. For example, the factory did not fully contribute to the social insurance fund for the workers; everyday they worked 2–4 hours of uncompensated overtime; they enjoyed no paid leave, maternity leave and so forth. Moreover, the NGO staff reminded the workers that according to the Labour Contract Law, firms need to inform and consult enterprise trade unions in regards to important matters such as massive lay-offs, dismissals, and changes in employment conditions. The NGO staff advised them to form a workplace trade union so as to acquire greater power over the factory on issues related to compensation.

Following the NGO's suggestions, in September 2011 You Yang and other core workers initiated a joint letter to the district trade union, requesting to join the workplace trade union as members. More than 90 workers signed the petition (out of 300 workers in the factory). In the letter, they wrote:

> The current trade union representatives were appointed by management rather than being elected by the workers. The enterprise trade union exists only in name and not in practice (*mingcun shiwan*). Moreover, the trade union does not have a single member. To safeguard worker rights, we now urgently request to join the trade union.

The district trade union gave no response to the workers, who then sent the joint letter to the Shenzhen city trade union and went to discuss matters with its officials. The officials replied that the district trade union was handling their case and directed them to contact it. Therefore, You Yang and other workers went to the district trade union's office, where officials alleged that a trade union already existed in their factory, and they should apply for trade union membership from that trade union. The workers responded that they were unknowledgeable about the identity of the enterprise union chair, the identity of committee members, and the number of union members. The district union official stated that he needed some time to further investigate the matter.

Later, the district union officials communicated to the workers that it would help establish a trade union in their factory soon. On the 19th October 2011, the factory called a meeting about the formation of a workplace union, to which none of the workers who signed the above-mentioned joint letter were invited. Only upon workers' opposition were two of them allowed to sit in the meeting. In the meeting, the district union officials explained the procedures for forming workplace unions. In addition, they handed out membership forms to the attendees, who would supposedly distribute them to workers that were interested in joining the union.

On the 21st October, the worker representatives from the Development Department and the Quality Control Department submitted 98 union application forms to the district trade union, while the director's office submitted 37. On the same day, management transferred some workers that had applied for union membership to new, inferior, less-skilled positions. The workers took this as revenge from the factory for their activism.

Ten days later, management posted a notice announcing the suspension of duties for five workers, who were the most active in pushing for reactivation of the workplace union. To block them from influencing other workers, management did not allow these five workers to reenter the factory.

Later in November, more than 30 workers each paid 400 yuan to hire a lawyer to handle their case. However, the lawyer did not do much for them; You Yang recalls, 'Everything was ok for him before we paid him; he told us he was optimistic and had great confidence. But in reality, he did not help us much.' The lawyer only met with the workers twice, giving them the same suggestions made by the NGO staff: organize a factory union. With the excuse that not all workers paid him had agreed to disclose their authorization of his representation to the factory and government agencies (due to the workers' fear of revenge), the lawyer ultimately did not help the workers write any letter to the factory or government agencies, not to mention negotiate on behalf of the workers. In retrospect, You Yang realizes that the lawyer could have represented the workers who were willing to disclose their identities, but the lawyer chose not to do so. You Yang thinks that the 12000 yuan paid to the lawyer was 'misspent'.

In late November, the factory and district trade union notified workers that they would soon organize elections for factory union representatives, but they did not specify the date. In China, enterprise trade union elections, if even held at all, usually first let members elect union representatives, who then elect the trade union committee members (Hui and Chan 2015). On the unannounced election day, union members in each department voted for a certain number of union representatives. After collecting the ballots, district union officials did not count the vote inside the factory; instead, they wished to do the tallying at the union office. Worried that the district trade union might play tricks, You Yang and other workers opposed this arrangement. Afterwards, two workers were allowed to go with the union officials to their office to witness the vote-counting. At the end, 19 union representatives were elected, 14 of which were rank-and-file workers and 5 were managerial staff.

A few days after announcing the election results, the factory posted a notice stating that the trade union preparation committee, which was responsible for conducting and monitoring union elections according to legal guidelines, had just been organized and that its five members were all managerial level staff. The workers were resentful because, first, according to the 1992 Temporary Regulations on the Elections for Grassroots Trade

Unions and the 2008 Measures for the Implementation of the Trade Union Laws in Shenzhen, the union preparation committee must be formed prior to the election of union representatives rather than after the election. Second, the factory did not explain how the preparation committee was selected, and why it solely consisted of the managerial staff. You Yang and other workers went to the district union enquiring about this issue. The officials did not give them a convincing answer, reiterating that the preparation committee members had to be well educated (*zhishi hua*), young (*nianqing hua*), and members of the CCP. The workers put themselves forward as candidates of the preparation committee members, but the district union officials insisted that ordinary workers were not qualified and that 'you [they] can't do things as you [they] like'.

As their resistance mounted, You Yang discloses, some workers disagreed with the approach of hiring the lawyer and filing a lawsuit against the factory for it was time-consuming. They believed that the factory was illegal in many respects and that if the workers took collective action, the company would bow to their pressure. Therefore, in mid-December, shortly before the Lunar New Year, they mobilized the workers to petition (*shangfang*) the Shenzhen Labor Bureau, the Shenzhen Trade Union, and the Letter and Visits Office of the Shenzhen Party Committee. Later in their last move, a hundred workers petitioned the Letter and Visits Office of the Shenzhen government; this aroused great concern from the government. City government officials invited workers' representatives to converse in their offices; district government representatives were also present, and they promised to handle the case properly and persuaded the workers to return to the district. The government officials even arranged two coaches to send the workers back to the factory.

After returning to the factory, the managers, Labor Bureau officers, district government officials, and worker representatives immediately held a meeting. The boss proposed to pay workers 75% of the compensation they demanded, stressing that there was no room for negotiation. The workers representatives agreed to the company's offer. Upon receipt of their compensation, You Yang and around 100 workers resigned. Being relieved from workers' pressure, union elections in the factory stopped altogether.

For You Yang, labor laws have not helped them much, and he is skeptical towards the officially promulgated idea of legal rights-defense. In his opinion, labor laws fail to protect workers due to misbehavior of problematic government officials. In his case, officials from the Labor Bureau, higher level trade unions, and the Shenzhen city government were in support of his boss because 'he pays taxes to the government'. He comments:

> If workers don't make their issues big (*naoda*), the government officials will just ignore you. In our case, they always stood on the side of the boss, saying that he had health problems and his business was not doing well, and they always asked us to be cooperative. There may be some good government cadres who care about the well-being of workers, but not any that we have encountered.

He adds, 'We could not have gotten any compensation by simply following the laws and not taking any collective action. Those workers who were compelled to quit their jobs but took no action, received no compensation, and those who resigned after us got nothing either'. You Yang summarizes that they deployed a two-track strategy in their struggle. The first strategy was rights-defense through organizing (*zuzhi weiquan*). This means mobilizing and consolidating workers in the name of forming a trade union, thereby pressuring the factory with the collective power of workers. The second strategy was rights-defense through laws (*falv weiquan*), which means seeking help from a lawyer and following legal procedures to complain about their boss. In his opinion, rights-defense through organizing is more effective than rights-defense through laws, but still they cannot completely neglect the laws:

> Even if you take the route of rights-defense through organizing, legal knowledge is indispensable because your collective actions are still related to laws; otherwise, it's difficult to succeed.

From You Yang's point of view, labor laws provided useful resources to their rights-defense through organizing; the Trade Unions Law was the ground upon which their actions took place. At the same time, he is cautious of not crossing the legal boundaries. He explains that if workers were legally insensitive, their actions might easily violate laws, and they thus, would be jailed by police. In such a situation, rights-defense through organizing would no longer be effective because 'the hardcore worker-activists would be arrested for breaching the laws, and then the whole core would collapse, and the struggle would be forced to an end'. You Yang demonstrates an understanding of the double-edged blade of the legal system. On the one hand, he recognizes that workers' collective actions utilizing labor laws are more powerful than simply exhausting legal channels in wringing compensation from employers. On the other, he believes that workers cannot unrestrainedly transgress legal and political constraints. Therefore, he consciously kept their actions within legal boundaries so as to make their struggle sustainable and achievable.

You Yang discloses that his fellow workers initially were not united because many of them did not know their rights, the functions and missions of trade unions and so forth. However, as their struggle developed, they became highly unified and better organized. More than 30 workers met among themselves once every few days, exchanging updates, discussing their actions and plans, and building up consensus. Around 20 core workers each contributed 100 yuan to set up an action fund supporting transportation fees and other expenses related to their actions. This is not a large amount of money, but You Yang considers it an indication of the commitment of the workers to the struggle. He recalls, 'The core workers knew that if they did not unite together, they would be the next ones to be forced to quit their jobs by the factory.' In other words, they realized their shared interests vis-à-vis the employer and understood that if they did not join hands together, their interests would be undermined. You Yang is highly committed to the struggle and even prepared himself for the company's revenge, 'At that time, I did not think too much. Of course, I knew revenge was possible, but I could not worry too much. Actually in the later stages, I anticipated that the factory would terminate me.'

4 Ambivalent Workers

Rather than being clearly affirmative or critical, some interviewees hover between the two. They partly accept the official legal discourses, yet partly disapprove of the legal practices, expressing ambivalent opinions towards the labor law system, the state, and the economy. They usually believe that what legal discourses advocate are somehow good for workers, but at the same time, they criticize the labor law system for having many loopholes, which they think are caused by the misbehavior of some government officials. They have not rendered active consent to legal hegemony but are in a state of uncertainty and submissiveness.

4.1 *Workers Without Labor Dispute Experiences*

Ah Xi is a 40-year old worker who has finished primary schooling. He has worked in the cities for more than 10 years and has now been hired by a small electronics company in Shenzhen.[27] He has a fair knowledge of labor laws and is aware of key legal regulations, such as those regarding social insurance, labor contracts, overtime compensation, minimum wage, and so forth. He has not encountered any labor disputes but has heard many stories from friends who have been treated unfairly at work. For example, one of his friends was denied proper compensation after a work accident; another one was forced to work unpaid, overtime work. When asked if labor laws could protect workers, he replied, 'Yes, they certainly do. Otherwise what would be the use of having a government?' However, when faced with the question about whether labor laws are skewed towards workers or employers, he became less affirmative. He responded, 'It depends on the situation. But society is presently like this, whoever has money is the big brother [*laoda*]. The laws have some loopholes.' By 'big brother', he is referring to wealthy and powerful employers who take advantages of legal loopholes in one way or another. Our conversation continued as follows:

Researcher: Has the government offered enough protection to workers?
Ah Xi: Um… I have never seen any government cadres inspecting my factory. Only the fire department has come a few times.
Researcher: So the government is biased towards employers?
Ah Xi: I am not sure about that.
Researcher: Which areas should the government improve?
Ah Xi Labor inspection. They should inspect factories more frequently.

Unlike the critical workers in this chapter, Ah Xi reveals a more positive opinion of labor laws and tends to regard them as providing some protections to workers ['yes, certainly they do. Otherwise what's the use of having the government?']. Nevertheless, unlike the affirmative workers in Chap. 4 who show little doubt about the labor law system, Ah Xi realizes that the rich can easily manipulate legal loopholes to their advantage. Concerning his position about the government, he believes the purpose of having the government is to protect workers, but at the same time, he knows that many government officials favor employers, and thus, fail to carry out labor inspections properly. Femia notes that some workers 'possesses a "contradictory consciousness": his [their] perceptions and evaluations of social life exhibit inconsistency and superficiality, which express the gap between the dominant interpretation of reality and his [their] own objective situation' (1987, 185). Ah Xi's ambivalence and mixed feeling towards the labor law system and the government is due to, on the one hand, the common sense reproduced by the ruling class regarding the juridico-political system and, on the other, the reality that he has witnessed and experienced (i.e., the rare inspection of factories by government officials) and the stories of exploitation from his friends.

Ah Kong is in his early 20s.[28] After finishing tertiary education in Hubei, he came to work in Shenzhen one and a half years ago. He is now employed at an electronics factory, taking care of warehouse logistics. His basic monthly salary is the same as the city's minimum wage. Including overtime payment, every month he earns less than 3000 yuan. When asked if labor laws are skewed towards employers or workers, he said the laws are fair, but the critical issue is whether government officials are fair.

Researcher: What do you think about labor laws? Can they protect workers?

Ah Kong: Protect workers? Um…I don't know what to say. If you say they don't protect workers, that's not true; they offer some degree of protection. But are they comprehensive? Certainly not. How can I put this? Ummm…they protect some things but not others.

Researcher: What do you think about legal rights-defense? Do you think workers can defend their legal rights?

Ah Kong: If the idea of legal rights-defense could be effectively enacted, it would be good for workers; these are their rights as citizens. However, in reality you cannot implement them that easily. You cannot easily change *guanxi* politics; money makes everything, right?

Researcher: What do you think about the rule of law?

Ah Kong: The rule of law means that things have to be done in accordance to laws. Under the rule of law, present-day society is not as chaotic as in the past.

Researcher: Is the rule of law well-established in China?

Ah Kong: Yes, it is; otherwise our society would become chaotic. However, some peoples' rights aren't being protected… The laws are ok [*hai keyi*], some of them are quite fair and just.

Ah Kong's ambivalence in regards to the labor law system is manifested in his simultaneous endorsement and disapproval of the state-constructed notions of legal rights defense and the rule of law, as well as the legal practices associated with them. First, he holds that the notion of legal rights defense offers some protection to workers and that some laws are fair and just. However, at the same time, he finds it difficult to defend one's legal rights because government officials are closely linked to the businesses ['You cannot easily change the *guanxi* politics; money can make everything, right?']. Second, Ah Kong approves of the rule of law for preventing society from falling into chaos, but at the same time, he realizes that some peoples' rights are not well protected under the rule of law. Ah Kong's comment on social chaos resonates with the state-promoted ideology of 'social stability', which stresses that socio-economic and socio-political 'stability' are prerequisite for economic growth and social prosperity (Breslin 2007). This ideological construction plus the political and social turmoil in the pre-reform era (such as the Cultural Revolution) have made many Chinese people prefer 'social stability' as articulated by the party-state over social chaos, as is associated with the country's turbulent contemporary history.

In brief, the discrepancies between legal rights-defense and the rule of law as legal ideals and as actual legal practices have not led to Ah Kong's full rejection of these notions as the critical informants have; he wavers between showing both appreciation for and doubts over the labor law system.

4.2 *Workers with Individual Labor Dispute Experiences*

Originally from Guizhou, Gui Nan has worked in Shenzhen for 9 years.[29] He is in his late twenties and has a job at a logistics company at the time of our interview. In 2010, he and his wife were recruited by a dispatch company, which sent them to work in a small factory in Shenzhen. The dispatch company paid Gui Nan an hourly wage of 6 yuan with a maximum limit of 10 hours per day. Within these 10 hours, he had to produce a designated amount of products. If he had to work overtime to accomplish the task, his boss would pay him no compensation. To add insult to injury, the dispatch company paid him no wages after he had worked in the factory for more than a month.

Gui Nan complained to the street-level Labor Bureau. The bureau officer required him to support his claim with evidence, such as the dispatch company's license, wage slips and so forth, none of which the company had ever given him. The officer said he would not be able to help much and directed Gui Nan to apply for labor arbitration. Gui Nan told me, 'At that time, I knew nothing about labor arbitration or how to fight for my interests.' Feeling frustrated, he went to talk to the dispatch company's manager and had a fierce quarrel with him. At the end, the manager only agreed to give him 1000 yuan, which barely covered what the company fully owed him. However, as Gui Nan had no plans to stay with the company, he just hoped to resolve the dispute as soon as possible, so he accepted the money and quit. Gui Nan's decision was not unique; as explained earlier, many workers give up pursuing their legal rights because of time-consuming legal procedures.

Gui Nan's assessment of the labor law system vacillates between dissatisfaction and affirmation. At one point of our interview, he condemned labor laws for their improper implementation and the lack of supervision over firms. He observes:

> Labor laws certainly cannot give workers enough protection. *The legal supervision over factories is unsatisfactory.* Many small domestically owned factories infringe on labor rights, yet nobody oversees them. Many local factories have horrible working conditions, but *when workers complain to the Labor Bureaus, they always shirk their responsibilities.*

On other occasions, however, Gui Nan shows approval of the labor law system, noting that 'the laws are well observed by some factories. For example, many foreign-owned enterprises observe labor laws well, and some local governments properly enforce them.' He comments that Chinese labor relations are generally 'acceptable', stating, 'Our country is developing rapidly, hence some things are not well established. But generally speaking, there has been progress.' Similar to the affirmative workers in Chap. 4, Gui Nan's opinion of the labor law system is principally grounded on the level of implementation rather than the actual legal contents. The uneven enforcement of labor laws across different types of factories (such as small versus large, foreign-owned versus domestic) contribute to his occasional denouncement and intermittent approval of the labor law system.

Gui Nan complains to me about soaring inflation and low wages in the cities, which all create huge pressure for him. When asked if workers benefit from economic development, he reveals an uncertainty and submissiveness.

He agrees that workers cannot enjoy economic prosperity, but he seems to have accepted the unfairness embedded into the socio-economic system. He imparts, 'Injustice and unfairness are everywhere in society. Wherever you go, you can feel it. But what can we do about this? The second-generation of the high-ranking government officials are very rich, but they were born to inherit this wealth; it's not a matter of fairness or not, right?' Gui Nan has revealed a strong sense of resignation towards the injustice facing workers.

Talking about the challenges to workers' rights-defense, Gui Nan notes that workers are not sufficiently united in their resistance, or they have not yet developed a rights-awareness—'many of them think it's fine as long as they have something to eat and wear'. That said, he observes that some workers, having worked in cities for a long time, have become increasingly conscious of their rights and have learned more about labor laws and rights-defense. Another obstacle to workers' rights-defense is, suggests Gui Nan, that they do not know how to assert their rights, for instance which government departments should be approached when problems arise. In these cases, he says, some workers simply give up their rights, but some will take extra-legal actions, such as road-blockages, rallies or committing suicide. He opines:

> From a legal point of view, I think *these [extra-legal] actions are not appropriate. But workers have no other means (qiuzhu wumen)*; there is nobody to help them, and they don't know what to do. A strong fire burns inside their hearts, and *therefore, they resort to these 'extreme' actions*; *they are forced by the circumstances* (bichu lai)!

Gui Nan's comments illustrate the legal influence on workers' self-understanding of resistance. Labour laws do not simply define what is right and what is wrong in the eyes of some workers (such as Ah Wen from Chap. 4), they also guide workers' perceptions of what forms of rights-defense activities are appropriate and what are not. Like the critical worker Shu Ren who was elaborated upon in the previous section, Gui Nan has partially submitted to legal logic, concurring that workers' actions should conform to laws ['From the legal point of views, I think these [extra-legal] actions are not appropriate']. However, in his opinion, since labor laws cannot always do workers justice, workers are forgivable for taking 'extreme' extra-legal actions. Similarly, another interviewee notes, 'Rights-defense is about safeguarding your rights within the legal arena.

Ordinary people don't want to take extreme actions, they are forced to do so. I stand up for my rights only because my boss is too unfair (*tai guo-fen*).'[30] Consciously or unconsciously taking legal channels as a normative means for rights-defense, some interviewees try to justify the extra-legal actions of workers by highlighting employer unfairness and worker helplessness. In this way, they have, though unintentionally, reinforced the legitimacy of legal vehicles and the illegitimacy of extra-legal means in resolving labor conflicts.

Jian Hua is in his late thirties. He suffered an occupational accident when working for an electronics factory in Dongguan in 2012.[31] According to law, during his period of medical treatment, his boss should have paid him a monthly salary equivalent to his average wage from the year prior to the accident (which was around 3000 yuan), but in reality, he only received the city's minimum wage (which was 1100 yuan). In addition, Jian Hua was a skilled worker earning around 4000 yuan per month prior to the work injury, but afterwards, his manager downgraded him to a position of an ordinary production worker (whose salary was only about 2000 yuan including overtime payment). This violated the terms and conditions stated in the labor contract signed between Jian Hua and the factory.

Jian Hua attended a mediation session organized by the mediation committee in his factory, but he could not reach an agreement with his employer who insisted that paying him the minimum wage was legal. His boss offered him a lump sum compensation to settle the dispute, but the amount was less than what he was entitled to. Therefore, Jian Hua turned down the proposal:

> My boss is not following labor laws; he bargained with me as if we were at the marketplace. The lump sum he offered me was much less than what laws prescribe. Therefore, I did not accept his offer and decided to take legal actions to resolve the dispute.

He then applied for arbitration at the Labor Bureau, and his case was to be heard 10 days after our interview. He shows great confidence in arbitration, trusting that it would do him justice. He tells me assuredly, 'If your claims have legal grounds, you will win the case. On the contrary, if they are unreasonable and lack evidence, then you will lose the case'. Similar to Ah Wen from Chap. 4, the normalizing mechanism of the labor law system induces Jian Hua to believe that legal prescription and court rulings must be right and unimpeachable.

The impact of the normalizing mechanism is further manifested in how Jian Hua perceives 'fairness' and 'exploitation'. When asked if some employers are exploitative, Jian Hua replies, 'I have not seen any exploitation in the factories where I have worked before. They are usually big companies, and they *comply with labor laws and are quite fair*. But I don't know what happens in other factories and whether they breach laws.'[32] For him, the definition of 'exploitation' and 'fairness' are associated with legal standards; 'exploitation' refers specifically to illegal treatment of workers and 'fairness' equals being legally-compliant. As long as employers follow labor laws, they are not exploiting workers and are being fair.

Jian Hua knew little about labor laws before his work injury and had only come across some sketchy legal information on TV. When he studied in vocational secondary school, there was a class on laws, but back then, he deemed it unnecessary to grasp legal knowledge. Having suffered a work injury and experiencing the dispute, he realizes that 'many things in reality are closely linked to laws'. Therefore, he now 'tr[ies] hard to learn labor laws' and 'rel[ies] more on the laws'. As stressed in Chap. 4, worker susceptibility towards legal hegemony is not stagnant; changing life experiences may trigger a change of their position among the five categories. Jian Hua used to be indifferent to labor laws, but the conflict with his employer propelled him to be more legally-conscious.

Commenting on whether labor laws offer workers adequate protection, at one point, Jian Hua reveals some confidence in the laws, without which he believes he might not be able to wrest any compensation from the factory.

> *Labor laws are fair; workers can use them to defend their rights* because they stipulate what you can do if your legal rights are violated. I think they are fair as far as my case is concerned. *Without them, I would have been left with no means to make my boss accountable for my injury.*

That said, at another point, Jian Hua manifests a degree of criticism towards the labor law system.

> Labor laws, especially those related to work injuries, are loosely enforced. If they are not strictly implemented, employers won't follow them because it would cost them nothing to disobey the laws. Many law enforcers do not do

> their jobs well (*bu daowei*). *If they seek to cover up the faults of enterprises, the laws are just empty words.*

Jian Hua's ambivalence towards the labor law system can be explained by the fact that, on the one hand, he (like Ah Wen from Chap. 4) has lived through the period when the Labour Law, Labour Contract Law, Social Insurance Law, Provisions on Minimum Wage, and so forth were not yet enacted. He, thus, has experienced the differences between an absence and a presence of labor laws, and has profoundly felt the benefits of having legal vehicles, which were unavailable to workers in the past, to pursue his interests. However, as official legal discourses have induced high expectations from workers in the labor law system, workers also quickly show frustration and disapproval when witnessing the discrepancies between the legal ideals and the legal reality.

When Jian Hua was hospitalized, a lawyer came to promote his business to him and other work injury victims, encouraging them to seek his legal assistance. After being released from the hospital, Jian Hua went to consult the lawyer in his office for an hour, which cost him 100 yuan. If Jian Hua would have asked this lawyer to handle the case, he would have needed to pay a service charge. Jian Hua found the legal consultation provided by the lawyer unhelpful:

> The legal consultation was not very useful. If I would have used the consultation fee to buy books on labour laws, which only cost 40 yuan, I would have benefited more. What the lawyer said was the same as what the books tell me; I think the 100 yuan was wasted.

Later Jian Hua got in touch with a labor NGO and attended classes on labor laws. He discloses that had he known the NGO earlier, he would not have spent any money on consulting a lawyer. He thinks positively of the NGO, which has 'offered [him] immense help' and 'enlightened [him] about labor laws'. Now he is highly active in the NGO, often visiting hospitalized, injured workers together with its staff and giving them advice on how to handle their cases. In the same way as Ah Rong from Chap. 4, Jian Hua has developed a sense of class empathy for workers who share similar exploitative experiences. Having encountered the obstacles in rights-assertion and gaining the support of the NGO in this process, he realizes that many workers are as helpless as he is and that 'it is my[his] responsibility to help other workers in need'.

Jian Hua stresses that workers contribute considerably to the Chinese economy and that 'if workers do not produce, enterprises cannot survive'. He thinks that workers have benefited from economic development; in the past, there was no electricity or even proper roads in rural areas, but now peasant-worker living standards have improved and their wages have grown. That said, he admits that sometimes workers are not fairly treated, for which enterprises should bear the major responsibilities because they have failed to observe labor laws. He also suggests the government has responsibility for not monitoring factories rigorously. In his opinion, local governments are biased towards employers and are quite corrupt, but the central government is better.

4.3 Workers with Collective Labor Dispute Experiences

Chang Shan, in his early twenties, was hired by a motor parts supply factory in the PRD where workers walked out in 2010, demanding an 800 yuan wage increase and democratic trade union reform.[33] As a student from a vocational secondary school, he initially came for an internship in the factory in 2007 and was hired on as a formal worker after graduation. Later, he was promoted to deputy group leader, a low-level supervisory position. The strike in his factory was initiated by rank-and-file workers, but he highly supported it and later became an active leader. He recalls:

> Initially, many supervisory staff in our department did not dare to join the strike. But I had close relationships with the rank-and-file workers, and I found their demands very reasonable. I started to work in the factory in 2007; my wages had increased by only around 20 yuan over the course of 4 years. *Our wages were too low; therefore, I gave my full support to the strikers.* If we did not go on strike, the company might only give us a thirty yuan pay rise.

During the course of the strike, management threatened workers, saying that strikes were illegal in China. Chang Shan verified this allegation through researching laws and consulting a legal scholar. He found out that Chinese laws do not spell out whether strikes are legal or illegal. Neither the Constitution nor other laws explicitly prohibit worker strikes. Neither do they prescribe what makes strikes legal or illegal. In other words, there exists a legal grey area concerning worker strikes. That said, during the strike Chang Shan and other strike leaders kept reminding workers that they should stage a 'civilized strike' [*wenming bagong*], and that they should not destroy any machines or property, or injure anybody. As the legality of strikes is an ambiguous legal matter, Chang Shan thought their strike should be carefully staged so that the police would have no excuse to arrest strikers.

At first the company refused to negotiate with the strikers, but later, it arranged a negotiation meeting with Chang Shan and other worker representatives due to rising social pressure. Finally, it conceded to a monthly wage increase of around 32.4% for formal workers and about 70% for student interns. Subsequent to the strike, the provincial trade union stepped in to push forward workplace trade union elections and annual wage negotiations in the factory.

Chang Shan did not learn about any labor laws in school, but he would research them when unsure. To prepare for the strike negotiations, Chang Shan spent great effort to study the laws associated with collective consultation. His evaluation of the labor law system swings between endorsement and disapproval. On the one hand, he finds labor laws 'more or less just' and 'protective of workers', though employers often exploit legal loopholes, and implementational problems of labor laws are easily identified. He notes that if strikers' demands were to have legal grounds, they would be 'more confident' (*diqi zu yidian*). Taking trade union member rights as an example, he comments:

> It is good that the Trade Union Law has spelt out union members' rights and obligations. In the past, I did not know what rights I had as a union member, but during the strike I found out that the Law has ensured our rights, such as the right to recall incompetent union officials. This has emboldened us (*danzi dale*) and given us greater confidence.

On the other hand, Chang Shan is skeptical of the rule of law, suggesting that it only protects the rich, not the poor. From the news, he has learned that some rich people kill the poor and pay someone else to go to jail in their place; he criticizes that 'the rule of law does not exist in any genuine sense'. In addition, he realizes there is a gap between labor laws as written on paper and labor laws as enacted in reality. He is disappointed with the 'invisible administrative intervention' from the managers and higher-level trade unions on the post-strike trade union reform in his factory:

> According to the Trade Union Law, union members have the right to recall the chair if he [she] does not fulfill his [her] duties. However, in reality, it is difficult to do this. First, will the company and higher-level trade unions agree to the recall? Second, will they approve the person supported by the majority of members to be the new chair? All these are not legal questions. If the chair only has workers' support but without approval from the company and the government, he [she] would come under great pressure.

In the post-strike trade union elections in his factory, management and higher-level union officials deliberately excluded a popular strike leader from running in the elections and thus, from being elected. They dissuaded workers from voting for this strike leader at the departmental-level elections; the trade union election preparatory committee, which was dominated by managerial staff, voted her down as a candidate for election to the trade union committee. Moreover, management and higher-level trade unions backed a high-ranking staffperson to be the chair, who commenced working at the factory only after the strike. Many workers felt that he was 'designated' to be the chair, though formal elections were held. In theory, labor laws have enshrined the trade union rights of workers, but, as Chang Shan highlights, the extra-legal influence imposed by the company and higher-level union officials has hindered workers from truly upholding their legal rights.

Chang Shan's assessment of the Chinese government also manifests an air of ambivalence. On some occasions, he says they are neutral but in others, he suggests they are pro-business. On the one hand, he opines that the government does not necessarily favor enterprises and that their principal concern is maintaining social stability (*weiwen*); if workers do not cause trouble (*nao dashi*), the government would tolerate protests. In the post-strike trade union elections and collective wage negotiations in his factory, suggests Chang Shan, the local government and higher-level trade union officials were neither on the side of the company nor on that of the workers. In other words, he believes they were 'autonomous' from the company.

> The provincial trade union official [that intervened in the post-strike industrial relations in the factory] tried not to offend either the company or the workers. He stressed that the enterprise had to survive and the workplace union should not request too high of a wage increase. Moreover, *he accentuated that the company and the workplace union should compromise with each*

> *other in order to find an equilibrium, and that this would lead to a mutual victory* [*shuangying*]. I think *he has not taken any sides.*

On the other hand, he underscores that the provincial and city government are not necessarily 'good' because they often focus only on the GDP and 'neglect the well-being of the people'. Because they endeavor to attract businesses to their cities, complains Chang Shan, they are unwilling to improve worker welfare, such as social insurance and minimum wages, or to enforce labor laws stringently. However, he thinks the central government is 'good', and its policies and laws are 'pro-labor'. For him, 'a lot of people approve' of the central government, but many local governments do not follow its orders:

> The policies and laws made by the central government are good, but they are not implemented effectively because 'the emperor is far away in the high mountains'. *The local governments have not executed the central government's laws and policies seriously.*

Being affected by the transmuting mechanism of legal hegemony, Chang Shan attributes workers' plight to local governments, which are responsible for capital accumulation at the local level, rather than to the central government which has been forcefully driving economic reform at a broader level. As a result, the legitimacy of the central government or the party-state en bloc remains unchallenged.

Chang Shan also expresses vacillating views about Chinese economic development. On the one hand, he complains that the economy has developed too rapidly and that the local governments have blindly pursued GDP at the expense of workers. He reckons that 'without workers' sacrifice, China would not have achieved the progress that it has made'. On the other, he expresses appreciation for the economic growth. He recalls that he was able to eat meat only once a week when he was young, but now, as society becomes more prosperous, he and his family in the rural village can afford to eat meat every day. He opines, 'It is everyone's responsibility to help pursue a higher GDP. Our country comes first, and then our family; we need to have a strong country before we are able to have a stable family. If our country is strong, we won't need to be afraid of other countries.' Like Xiao Mei in Chap. 4, he reveals strong nationalist sentiments, believing that his well-being is closely linked to the country's economic development. He discloses that he does not mind working hard, as long as he witnesses the changes of the country. Overall, he endorses the central government's development strategies:

> China has only opened up for a short period of time, but the GDP has gone up swiftly. If we do not sacrifice workers' well-being, China's reform would go very slowly, and our country might not be as strong as it is. I can sacrifice for my country, though only for a certain amount of time.

5 Conclusion

Having actively endorsed the labor law system and internalized the values and ideas it reproduces, the affirmative workers in Chap. 4 have conferred active consent to legal hegemony. In contrast, the indifferent, critical, and ambivalent workers in this chapter render passive, not active, consent to legal hegemony. Some of them demonstrate a feeling of impotence and resignation; some are only partially assimilated to the legally mediated capitalist worldviews and demonstrate varying degrees of criticism over the labor law system, the state, and the capitalist economy.

For the indifferent workers, the labor and social policies (such as the household registration system) and their personal attributes related to age, education, and gender role, have tied them to their rural origins. They feel alienated in the cities and consider their work life there transitory; hence, they see labor laws and socio-economic development as irrelevant to them. If there are any problems with their bosses, they would opt to quit their jobs, rather than resorting to legal or extra-legal channels to resolve issues. Their rejection of the legal frame of reference is not a result of conscious reflection, but that of social alienation created by the state's economic and social policies. The social exclusions that the indifferent workers experience in cities have impeded the labor law system from securing their active consent. However, this does not necessarily mean that they are insusceptible to legal hegemony. Although they have not actively consented to the legally mediated worldviews, they have passively submitted themselves to the status quo and capitalist values normalized by the labor law system. Due to the legal labor contract system, both Ah Qing and Ah Ying believe that they are 'free' to withdraw from employment relations whenever they like. As they are full of apathy and submissiveness, the indifferent workers are not a serious threat to the capitalist social and economic order.

Workers that have experienced individual or collective labor disputes seldom fall into the indifferent category for they usually find labor laws relevant to their rights-assertion in one way or another. Most, if not all, of them have actively acquainted themselves with legal knowledge during the course of championing their rights. Some of them have already paid attention to labor laws prior to their disputes. Some, however, only started to become conscious of legal regulations subsequent to the outbreak of labor disputes (such as Xin Xin and Jian Hua). While pursuing their rights, many of them have gained deeper legal knowledge and developed particular views of the labor law system. None of them find labor laws irrelevant to them. In other words, the labor–capital conflicts have transformed some workers from an indifferent mode into other modes.

The critical workers discredit the labor law system, including the relevant legal discourses and practices. The exploitative experience incurred by my informants has shaped their attitudes towards labor laws. Some critical workers were treated unfairly or illegally in workplace, but they did not report their grievances to managers or the government. This was either because they thought it was useless (Chen Fei), or they believed labor contracts were 'fair' and 'equal' deals with employers, and thus, they should simply quit their job if they felt unsatisfied (Zhang Lin). Although this type of critical worker has not engaged in any open disputes with their bosses, the unfair treatment they have encountered makes them critical of the labor law system, which they deem unable to protect workers due to implementational deficits.

For the critical workers that have experienced individual labor disputes, they sought to address their grievances through legal channels, but met substantial difficulties. They, therefore, have become skeptical of legal discourses such as rights defense according to laws and the rule of law. In spite of their disapproval for the labor law system, they are not completely immune to its double hegemonic effects. Their criticism of labor laws is confined within the capitalist-legal logics, usually targeting implementational issues rather than unbalanced power relations inherent in the laws. This, indeed, echoes what Femia highlights: 'while the masses may be dissatisfied, while they may sense the contradiction between the positive official definition of reality and the starkness of their own subordination, they are unable even to locate the source of their discontent, still less remedy it' (1975, 33–34). Many of these kinds of critical workers hold that the central government has good intentions to protect workers with labor laws; they attribute the failures of the labor law system to the faults of local governments who do not effectively enforce labor laws, have strong connections with the businesses and/or benefit tremendously from the presence of these firms (see Zhang Lin, Chen Fei, Shu Ren, and Xin Xin). The concealing mechanism of legal hegemony convinces this group of workers that the existence of numerous labor laws is proof that the central government is pro-labor and autonomous from businesses. Moreover, the transmuting mechanism of legal hegemony helps shift worker criticism from targeting the party-state as a whole (which has been engineering capitalist reform at the macro level) to local government officials (who are delegated the task of capital accumulation at the local level). In addition to buttressing the party-state, legal hegemony is able to normalize the capitalist logics with regard to this type of critical worker. A few of them, though not all, believe that employers are above reproach were they to pay workers wages according to labor laws; some say they would do the same if they were to hire workers one day (Fu Shan). For these workers, labor laws are a legitimate yardstick to measure employer behavior. Since labor laws approve of and normalize wage-labor, surplus value extraction, and maximization of profits by capitalists, some critical workers find these capitalist practices unproblematic.

The critical workers that have encountered collective labor disputes discredit the labor law system for similar reasons held by critical workers that have experienced individual labor disputes. Yet, the former's attitude towards rights defense are distinct from the latter's. For the critical workers that have undergone individual labor disputes, legal hegemony still shapes their understanding of the appropriate form of rights defense (see Shu Ren). They see rights defense as an action that ought to be carried out within the legal arena; hence, they try to justify extra-legal worker actions by stressing the legality of their demands and the lack of alternative means to redress their legitimate grievances. Some of them (see Xin Xin) still have confidence in legal rights defense, even though they were frustrated by their own experience and know it is not easy. In contrast, the critical workers that have experienced collective labor disputes seem to be less convinced of the approach of legal rights defense (see You Yang). They realize the limitations of solely utilizing legal channels in advancing worker interests and understand that if workers do not make their complaints a big issue, the government will not give them proper attention even if their demands are legally grounded. They believe that utilizing labor laws to consolidate workers' collective power into extra-legal forms is more effective than pursuing individualized legal channels in pushing the government to take corrective actions.

For the ambivalent workers, they simultaneously approve and discredit the labor law system. On the one hand, they consider the labor law system fair and protective of workers. On the other, they reproach it for improper legal implementation and lack of supervision over firms. The uncertain attitude of ambivalent workers towards the labor law system is rooted in the discrepancies between the legal ideals promoted by the party-state and the legal reality they witness. Some ambivalent workers believe in the party-state-constructed ideology that the government is pro-labor and autonomous from businesses, but at the same, they are aware that some government officials are biased towards the rich and that some firms manipulate legal loopholes to their advantage (Ah Xi). Some ambivalent workers feel the benefits, however minimal, from the establishment of the rule of law and a proper legal system, which help maintain 'social stability' (that was absent during the political and social turmoil in Maoist China); yet they notice that workers' rights are not fully respected (Ah Kong). As labor laws are unevenly applied across the country, some factories better observe them while some ignore the law; therefore, some ambivalent workers occasionally discredit the labor law system, while at times they will also show appreciation (Ah Xi).

Although the ambivalent workers do not give their full consent to the labor law system, it still exercises a certain degree of hegemonic effect on them. Due to the normalizing mechanism of labor laws, some ambivalent workers hold that what labor laws prescribe and whatever the courts decide must be right and indisputable (Jian Hua). For some of them, 'fairness' and 'justice' mean observing legal standards. Moreover, similar to some critical workers that have had individual labor dispute experiences, they consider rights defense via legal channels an appropriate form of labor activism, believing that workers' resistance should be carried out within legal boundaries (Gui Nan); but, at the same time, they try to justify 'extreme' actions by workers. Also, some of them express greater confidence when their demands have legal grounds (Chang Shan). Furthermore, due to the transmuting mechanism of legal hegemony, most of the ambivalent workers think that the central government is pro-labor, and that it is the corrupt local governments that have failed to enforce labor laws rigorously. They do not challenge the legal content or the rule-setters that favor the capitalist mode of production.

Two last points must be noted in regards to the critical and ambivalent workers. Despite their skepticism over labor laws, labor laws have helped some of them overcome hierarchical relations at the workplace so that they were able to negotiate with their bosses on equal footing (Shu Ren and Jian Hua). Labor laws also embolden some workers to talk to government officials audaciously and hold them accountable for their failure in legal implementation. As elaborated in Chap. 3, the labor law system has turned workers from class actors into juridico-political subjects so as to mask capitalist domination; but it somehow has bestowed workers with a feeling of 'equality' with their bosses, fuelled their rights defense and assertion, and given them courage to confront employers and government officials. Because of this kind of legal impact, some scholars argue that laws have paradoxically become 'political resources' that Chinese workers can utilize to defend their interests (Chan 2012, 325). Some scholars also hold that the proliferation of labor laws, the party-state's emphasis on the rule of law and the rights discourse have emboldened aggrieved groups to 'fight the power' (Diamant et al. 2005; Chen and Xu 2012, 90) and help raised rights consciousness and legal consciousness of workers (Chen and Tang 2013, 576). It has even led to the mushrooming of 'rightful resistance' in China (O'Brien and Li 2006), in which the claims of protesters are based on laws, policies and official rhetoric while they carry out some disruptive (but not unlawful) collective action in order to curb the power of government officials. All these observations echo Thompson's argument (1977) that legal rhetoric has been proactively adopted by the subordinate class to protect their interests and to refrain the ruling class. However, Poulantzas reminds us that workers only enjoy an abstract and formal equality and that '[i]n this sense and this alone does modern law set the limits of the exercise of power and of intervention by the state apparatuses' (2000, 92).

Finally, most critical and ambivalent workers, like the affirmative workers, view Chinese economic reform in a positive light and have endorsed the developmental strategy of letting some people become wealthy first, even though they are aware that the well-being of workers is being sacrificed (see Chang Shan). They approve of economic development because it has brought them job opportunities and better living standards in comparison to the pre-reform period (see Jian Hua), and it has made their country strong vis-à-vis other countries. Despite their general approval of economic development, they, nevertheless, complain about low wages, unequal social benefits among migrant workers and urban citizens, and the widening income gap. Still, some workers reveal a sense of resignation towards unbalanced economic development (Gui Nan). A few workers (like Xin Xin) have displayed disapproval towards economic development, criticizing it for being beneficial to the rich and the government only. They understand that workers help the rich to create wealth but barely enjoy the fruits of economic prosperity.

In brief, although the indifferent workers have manifested apathy and resignation to the labor law system, and both the critical and ambivalent workers do not place complete trust in it, it is still able to secure their passive consent because their worldviews and actions are somehow constrained by capitalist-legal boundaries.

Notes

1. Interview T1.
2. See http://www.chinadaily.com.cn/cndy/2012-06/15/content_15503891.htm accessed 2nd February 2014.
3. Interview G1. Also see 2010 at http://big5.xinhuanet.com/gate/big5/jx.xinhuanet.com/news/2009-12/10/content_18459005.htm, accessed on 12th July 2014.
4. Interviews with over 25 representatives from overseas business chambers in China between April and July 2011.
5. Interview G1. Also see http://www.clb.org.hk/en/content/wage-arrears-cases-continue-dominate-worker-protests-November, accessed on 24th July 2014.
6. A labor NGO staff in Shenzhen shares with me that most factories want to hire workers of age from 18 to 25.
7. Interview T2.
8. See http://finance.sina.com.hk/news/-33452-6821719/1.html, accessed on 26th July 2014.
9. Interview R2.
10. Interview E1.
11. Interview R3.
12. Interview R4.
13. According to the Report on the Social Development in China 2014 (Zhongguo Minsheng Fazhan Baogao 2014) by the Institute of Social Science Survey of the Beijing University, the top 1% of the wealthiest families own more than one-third of the total wealth in China while the poorest 25% own only 1% of the national wealth. See http://hk.apple.nextmedia.com/realtime/china/20140726/52732681, accessed on 27th July 2014.

14. Interview R6.
15. See http://www.worldlabour.org/eng/files/Dispatch%20labour%20a%20preliminary%20study%20%28chinese%20report%29.pdf, accessed on 25th July 2014.
16. Interview R14.
17. For example, the 2008 Labour Contract Law, the 2013 Measures for the Implementation of Administrative License for Labor Dispatch, the 2014 Temporary Regulation on Dispatch Labour.
18. See http://finance.sina.com.cn/chanjing/gsnews/20130206/151614521283.shtml, accessed on 25th July 2014 and http://www.worldlabour.org/eng/files/Dispatch%20labour%20a%20preliminary%20study%20%28chinese%20report%29.pdf, accessed on 25th July 2014.
19. http://www.clb.org.hk/en/content/wages-china, accessed on 5th April 2014.
20. http://big5.cntv.cn/gate/big5/news.cntv.cn/special/opinion/laborsalary/, quoting the figures from the national statistic bureau, accessed on 5th April 2014.
21. Interview F1.
22. Interview H1.
23. http://big5.cntv.cn/gate/big5/news.cntv.cn/special/opinion/laborsalary/, accessed on 5th April 2014.
24. Interview R10.
25. See http://www.infzm.com/content/92430, accessed 11th July 2014.
26. Interview R11.
27. Interview P2.
28. Interview P1.
29. Interview P5.
30. Interview Q15.
31. Interview P3.
32. Interestingly, even though his last employer did not pay him compensation according to the labor laws and he had to resort to the legal channel to solve the disputes, he still considered his boss not exploitative.
33. Interview P8.

References

Allen, Steven G. 1984. Trade Unions, Absenteeism, and Exit-Voice. *Industrial and Labor Relations Review* 37 (3): 331–345.

Blecher, Marc, and Vivienne Shue. 1996. *Tethered Deer: Government and Economy in a Chinese County*. Stanford: Stanford University Press.

Breslin, Shaun. 2007. *China and the Global Political Economy*. New York: Palgrave Macmillan.

Chan, King Chi Chris. 2012. Class or Citizenship? Debating Workplace Conflict in China. *Journal of Contemporary Asia* 42 (2): 308–327.

Chen, Feng. 2004. Legal Mobilization by Trade Unions: The Case of Shanghai. *China Journal* 52: 27–45.

Chen, Feng, and Mengxiao Tang. 2013. Labor Conflicts in China: Typologies and Their Implications. *Asian Survey* 53 (3): 559–583.

Chen, Feng, and Xu Xin. 2012. "Active Judiciary": Judicial Dismantling of Workers' Collective Action in China. *China Journal* 67 (January): 87–107.

Diamant, N., S. Lubman, and K.J. O'Brien. 2005. *Engaging the Law in China: State, Society, and Possibilities for Justice*. Stanford: Stanford University Press.

Femia, Joseph V. 1975. Hegemony and Consciousness in the Thought of Antonio Gramsci. *Political Studies* 23 (1): 29–48.

Femia, Joseph V. 1987. *Gramsci's Political Thought: Hegemony, Consciousness, and the Revolutionary Process*. Oxford: Clarendon Press.

Freeman, Richard B. 1976. Individual Mobility and Union Voice in the Labor Market. *American Economic Review* 66 (2): 361–368.

Gallagher, Mary E. 2004. "Time is Money, Efficiency is Life": The Transformation of Labor Relations in China. *Studies in Comparative International Development* 39 (2): 11–44.

Hirschman, Albert O. 1970. *Exit, Voice, and Loyalty: Responses to Decline in Firms, Organizations, and States*. Cambridge, MA: Harvard University Press.

Hui, Sio-Ieng Elaine, and King-Chi Chris Chan. 2015. Going Beyond the Union-Centred Approach: A Critical Evaluation of Recent Trade Union Elections in China. *British Journal of Industrial Relations*.

Lubman, Stanley. 1999. Bird in a Cage: Chinese Law Reform after Twenty Years. *Northwestern Journal of International Law & Business* 20: 383–424.

McNally, Christopher A. 2008. The Institutional Contours of China's Emergent Capitalism. In *China's Emergent Political Economy: Capitalism in the Dragon's Lair*, ed. Christopher A. McNally. London: Routledge.

McNally, Christopher. A. 2011. China's changing guanxi capitalism: Private entrepreneurs between Leninist control and relentless accumulation. *Business and Politics* 13 (2): 1–28.

O'Brien, Kevin J., and Lian Jiang Li. 2006. *Rightful Resistance in Rural China*. Cambridge, NY: Cambridge University Press.

Pearson, Margaret M. 1997. *China's New Business Elite*. Berkeley: University of California Press.

Poulantzas, Nicos. 2000. *State, Power, Socialism*. London: Verso.

Pun, Ngai, and Lu Huilin. 2010. Unfinished Proletarianization: Self, Anger, and Class Action among the Second Generation of Peasant-Workers in Present-Day China. *Modern China* 36 (5): 493–519.

Silver, Beverly. 2003. *Forces of Labor: Workers' Movements and Globalisation Since 1870*. Cambridge: Cambridge University Press.

Thompson, E.P. 1977. *Whigs and Hunters: The Origin of the Black Act*. Harmondsworth: Penguin.

Wang, Haiyan, Richard P. Appelbaum, Degiuli Francesca, and Nelson Lichtenstein. 2009. China's New Labour Contract Law: Is China Moving Towards Increased Power for Workers? *Third World Quarterly* 30 (3): 485–501.

Wedeman, Andrew. 2005. Anticorruption Campaigns and the Intensification of Corruption in China. *Journal of Contemporary China* 14 (42): 93–116.

Wong, Linda. 2011. Chinese Migrant Workers: Rights Attainment Deficits, Rights Consciousness and Personal Strategies. *China Quarterly* 208: 870–892.

Xu, F. 2009. The Emergence of Temporary Staffing Agencies in China. *Comparative Labor Law and Policy Journal* 30 (2): 431–462.

Xue, Hong. 2008. Local Strategies of Labor Control: A Case Study of Three Electronics Factories in China. *International Labor and Working-Class History* 73: 85–103.

Yang, Mayfair Mei-hui. 2002. The Resilience of Guanxi and its New Deployments: A Critique of Some New Guanxi Scholarship. *The China Quarterly* 170: 459–476.

CHAPTER 6

Workers' Refusal to Consent

1 Introduction

In Chaps. 4 and 5, I illustrate, respectively, in what ways the affirmative workers have granted active consent to legal hegemony and in what ways the indifferent, ambivalent, and critical workers have rendered passive consent to it. In this chapter, I focus on the radical workers who are rather insusceptible to legal hegemony, refusing to consent to the values and worldviews it promulgates.

2 Radical Workers

2.1 *Workers Without Labor Dispute Experiences*

It is uncommon for the workers-informants that have not encountered any labor conflicts to develop a radical attitude towards labor laws and the socio-economic and political worldviews that they reproduce. Wang Lin is one of the few exceptions. She is 25 years old and has obtained a university degree.[1] She is an assistant to a division head in a Japanese car factory in Guangzhou, earning around 5000 yuan per month. Compared to other interviewees that have not experienced any overt industrial conflicts, she knows more about labor laws. In our interview, she keenly explained to me some legal differences between Guangzhou and Shenzhen. She has taken great initiative to look up information on labor laws and politics through, for example, TV news, web surfing, online fora and so forth. She even

E.S.I Hui, *Hegemonic Transformation*, Series in Asian Labor and Welfare Policies, DOI 10.1057/978-1-137-50429-6_6

applies the technique of '*Fanqian*' (which means using a Virtual Private Network, or VPN) to gain access to foreign websites banned by the Chinese government, believing that many Chinese online sources are unreliable. She notes that labor laws offer workers some degree of protection; hence, she is motivated to gain legal knowledge so that she would know what to do if her boss were to act illegally. However, she has also formulated radical opinions on labor laws, the state and the economy.

Researcher: Have you heard of rights-defense according to laws?

Wang Lin: Yes, but the laws guiding rights-defense are very broad and vague. Therefore, only those who have power [*quan*] can defend their rights. If you don't have any power, you can't do so.

Researcher: What difficulties are there for ordinary people to defend their rights?

Wang Lin: First, the legal system has defects [*bu wanshan*]. Second, *guanxi politics* [the politics of personal connection] are too deep-seated in China. If we do not eradicate these two problems, rights-defense is difficult for ordinary people.

Researcher: What legal defects are you referring to?

Wang Lin: There exist many legal loopholes of which businesses have taken advantage. Labor laws only spell out the general rules, but their specific details are subject to the interpretation and manipulation of some people. In my opinion, the legal defects are linked to defects in the [political] system [*tizhi bu wanshan*]; there isn't a big difference between having laws or not.

Researcher: What do you mean by the 'defects of the [political] system'?

Wang Lin: For example, if Jiang Zemin's son killed somebody, he might be sentenced to jail for only 5 years; but if an ordinary person were to do something like that, he would need to compensate a life with his life. This example shows that the *guanxi* network in China is too complicated, and that the legal system is not well developed and has many loopholes.

Researcher: What do you think about the rule of law?

Wang Lin: I really think laws should be something useful to ordinary people. Now, the mandate of laws does not come from the people; they are used to govern [*zhili*] and manage [*guanli*] us. Laws are made by administrators [*guanli renyuan*];

what's the use for us? Ordinary people should be the point of departure for laws; only when people believe that certain rules are protective, only then should they be turned into laws. What's the point of making laws that don't protect us? Right now, we don't know who makes the laws and what their purposes are.

Researcher: Do you think labor laws are neutral, or do they favor businesses?

Wang Lin: I have read through some labor laws; theoretically speaking, some of them seek to protect workers, but in reality, they end up being utilized differently from their intentions when originally implemented.

While the affirmative workers in Chap. 4 and some ambivalent workers in Chap. 5 approve of the discourses of legal rights-defense and the rule of law, Wang Lin is highly skeptical of these notions, hinting that unequal social power relations make the rights-defense of ordinary people difficult ['If you don't have any power, you can't do so']. She critiques *guanxi* politics in China for leading to lax legal enforcement; she does not only blame individual government cadres for this, but also the *tizhi*, the political system. She recognizes that the legal and political spheres are intricately related, and that the latter contributes to the former's defects ['the legal defects are linked to the defects of the [political] system']. She considers the current legal system dominated by the political system rather than responding to people's needs. In contrast to the workers that see labor laws as authoritative yardsticks for judging employers and the government, Wang Lin regards the objectives of laws to be 'managing' and 'governing' the people.

As Wang Lin hints, the legal system is inseparable from the state and power relationships in society. Our conversation on the party-state and China's economic development continues below.

Researcher: Do you think the government is neutral or…?

Wang Lin: For sure it is biased towards businesses. The Chinese government's economic performance depends heavily on them; companies pay much more taxes than individuals do.

Researcher: Is it the central government or local governments that are biased towards businesses?

Wang Lin: The central government leans towards whoever has money… that's my feeling. Ordinary people's rights-defense activities are very difficult. If the media were to report their issues and everybody knew about them, then local governments would no longer be able to shelter the businesses, and they would have no choice but to follow normal procedures. But if workers' issues are not reported on or made big, nobody would know what the government would do.

Researcher: Some people suggest that if the Chinese people could elect their own government, they would be better protected. What do you think about this?

Wang Lin: Like the election system in the USA?

Researcher: Yes, or like grassroots elections in some Chinese villages.

Wang Lin: It certainly would be better. However, there is a population of 1.4 billion people in China; it would be difficult to do this.

Researcher: Why would it be difficult?

Wang Lin: Even if we were to change the government officials, they would always be from the CCP as only one party exists in China. Nobody can supervise and monitor them; even if there would be, they'd still be from the CCP. It is 'self-supervision' [*zijiren jiandu zijiren*]. Nothing good comes out of this. Even if we have a vote, it's useless [*mei youyong*]; those elected are always from the few [political] circles that exist. Elections are useless unless two or three political parties are allowed to compete in elections. Only in this situation can poorly performing government officials be kicked out of office. Only then can we truly achieve the purpose of democratic elections. Nowadays in China, even if all the people were to have the right to vote, those elected would be from the CCP. What's the use of that? It's useless.

Researcher: What do you think about China's economic development?

Wang Lin: The economy has developed rapidly, too rapidly. China's economy has integrated globally [*yu guoji jiegui*], but when will our wage levels be synchronized with global standards? It's true that China is getting rich, but the money has gone to the government and the rich, not to ordinary people.

Researcher: Do you think workers can share in the fruits of the economic development?

Wang Lin: No. It [economic development] is useless. China's economy grows speedily and prices increase quickly, but ordinary people's wages can't catch up with inflation. The money goes to the government, and it's kept by the government. Ordinary people don't know how the government spends the money, but we know for sure it is not spent on the people.

Wang Lin's comments on the party-state and economic development are substantially distinct from the workers in the previous two chapters. Instead of seeing the party-state as neutral or inclined towards workers, she underscores the symbiotic relationship between the government and the capitalists—the party-state depends on business investments for taxes and economic growth ['The Chinese government's economic performance depends heavily on them; companies pay much more taxes than individuals do'] while the wealthy class gains socio-economic privileges under the shelter of the government ['If the media were to report their issues and everybody knew about them, then local governments would no longer be able to shelter the businesses, and they would have no choice but to follow normal procedures. But if workers' issues are not reported on or made big, nobody would know what the government would do']. Unlike some affirmative and ambivalent workers, she does not thank capitalists for job creation or see the fast-growing economy as an object of national pride. Instead, she feels that the economy has been developing too rapidly and that workers barely benefit from it. For Wang Lin, peoples' livelihoods cannot be improved by simply changing the laws (because they are dominated by the political regime), by replacing the government with another CCP faction, or by simply giving people the right to vote. The root of the problem lies in the current political system which bars competition among candidates that hold different political beliefs.

Although she has no labor dispute experiences, Wang Lin is able to cultivate radical positions towards legal hegemony probably because of her relatively higher education which allows her to think independently. Moreover, she is interested in political issues and is motivated to learn critical information about the country and society through the internet. As a young migrant worker, she is well equipped with technological knowledge (Qiu 2009) which permits her to access websites banned by the party-state. This might also have contributed to the formation of her radical positions.

2.2 *Workers with Individual Labor Dispute Experiences*

Lin Xia is 20 years old.[2] When studying in vocational secondary school, she had an internship at a hotline center for a telecommunication company in Guangzhou. Under the current educational system, students from vocational schools must complete internships for a period of 1 year or more during their 3 years of study in order to obtain academic qualification. The disproportionately long internships are results of the state's effort to channel cheap, young, and semi-skilled labor into secondary industries. Many factories abuse this system by offering student interns wages, benefits, and working conditions below legal standards while assigning them the same duties as normal workers. Yet these factories are not violating any labor laws because student internships are regulated through the Education Law; the labor law system does not consider student interns to be workers, they are thus denied proper legal protection, though they produce surplus value for factories in the same ways as normal workers. News about the ill-treatment of student-interns is widely reported in China; the most notable cases are related to Nanhai Honda and Foxconn (Chan and Pun 2010; Chan and Hui 2012).

When this telecommunication company came to recruit student interns in Lin Xia's school in Guangxi, it promised them basic monthly salaries of 1200 yuan plus commission. However, when she and other students went to the office in Guangzhou, the manager asked them sign internship agreements that only offered them monthly salaries of 800 yuan. Initially she insisted on not signing the agreement; she called her teachers for help, but they did not follow up with her complaint. Later, her manager threatened her that if she did not sign the agreement, she would not be able to complete the internship, and thus, could not graduate from school. In the end, she bowed to the pressure. After working there for three months, she quit and found another job at a trading company as a replacement for her internship. In 2012, she graduated from vocational secondary school and was hired by an automobile factory in Foshan as a production worker.

Having learned some legal knowledge in school, Lin Xia says she knows 'what labor contracts are, what they should cover, and what is considered illegal'. When she first entered the automobile factory, the managers further explained labor laws connected to holidays, rest days, and the other labor rights. When I asked for her opinions on labor laws, she responded:

> *Many policies and laws are made within a small circle of the government. Labor laws are made to employers' advantage.* Take statutory holidays as an example; workers are only entitled to 11 days of paid statutory holidays every year, which is absolutely insufficient. The labor law system does not consider the situation of workers; it only serves the capitalists. *Employers think that if workers have too many statutory holidays, nobody would work for them, and they would need to pay more, and thus earn less.*

Different from the affirmative, ambivalent, and critical workers whose criticism of the labor law system focuses on the enforcement level, Lin Xia sharply points out the ingrained inclinations of labor laws towards the capitalists ['Labor laws are made to employers' advantage'] and the undemocratic nature of legislation in China ['Many policies and laws are made within the small circle of the government']. In addition, she criticizes the slogan of rights-defense in accordance with laws:

> Rights-defense? Who defends our rights? Who helps us? *The government? It doesn't care about us.* When workers are in need, where is the government? We know we should defend our rights, but who should we appeal to? The road of rights-defense in China is very long; it takes years. During the process, one encounters lots of frustrations and difficulties. *Right now, the problem is not that people do not know their rights, it is that they don't know who can help them.*

In contrast to Qing Fa from Chap. 4 who views workers' determination and persistence as key to rights-defense, Lin Xia censures the government for not providing proper assistance and infrastructure for workers' rights-defense. Instead of attributing unsuccessful rights-defense to the poor psychological qualities of individuals, she believes the government is obligated to handle worker grievances and facilitate their rights-defense ['When workers are in need, where is the government?']. The government should 'serve the people', opines Lin Xia, but the Chinese people do not exercise any power over the government. She also criticizes trade unions for failing to aid workers' rights-defense: 'they only organize recreational activities and from time to time give workers small gifts and coupons'.

Compared to Ah Wen from the affirmative group (Chap. 4), Jian Hua from the ambivalent group, and Fu Shan from the critical group (Chap. 5), the normalizing mechanism of legal hegemony has exerted a less remarkable impact on Lin Xia. She does not take labor laws as the benchmark for measuring fairness or exploitation. Instead, she uses the gap between how much workers gain and how much factories earn, i.e., the surplus value appropriated by capitalists, as an indicator. She stresses:

> *My company uses all kinds of excuses for not giving us a decent wage increase* and fair annual bonus. But actually, the money it earns from selling just one transformer would be enough for granting all production workers a yearly bonus equivalent to two months of salary for them. They think we don't know mathematics. *Capitalists are capitalists; they always put their own interests as the top priority. It's so unfair that we work so hard but earn so little in comparison to them.*

Lin Xia knows clearly how much the factory's products are sold for, how much workers are paid, and thus how much her employer earns. Therefore, even though her boss offers wages higher than legal minimum rate, she is unsatisfied and feels the wages are unfair. She is asking for decent wages and a fairer distribution of profits between workers and employers rather than the legal minimum wage.

Most likely due to her acute awareness of capitalist exploitation, Lin Xia expresses deeper discontent towards Chinese economic development in comparison to the other types of workers. Instead of approving of the strategies of 'let some people get rich first', she decries uneven development and the grave wealth disparity within the country, 'The government has allowed people from the urban areas to become wealthy first and invests a lot in the coastal areas; therefore, people want to leave underdeveloped areas and rush to the more developed ones. As a consequence, there is a great disparity between different regions.'

As pointed out by some studies (Pun and Lu 2010; Chan and Hui 2012), the second generation of migrant workers are less tolerant of unjust treatment at work in comparison to the older generation. Belonging to this new generation of workers, Lin Xia is more radical in response to her experience with unfairness. Moreover, in contrast to workers in some low-skilled industries that have usually only finished primary or junior secondary school, Lin Xia is comparatively well educated. Having worked in the automotive industry, which has been an important pillar of the Chinese economy, and possessing semi-skilled labor in production, her marketplace and workplace bargaining power are relatively bigger; hence, she is more confident and vocal.

Xiao Bao came to work in the cities in 2002.[3] When she studied in vocational secondary school, her teachers always stressed the 'professional etiquette' of workers, teaching them to be legally compliant when working in cities. Xiao Bao discloses:

> The teachers told us to be obedient and loyal to companies, and to follow managers' orders. But having worked in the cities for some time and witnessing all kinds of unfairness facing workers, such as work accidents, long work hours, and exploitative wages, I realize that nobody has ever told us what to do if our employers were to violate labour laws.

The discrepancies between what her teachers taught her and how factories operate in reality disillusion Xiao Bao. She witnesses and experiences unequal power relations between workers and employers, which leads her to reflect on the 'unreasonable distribution of profits' (*fenpei bu heli*). She questions why managers and employers who do not produce commodities earn far more than workers do. Similar to Lin Xia, for Xiao Bao, fairness is not the mere fulfillment of legal standards but is related to how profits are distributed between workers and employers.

Xiao Bao started out as a production worker in a state-owned enterprise in Shenzhen; after 2 years, she was promoted to be a clerk. In 2002, she came to know a labor NGO close to her factory called Sunrise. At first, she went to Sunrise just 'for fun' (*qu wan*), reading books from its library and chatting with other workers. Later, as she experienced more social injustice and understood Sunrise's mission better, she became an active volunteer in the NGO and strongly identified with it. Through Sunrise, Xiao Bao realized 'what workers should do if their rights are infringed upon'. She recalls:

> In one of Sunrise's meetings, its staff said workers can help improve society; then, I wondered how we had anything to do with social progress. The staff explained that workers form society and contribute to its positive development; therefore, we have the power to change it, and each one of us is closely linked to social progress.

In this factory, if workers resign a month prior to completion of their employment contracts, the manager deducts 350 yuan from their 590 yuan monthly wages; if they resign less than a month before the contract ended, 700 yuan would be deducted.[4] In addition, workers only receive 80% of wages owed to them if they cannot complete their contracts. In the early 2000s, this kind of illegal practice was highly common in China. Xiao Bao was unaware that the factory had contravened labor laws until Sunrise staff informed her. At the time, she had many opportunities to talk to workers who planned to quit as she was responsible for handling documents related to their resignations. She would tell them about the company's illegal policy, encouraging them to talk to the manager in groups to retrieve their money from the factory. Inspired by Sunrise, Xiao Bao demonstrates a consciousness of labor–capital conflicts, as well as a concern for other workers facing injustice.

Xiao Bao did not like her job, which was to discipline workers and fine them (5–20 yuan) for inappropriate behavior and non-compliance with dress code, such as not cutting their nails, not drying their hands after washing up, not wearing socks, and so forth. She felt depressed and unhappy with her disciplinary role, and found vast inequality embedded in labor relations. Therefore, she resigned after working in this factory for 3 years. As per practice, her manager deducted a portion of money from her final month's salary. She then went to negotiate with him, and finally, got 300 yuan back. During the process of her rights-defense, she tried to seek help from the enterprise trade union, but it was not responsive and so she turned to Sunrise for support.

After quitting this state-owned factory, Xiao Bao worked in a Taiwanese-owned electronics factory as a clerk in 2005. Encouraged and supported by Sunrise, she decided to join the workplace union and run in the union official elections. However, only two people, including Xiao Bao, joined the election, and there were not enough candidates to form a proper trade union. At the end, the company dissolved the trade union altogether. Xiao Bao wrote a letter of opposition to the deputy CEO but received no response.

Xiao Bao learned in Sunrise what trade unions ought to do and what their objectives should be, but she realized that in reality, many trade unions do not perform their duties of serving worker interests. This motivated her to run for the election so as to arouse workers' awareness of the proper role of trade unions and to initiate reform of her enterprise union. Xiao Bao explicates:

> I think the labor movement in China needs trade unions as a vehicle to organize workers collectively. Workers need to realize that collective power can make a change. Without this vehicle, it is difficult to build up a strong

> labor movement. However, workers' trade union consciousness is still very low; they don't know that unions should represent them and have not developed an awareness that they need to monitor unions. Right now, the Chinese unions remain welfare providers rather than being vehicles to fight for the real interests of workers.

In fact, some labor NGOs in the PRD have adopted the same strategy concerning trade unions. Since independent unions are forbidden in China, labor NGOs cannot openly advocate for them. Instead, these NGOs believe that exposing the discrepancies between the ideal functions of unions and their actual performance can heighten workers' consciousness of their rights as union members. They also believe that encouraging workers to exercise their union members' rights actively might be able to pressure official unions to reform.

Xiao Bao discerns a huge gap between what labor laws should be and what they are in reality. She gauges that labor laws do not protect workers.

> Many factories do not abide by the laws. I don't think labor laws offer workers much protection. Although it has become more common for employers to sign labor contracts with workers, it is still difficult to make them follow contractual terms and labor laws; they always manage to get around the laws. *The rule of law is deceiving. Labor laws are tilted towards the capitalists*; the government seldom punishes employers operating illegally, but, instead, allows them to continue their unlawful practices.

She stresses that some new laws have made workers worse off while benefiting employers. For instance, the 1988 Regulations Concerning the Labour Protection of Female Staff and Workers spelt out that employers must not assign women workers certain tasks during their menstrual period,[5] but this stipulation has been removed from the 2012 Special Provisions on Labour Protection for Female Employees.[6] This has deprived women workers of certain protections and permits employers to exploit their labor fully. Unlike the affirmative, ambivalent, and critical workers, Xiao Bao does not simply associate problems with the labor law system to irresponsible government departments or corrupt officials; neither do her criticisms focus solely on legal implementation. Instead, she views the labor law system and the process of legislation as inherently biased towards the capitalists ['*The rule of law is deceiving. Labor laws are tilted towards the capitalists*']. For her, the rule of law is deceiving because it has established rules that favor employers and tolerates their illegal practices.

Xiao Bao worked in the Taiwanese factory for a year before she became a staff-person at Sunrise in 2005. She is now responsible for activities related to women workers, including visiting women workers in their dormitories and hospitals, organizing focus groups, and so forth. She explains that Sunrise helps workers in a number of ways. First, it informs workers of labor laws and labor rights through classes on labor laws and focus group discussions. It helps workers to 'understand how they have been discriminated against and oppressed in the workplace and society'. Second, Sunrise provides a platform for workers from different factories to share their frustration and grievances at work, and to discuss ways of dealing with them. Also, it endeavors to promote mutual support and solidarity among workers. Third, it aims to boost workers' confidence, encouraging them to express what they think and to strive for what they deserve. For example, a woman worker was accused of sleeping with a boy in her dormitory in the daytime; the company fined her 300 yuan and denounced her in a public notice as a filthy, disgusting animal (*zhugou buru*). The woman worker felt humiliated and was extremely upset. With the encouragement and support given by Sunrise, she exposed this issue to the media.

Fourth, Sunrise helps workers to defend their rights and strengthen their 'capacity for action' (*xingdong li*). The staff always discuss 'the strategies and actions' for redressing a variety of workplace issues with workers. With Sunrise's support, some workers have taken collective action to improve their working conditions. In one case, five women workers initiated a petition among their fellow workers to demand a high-temperature subsidy from their factory. In another case, a group of women workers, who were dissatisfied with the poor quality of meals offered by the factory (which mainly consisted of sour green beans), collected more than two hundred signatures from co-workers to demand better food. Fifth, increasingly more NGOs, including Sunrise, try to intervene in workers' collective actions, such as strikes. However, due to the suppressive political environment in China, their intervention is usually carried out in a low-key manner.

2.3 *Workers with Collective Labor Dispute Experiences*

Zhi Wan is responsible for management of facilities at a factory located in Panyu city-district of the city of Guangzhou.[7] He is over 30 years old and has completed the vocational secondary school. Having self-studied labor laws since 2006, he passed the legal examination and obtained a lawyer's practice certificate. He is active in providing legal advice to other workers and representing them in courts and arbitration as an agent ad litem. In his opinion, the living standards and material life of the Chinese people have improved; now, most people own electronic appliances, cell phones and so forth. However, he notes, it is still unsatisfying in terms of peoples' spiritual and psychological development. For example, due to the discriminatory household registration system many migrant workers' children are left behind and raised in villages by their grandparents while their parents have to work in the cities; this, he suggests, has detrimental impact on the growth of the next generation.

Zhi Wan has been active in the labor movement for some years, and has rich experiences in both individual and collective rights-defense. With the support of a labor NGO, he and some workers have formed a 'volunteer group' in Panyu, aiming to promote worker rights. Since 2011, they have initiated a series of legal actions to challenge the legality of the minimum wage standard in Panyu. According to the Provisions on Minimum Wage, each province should set the minimum wage rate in different cities under its administrative rule. Guangdong province has a four-tier minimum wage standard. The first tier minimum wage rate is the highest one and applies to the biggest cities that are well-developed and have higher living standards; the fourth tier rate is the lowest and applies to the least developed cities within the province. Guangzhou, the capital of Guangdong province, has 12 regions which are subject to different minimum wage rates. In 2011, Panyu and four other city-districts were assigned the second-tier minimum wage rate (1100 yuan per month at the time) while the other 7 regions were given a first-tier rate (1300 yuan).

In 2011, Zhi Wan and his fellow workers found that the Notice on the Minimum Wage Standards issued by the Guangzhou Municipal Human Resources and Social Security Bureau (hereafter referred to as the Guangzhou Social Security Bureau) did not conform to the document issued by the Guangdong provincial government, which has greater authority. The provincial document stated that Guangzhou's monthly minimum wage in 2011 was 1300 yuan (i.e., the first-tier rate) and did not dictate that Panyu must implement the second-tier minimum wage, but the city document determined that Panyu should apply the second-tier minimum wage rate (which was 1100 yuan).[8] Zhi Wan and five other workers held that Panyu's minimum wage standard as decided by the Guangzhou Social Security Bureau was unlawful because city policies should not override provincial ones. Different from some affirmative, ambivalent, and critical workers that took labor laws as a yardstick for measuring fairness and justice, Zhi Wan and his fellow workers overcame the normalizing effects of the labor law system to challenge the legal standards concerning minimum wages. As will be elucidated shortly, they contested the legality of Panyu's minimum wage through various legal actions: (1) applying for disclosure of information from the Guangzhou Social Security Bureau; (2) applying for administrative reconsideration from the Guangdong Social Security Bureau; (3) applying for review of administrative documents from the Legislative Affairs Office of the Guangzhou Municipal Government (hereafter referred to as the Guangzhou Legislative Affairs Office); and (4) suing the Guangzhou Social Security Bureau.

According to the 2008 Regulations on the Disclosure of Government Information,[9] the government at different levels should operate in a transparent manner by disclosing information that is pertinent to the interests of citizens, legal persons, and organizations, that needs to be spread widely throughout society, that is related to the structures of government departments, missions, and work procedures, as well as disclosing policies and rules that are based on established laws (Article 9). The Regulations also grants citizens the right to apply for disclosure of the aforementioned information from ministries under the State Council, governments at different levels, and government agencies above the county level (Articles 13 and 20). Appealing to the Regulations, in June 2011, Zhi Wan and his team submitted a joint letter to the Guangzhou Social Security Bureau enquiring about the factors that it had taken into considerations for the determination of the Panyu's minimum wage level. It is worth noting that their endeavor reflects a rising trend in broader society. According to an official newspaper report, more people increasingly file administrative cases to demand the disclosure of government information.[10] For example, in Beijing, the number of these cases jumped from 10 in 2008 to 551 in 2012, witnessing a 55 fold increase within 5 years.

In July 2011, the Guangzhou Social Security Bureau replied to Zhi Wan and other workers, alleging that the information that they requested did not fall within the scope of its responsibilities, and thus, 'should not be disclosed by the Bureau'.[11] Dissatisfied, in September 2011, Zhi Wan and his team applied for reconsideration from the Guangdong Social Security Bureau regarding whether the Guangzhou Social Security Bureau's reply to their enquiry was appropriate. According to the 2007 Regulations on the Implementation of the Administrative Reconsideration Law, citizens have the right to apply for administrative reconsideration in situations whereupon their legal rights are infringed (Article 6). The Guangdong Social Security Bureau determined in December 2011 that its subordinate at the city level was unreasonable in claiming itself to hold no authority to explain why Panyu's minimum wage was 1100 yuan rather than 1300 yuan. It invalidated the Guangzhou Social Security Bureau's reply to the workers and ordered it to issue an appropriate reply.

In March 2012, the Guangzhou Social Security Bureau issued a new reply. It held that according to Article 13 of the 2008 Regulations on the Disclosure of Government Information, only when the information they request is related to their production, livelihood, scientific, and technological research can they apply for its disclosure. As they had not proved that they worked in Panyu and that their wages were at the legal minimum level, alleged the Bureau, they failed to prove that the information they requested was related to their livelihood or production, and thus, were not in the position to apply for the disclosure of information concerning Panyu's minimum wage. Shortly after its reply, a high ranking official from the division of wages and welfare (*gongzi fuli ke*) under the Guangzhou Social Security Bureau called them to arrange a meeting. In the meeting, this official promised them that the Bureau would disclose the requested information and that the minimum wage rates within Guangzhou would be unified soon. Later Zhi Wan and his volunteer group organized a seminar on minimum wages, inviting this official and a legal professor-cum lawyer from a university in Guangzhou to be the speakers. In the seminar, Zhi Wan had a heated debate with this official who denied what he promised in the private meeting with the workers.

Along with their legal actions based on the laws concerning information disclosure and administrative reconsideration, their third legal front was related to the review of administrative documents. In August 2011, they applied for review of whether the Guangzhou Social Security Bureau's notice was made according to the 2011 Provisions of Guangzhou Municipality on Administration of Normative Administrative Documents from the Guangzhou Legislative Affairs Office. This Provision specifies that any normative documents issued by the government at various levels or their agencies can only be promulgated upon approval from the Legislative Affairs Office at the corresponding level; otherwise, citizens have the right to not comply with them (Article 16). In addition, the normative documents prepared by the government departments must be approved by the corresponding government (Article 17). Therefore, in theory the notice issued by the Guangzhou Social Security Bureau on Panyu's minimum wage rate should have been reviewed and approved by the Guangzhou Legislative Affairs Office and the Guangzhou Government. However, this notice cannot be found in the Guangzhou government's online database—the 'administrative regulatory document full-text search system'[12]—which compiles all of the city's normative documents. Because of this, Zhi Wan suspects that this notice might not have been issued in accordance with legal procedures, and thus, should be considered legally null.

After investigating Zhi Wan and other workers' inquiries, the Guangzhou Legislative Affairs Office determined in October 2011 that the Guangzhou Social Security Bureau's notice was made in accordance with legal procedures—the Bureau had asked for the Guangzhou government's instructions, and the latter had then sought the agreement of other departments concerned. In addition, the Guangzhou Legislative Affairs Office stressed, in its reply, that Guangzhou has always used two minimum wage rates for its districts, which did not violate the principle underscored by the Guangdong government's notice that 'all Prefecture-level cities in principle should unify the minimum wage standard. Any districts [under the prefecture] that can afford it, may set a higher standard, and [if so] should file a report to the Guangdong Social Security Bureau'. Zhi Wan was unconvinced at all by the reply from the Guangzhou Legislative Affairs Office, rebutting that the Guangzhou Social Security Bureau's notice set a lower, rather than a higher, minimum wage standard for Panyu and other districts.

The fourth legal front initiated by Zhi Wan and his team took place in the courts. According to the Administrative Procedure Law, citizens can sue a government department when their 'lawful rights and interests have been infringed upon by a specific administrative act of an administrative organ' (Article 2). As the Guangzhou Social Security Bureau denied them access to information concerning Panyu's minimum wage, they filed an administrative lawsuit in May 2012 against the Guangzhou Social Security Bureau in the district court, requesting an explanation of the rationale behind its minimum wage policies. This reflects another rising trend of legal activism in China. It has been reported that an increasing number of people file lawsuits against government agencies in courts for failure to disclose government information. However, citizen's chances for winning these cases remain slim. For instance, in Beijing in 2012, only 17.6% of the plaintiffs won the case.[13] According to an NGO staff that I interviewed, more workers in Shenzhen have sued the Labor Bureau and the Social Security Bureau for not monitoring firms closely which eventually harms worker interests.[14] As a means of pressuring government agencies to resolve workers' issues, administrative lawsuits are a worker strategy for circumventing the long, drawn-out procedures related to labor mediation, arbitration, and litigation.

In August 2012, echoing the legal reasoning issued by the Guangzhou Social Security Bureau, the court ruled against Zhi Wan and his fellow workers, stating that they could not prove the information they requested was related to their production, livelihood, or scientific and technological research. Some workers from Zhi Wan's team, who were able to prove their working status in Panyu and their wages with their employment contracts, then applied for information disclosure from the Guangzhou Social Security Bureau once more in November 2012; the Bureau again refused to disclose the rationale of its minimum wage policies. In January 2013, these workers filed another administrative lawsuit against the Bureau. In March 2013, the court ruled in favor of the workers, ordering the Bureau to respond to their information disclosure request.

Although their campaign largely resorted to legal means, Zhi Wan and his team mobilized immense extra-legal resources to support their legal fronts. First, they sought to generate wider support and stronger solidarity among workers. Before commencing their legal campaigns, they organized a meeting with workers in 2011 to discuss the minimum wage policies in Guangzhou. They also went to industrial areas to talk to workers about the issue. Second, they tried to connect with academics. Upon referral from the labor NGO that had been supporting Zhi Wan and the volunteer group for many years, the legal scholars-cum-lawyers and law students from a university in Guangzhou gave vast support to their legal activism. They helped the workers conduct research, organize seminars, and render aid to their lawsuit against the Guangzhou Social Security Bureau. Zhi Wan notes that this labor NGO was a vital source of support to their campaign through provision of advice and resources. He also shows substantial appreciation to the assistance offered by the legal scholars and students.

Third, in hopes of mobilizing greater social support, they invited newspapers to cover their stories.[15] However, only two were willing to report their actions, while most of the state-owned newspapers in Guangzhou declined. Zhi Wan reflects that 'these newspaper work for the government rather than for the people'. Being denied wider access to mainstream media, they utilized Weibo, the Chinese equivalent to twitter, to spread news of their actions. The updates on their legal mobilizations, press releases, and so forth were posted onto Weibo, which was being followed by around 900 people.

Their last strategy was to petition the government. In 2012, during the period of the meeting of the Guangdong People's Congress, 16 workers petitioned Congress members. As of June 2013, the Guangzhou Social Security Bureau still has not replied to their request for information disclosure, telling them that it is considering appealing to a higher court concerning the district court's ruling. In spite of this, the Guangzhou government announced that starting in 2013, the minimum wage standards in all districts under the jurisdiction of Guangzhou would be unified; this means that Panyu's minimum wage rate would be raised to a higher standard. Regarding this as a triumph, Zhi Wan believes their series of actions has successfully pressured the government to change its minimum wage policies.

Zhi Wan and his team's campaign for a higher minimum wage in Panyu illustrates that labor laws are not simply instruments for class control, but also a terrain for class struggle. On the one hand, the Chinese ruling bloc seeks to mediate state–labor–capital relations in favor of capital accumulation through the labor law system; on the other, some workers, like Zhi Wan and his fellow workers, endeavor to advance their interests by strategically utilizing legal resources and invoking legal logics in order to constrain the ruling class with the same legal rhetoric it advocates. For the labor law system to exercise double hegemony effectively, it must, to a certain extent, appear to be just and independent from manipulation by upholding some of its logics because the legal forms of equity and universality are the basis upon which the ruling class's legitimacy is built. In other words, in order to maintain their legitimacy, the ruling class is subject to the rule of law as much as the ruled are. Thompson summarizes this dynamic well:

> One the one hand, it is true that the law did mediate existent class relations to the advantage of the rulers...as the century advanced the law became a superb instrument by which these rulers were able to impose new definitions of property to their even greater advantage...On the other hand, the law mediated these class relations through legal forms, which imposed, again and again, inhibitions upon the actions of the rulers....And not only were the rulers (indeed, the ruling class as a whole) inhibited by their own rules of law

> against the exercise of direct unmediated force…, but they also believed enough in these rules, and in their accompanying ideological rhetoric, to allow, in certain limited areas, the law itself to be a genuine forum within which certain kinds of class conflict were fought out. (Thompson 1977, 265)

In China, the ruling bloc apparently has not observed the labor law system fully, but neither has it neglected the rule of law completely. To maintain the authority of the legal system, hegemony of the party-state and the capitalist economy, the ruling class has, to a certain degree, subjected itself to the legal rules and logics with which it seeks to constrain the Chinese working class, as demonstrated in Zhi Wan's case. Understanding laws as an arena for class struggle, the struggles of Zhi Wan and his fellow workers further demonstrate that some laws and policies 'were defined and won in struggle against the dominant interests in society not bestowed on society by theory' (Hall 1980, 10).

When Zhi Wan first studied the law, he thought that they were fair and just, and that the society could attain equality through laws. However, having been involved with the labor movement for some time now, he has become disillusioned and strongly feels that the labor law system cannot do workers justice. In other words, he has shifted from the affirmative mode into the radical mode over the years. While some affirmative workers in Chap. 4 view labor mediation and arbitration as useful means for rights-assertion, Zhi Wan criticizes them for wasting worker energy and time:

> What's the purpose of establishing this system of labor arbitration? The government says it is to help resolve disputes quickly and timely. But a large percentage of workers who have gone through arbitration will resort to the courts eventually. So why make labor arbitration compulsory, making workers waste so much energy on arbitration? Why not allow them to bring their cases to courts directly?

In addition, Zhi Wan disapproves of the courts for their partiality. As a legal agent, he represented five other workers in the lawsuit against the Guangzhou Social Security Bureau. In court, the judge asked Zhi Wan, 'Have you ever thought about the consequences for getting involved with this lawsuit?' Zhi Wan took this as a threat from the court, which indeed acted on behalf of the government. In China, as explicated in Chap. 3, the courts are still subject to the government's influence because local courts are financially dependent on local governments, and their judiciary personnel are appointed by local party-members and the government (Liebman 2007). It is a common occurrence in which 'the courts are under enormous pressure to respond to political contingency' (Friedman and Lee 2010, 515).

In the past Zhi Wan used to attribute workers' plight only to unscrupulous employers, but now he realizes that the government serves as 'a protective shield for employers' (*baohu san*) and helps employers evade legal responsibilities. In his opinion, the government does not safeguard worker interests, only those of the capitalists; it grants capitalists numerous rights and privileges, but does not request them to fulfill their legal obligations.

> For example, the Labour Contract Law stipulates that employment contracts should clearly state workers' duties and work locations, but I have come across many cases in which these items have not been specified in contracts. Many employers simply put 'worker' as their duties. Because of this loophole, employers can assign tasks to workers arbitrarily, thus exploiting them fully.

> Both the local and central government are the same. *They always say labor laws protect workers;* then, at least they have to take a neutral position. But currently, *they are not even neutral; they are on the side of the firms.*

In contrast to workers who are influenced by the transmuting mechanism of legal hegemony and thus only blame local governments for being partial towards employers, Zhi Wan is critical of both the local and central government. He understands that the central government and the local government are no different; both of them do not safeguard worker interests or are not even neutrally positioned in labor–capital relations. He highlights that the governments and the capitalists are intricately linked, and that the party-state acts as the capitalists' 'protective shield'. The 'people' are supposed to monitor the government, he comments, but, "Who are the 'people'? When the people really monitor the government, they would say that we are crazy."

From Zhi Wan's point of view, it is difficult for workers to carry out rights-defense according to laws due to weak legal implementation and insufficient monitoring over the government.

> Legal rights defense eats up worker time and energy. Some workers spend a lot of time on court cases, but cannot get a cent even if they win their cases because *the courts do not enforce their rulings strictly* and allow employers to get away with it.
>
> Many workers can't afford resolving their cases through time-consuming labour mediation, arbitration and litigation; they then go to make trouble to arouse the government's attention (*naoshi*). In China nowadays, *if you make trouble you can get some compensation; if you don't make any trouble, you get nothing. Rather than creating 'social harmony', the current political and legal regime encourages workers to make trouble.*

Zhi Wan regards compulsory labor arbitration as a hindrance to workers' rights-defense. He rightly reveals that many court rulings remain unimplemented because employers can disappear or delay paying workers compensation without being penalized. He questions why the courts do not pressure employers to fulfill court orders, 'If somebody owes the judge some money, I am sure the judge would make them pay by any means necessary.' Zhi Wan's opinion somehow echoes the findings of many studies; the difficulties in implementing court orders in China are caused by the governments' protection of firms, weak punishment (Liebman 2007), and corruption of judiciary personnel (Lubman 1999).

Zhi Wan observes that workers' rights consciousness has heightened. Regarding Panyu's minimum wage being lower than some districts in Guangzhou, he notes that in the past workers accepted what the government decided without any complaint. Now, they are not only discontented, but also willing to take action to redress the inequality. He emphasizes that this case about Panyu's minimum wage does not simply concern individual workers, 'We do not struggle for our own sake, we struggle together as a group of workers in unity; this case is related to the interests of workers as a bloc.' Zhi Wan notes that many workers are active and willing to contribute to the legal campaign, offering help on their own initiative. This exhibits the gradual formation of their class consciousness and class identity.

Shao Jian works closely with Zhi Wan in the legal campaign pertinent to Panyu's minimum wage.[16] He is over thirty-years-old and has finished vocational secondary school. He started to self-study laws in 1997, and has represented workers in arbitration and litigation since 2003. In 2007, Shao Jian incurred a work accident, but his boss did not pay the medical expenses for him as required by law. Trying to hold him accountable, Shao

Jian resorted to legal channels, and the whole process took more than half a year. He is now active in providing legal advice to workers who are in need, and also in representing workers in courts or arbitration.

For Shao Jian, labor laws are unjust and of little use to workers.

> Corporations have a wealth of resources, such as lawyers and staff, so that they can easily exploit legal loopholes. Both firms and the government prefer workers to resolve disputes through legal means. But the laws kill us (*ba women gaosi*) because workers usually get little compensation or nothing at all out of the long and complicated legal procedures. Some of them give up their claims because they are unable to spend so much time on the legal process.

Like Zhi Wan, Shao Jian realizes the negative impact of the labor law system on workers' rights defense. Its time-consuming nature excludes the workers that could not afford to play the legal game; the government and businesses prefer workers to resolve labor disputes through legal means as this puts workers in a disadvantaged position. Moreover, contrary to the belief of some workers (see Chap. 4) that everybody is equal in front of the law, Shao Jian points out that in reality, workers and employers are not on an equal footing within the legal realm ['Corporations have rich resources, such as lawyers and staff, so that they can easily exploit the legal loopholes']. The businesses exercise greater leverage in the legal arena as they own a wealth of resources that enable them to manipulate legal loopholes while some workers do not even possess the time and money to play the legal game. For Shao Jian, rights-defense according to laws is 'not meaningful' (*mei shenme yiyi*). The term 'rule of law' sounds appealing, but he questions how many employers and government officials follow the laws in reality. He advocates that 'taking extra-legal actions and holding equal negotiations with employers are more effective ways of rights-defense'. A group of workers sought help from him because their factory had failed to contribute to their social insurance fund according to law. Although they had applied for labor arbitration, they decided to put greater pressure on the employer through extra-legal actions. In the end, the employer compensated them before the arbitration even began. For Shao Jian, labor laws are merely 'rhetoric' and 'only when workers initiate collective action can their interests be better safeguarded'.

Shao Jian suggests that trade unions are basically non-existent (*xingtong xushe*); they offer workers little help in their rights defense or are simply absent during labor disputes. In cases where they intervene, they often persuade workers to stop extra-legal actions rather than help them champion their rights. Therefore, he considers the trade union slogan of 'harmonious labor relations' to be sarcastic and ironic. He opines that harmonious labor relations are impossible in China, 'If capital–labor relations are unequal, and workers do not enjoy any bargaining status, it is hard to establish harmonious labor relations. To have harmony in the workplace, the official unions must function properly (*zuowei*), if not, they should allow workers to build their own trade unions.'

During the course of the legal actions regarding Panyu's minimum wage level, somebody came to talk to Shao Jian as a government representative, asking him questions and giving him pressure to ease their organizing. This was not the first time that he has come under pressure from the government or businesses. In 2009, Shao Jian and some workers from the jewelry industry sued their employer for labor disputes. Their employer then blacklisted them and posted their information onto the internal website of the Panyu Jewelry Manufacturer Association. Because of this, they faced tremendous difficulties in getting jobs in the jewelry industry.[17] They then filed a lawsuit against their employer, after which some undercover security police pressured them into stopping litigation. In China, it is common for the government to send undercover security officials to talk to people that are considered a threat to the political regime, such as political activists, staff of labor NGOs, human rights activists, strike leaders, etc. Most labor NGOs and right-lawyers I interviewed are regularly approached by undercover security officials. Facing this kind of political pressure, Shao Jiang does not feel threatened, 'I am very willing to take all these rights-defense actions. What I am doing is all legal. Of course, there is huge pressure for me to stop, but as *this is related to the well-being of all workers, I will definitely carry on*.' As elucidated in Chap. 2, the state always exercises coercion alongside consent-building to maintain the superiority of the ruling class. While the coercive side of the Chinese party-state is not so noticeable in the life and work experiences of the affirmative, indifferent, ambivalent, and critical workers, it is clearly manifested in that of the radical workers that attempt to take extra-legal collective actions to struggle for their interests. Government surveillance and other forms of coercion generally surface in the event that legal hegemony fails to tame defiant workers.

Mei Xia is in her early twenties.[18] She used to work in an automobile parts factory in the PRD where workers walked out in 2010 to demand an 800 yuan wage increase and democratic trade union reform. At first, she was a student intern in the factory and was hired as a formal production worker after graduation. During on-site training, she thought that the factory was good and that she would be able to learn something new. However, after formally starting her job, she found the work in assembly lines extremely boring and exhausting. Although workers' salaries in this factory were higher than the city's legal minimum wages, Mei Xia and her fellow workers considered them insufficient for a decent standard of living. They believed they deserved higher wages as they had worked hard to produce huge profits for the company. That was the reason that they went on strike.

Mei Xia was one of the leaders of the 2010 strike. She had close relations with the rank-and-file workers from her department, many of which were classmates in vocational secondary school. They always gathered together to share their grievances. When they were vexed by the management or discontented with their work, they often said to each other, 'One day, when I leave this factory, I will disrupt the assembly line so that the management will know I am not a coward'. The 2010 strike was kicked off by two workers from Mei Xia's department, who submitted their resignation letters before the strike began. They cut off the electricity supply to the production lines; then, many workers from the department stopped working and ran to the open area on the factory premises. The news quickly spread to workers in other departments who then joined the strike. Mei Xia confessed that initially, she and other workers did not plan seriously for a strike. They only wanted to let out their emotion and anger, and they simply wondered, 'Why are we working so hard for such low wages?' In Mei Xia's opinion, the management, who at first refused to talk to the strikers and unilaterally proposed to raise their living subsidy by only 55 yuan, had fuelled the resentment of strikers and made them even more determined to carry on with the strike. The antagonism between the workers and management, as well as the tenacity of workers in their resistance, intensified during the process of the strike. In Thompson's languages (1980), the workers developed a stronger class consciousness in the process of collective struggle.

During the strike, the company deployed various intimidation tactics to demoralize the strikers, such as videotaping the strikers and pressuring student interns to sign a document declaring that they would not lead, organize, or join any strikes. In addition, it kept alleging that the strike was illegal and had arranged legal experts to talk the workers into dropping the strike. Furthermore, in a meeting between the strike representatives and the CEO of the automobile group to which their factory supplied spare parts, this CEO warned the worker representatives that their strike was illegal and ordered them to resume production, threatening them that their actions would affect their friends and families and that they would not be able to bear the consequences for violating the laws. Mei Xia attended this meeting and was in quite a panic at the time as she knew little about the legal regulations for strikes. She had little knowledge of labor laws prior to the strike; both the vocational school she attended and the factory neglected to inform her about the laws. During the meeting, she consulted with supporters from some social groups through text messaging, and they told her that there was legal ambiguity concerning strikes. Initially, Mei Xia did not know how to respond to the CEO's accusations, but later she made up her mind:

> No matter how the CEO threatens us, we should have no fear. We should continue our strike. Although I know nothing about the laws, and am uncertain about what he says about strikes, I should not be scared. *As long as the workers are united and do not resume their work, the company can't do anything to us.*

Mei Xia then asked the CEO exactly which clause in which law forbade strikes, but the CEO could not give her a definite answer. All the representatives denied that their strike was illegal. Unsure of whether their strike was legal or not, labor laws were not the catalyst for Mei Xia's resistance as in the case of some affirmative, ambivalent, and critical workers. It was workers' unity and collectivity that gave Mei Xia, a subordinate worker, the courage to carry on the strike and emboldened her to overcome hierarchical relations in the workplace to challenge management's authority.

Subsequent to the meeting with the CEO, Mei Xia and other strike leaders studied the labor laws more closely. Mei Xia got in touch with a legal scholar, as well as a labor scholar and student, who reassured her that their strike was not illegal; this made her feel relieved. The labor scholar and student advised her and other core leaders on how to organize the workers, raise public support, and bargain with the company. The legal scholar later agreed to be the workers' legal consultant in their wage negotiations with the company. In the end, the company conceded to a monthly wage increase of around 32.4% for formal workers and about 70%

for student interns. Mei Xia highly appreciated the support rendered by the legal scholar, stating, 'He is a legal expert whose presence in the negotiations gave us confidence and helped our negotiations.' She remarks that they might have been unable to settle the strike smoothly without any help from the scholar.

Mei Xia distrusts the labor law system for 'it contains many legal loopholes that are abused by businesses'. For example, she points out, as long as companies pay workers the legal minimum wage, they do not breach any laws, and thus, cannot be penalized, even though their employees are poorly remunerated. She challenges, 'Is the minimum wage enough for a decent living? Whose interests does the government, who is responsible for determining the minimum wage, serve?' As illustrated in previous chapters, the labor law system, in particular the minimum wage policy, has normalized the capitalist system of wage labor in post-socialist China; some workers thus deem their bosses fair and above reproach for rendering them the minimum wage. Mei Xia, however, has overcome the normalizing effect of the labor law system and contests the idea that what is stipulated in the law must be correct and fair.

Mei Xia also condemns the idea of legal rights-defense because workers have to pay high costs for doing so:

> For workers seeking to defend their rights through legal channels, many need to give up their jobs as the legal procedures usually take a long time, maybe more than a year. Workers do not have much savings; they can't afford to have no job and spend most of their time on legal procedures. Therefore, many of them simply give up pursuing their rights through legal means.

In addition, Mei Xia points out that the rule of law in China is deceptive because the government does not respect laws. Since they want to retain investments in the city, local governments do not implement labor laws stringently, or they often help employers control workers through their administrative powers. Taking the strike in her factory as an example, she maintains that the district-level and town-level governments were backing the factory rather than 'being neutral' as portrayed in the news. The government officials kept pressuring the strikers to resume work. Additionally, during wage negotiations with management, they kept persuading the strike representatives to accept the company's offer, suggesting that it was already higher than the wages rendered by nearby factories. Moreover, after the strike ended, the government sent a student intern to investigate Mei Xia, trying to find out, for example, her work schedule, her financial situation, what she did in her spare time, etc. In order to give her greater pressure, her father who lived a rural village was brought by the government to the city to meet with the government officials. Furthermore, her communications were spied on by government officials and higher level trade union officials, who were aware of her communication exchange with supporters from various social groups.[19] She was invited to an academic conference in Beijing to share her strike experience, but a provincial trade union official tried to deter her from going. In addition, she was given an award by a newspaper that organized a ceremony to acknowledge the contribution of migrant workers to the country,[20] but she was stopped by the government from attending the award ceremony.[21] Mei Xia points out that outsiders and the public might think the government is neutral and does not take sides, but 'in reality, they are pro-business'. Mei Xia is able to see through the apparent autonomy of the Chinese government from businesses, and thus, does not consider the state neutral or standing apart from the society.

The above-mentioned examples of government pressure on Mei Xia illustrate their coercive tactics in taming worker activists. As reiterated, coercion and persuasion are both the ruling strategies of the state. The Chinese party-state's coercive tactic are exemplified in a number of labor disputes that have arisen recently; for instance, twelve hospital security guards in Guangzhou were detained for more than 50 days and convicted of 'disturbing the peace' for launching a protest in August 2013,[22] a worker-activist in Shenzhen joined a strike in May 2013, and was thus detained for over a year, facing criminal prosecution that was later dropped.[23] My fieldwork finds that the party-state is relatively tolerant with workers that only join protests or strikes, and do not directly organize them (like Liu Chiu and Cai Lin from the affirmative group). This type of worker seldom experiences the coercive side of the government. However, when it comes to strongly committed worker-activists, like Mei Xia, who have overcome legal hegemony to organize collective resistance, the party-state resorts to forceful means to curb their activism.

It is worth highlighting that Mei Xia's radical attitude towards the labor law system has developed out of her work and struggle experiences over time. At first, she knew nothing about labor laws; then, during the strike, the fleeting moment of desire to be lawful emerged when she was warned about the alleged illegality of the strike. However, during the latter half of the strike and subsequent to it, she developed a radical criticism of the labor law system, realizing that the laws were asymmetrically designed and executed.

Mei Xia reveals discontent towards Chinese economic development. Although China is the second largest economy in the world, she notes, its per capita GDP still ranks low, and the wealth gap in the country has continued to widen[24]:

> *Our economy has been developing at the expense of workers.* The government has attracted foreign investment with a cheap labour force; our growing GDP has been created in exchange for the sacrifice made by workers. Workers have contributed tremendously to our country, but they can't share in the fruits of development. The government has channeled them into work in the cities, but under the current household registration system, they are 'dumped back' into villages when they get old. Economic development has already reached a certain standard; the government should make sure that workers have enough social protections.

Mei Xia does not endorse the capitalist mode of accumulation as it is, criticizing that China's economic growth is built upon the sacrifice of workers, who can hardly share in the economic progress that has been made. She also denounces the governments for utilizing workers for economic development, but constraining them from enjoying proper social welfare and benefits with its household registration policies.

3 Conclusion

This chapter demonstrates that the radical workers have refused to render any consent, not even passively, to legal hegemony. Various hegemonic mechanisms embedded into the labor law system have failed to shape their worldviews and actions in favor of capital accumulation. The radical workers have overcome double hegemonic effects to formulate radical challenges to both the capitalist economy and the party-state. Concerning capital–labor relations, first, while many affirmative, ambivalent, and critical workers have taken labor laws as a benchmark to gauge the behavior of employers and as a reference for defining fairness and justice, the radical workers are relatively immune to the normalizing mechanism of legal hegemony that seeks to normalize wage labor, surplus value extraction, profit maximization, and other capitalist managerial practices. The radical workers do not consider the legal minimum wage to be fair. Instead, they are aware of the huge gap between how much workers make and how much their factories earn; therefore, they ask for fair distribution of company profits as wages. Some of them actively contest the legal minimum wage standards that they deem unfair through both legal and extra-legal actions, while some strive for fair wages through staging strikes. Moreover, they do not thank the corporations for creating jobs for workers, rather, they emphasize workers' contributions to both the huge profits of companies and China's high GDP.

Second, as expounded upon in Chap. 4, the labor law system has countervailed some adverse impacts imposed by the market economy on workers in such ways that some affirmative workers think that the economic system is not completely exploitative, and that the labor law system can redress their grievances and curb illegal labor practices of employers. In other words, for them the legal is autonomous from the economic. However, the countervailing mechanism of legal hegemony has not influenced the radical workers to such an extent. Some of them understand that the legal and the economic are not independent or autonomous from each other, that the law-making process and legal content are biased towards capitalists, and that workers and capitalists are on unequal footing in the presence of the law. Some realize the systematic problems of labor laws, pointing out that it reflects and reproduces unequal social relations. Some reject the mediation, arbitration, and litigation systems, which some affirmative and ambivalent workers praise, for wasting workers' time and energy. Due to these reasons, the radical workers distrust the notion of rule of law and legal rights defense. Overall, the radical workers condemn Chinese economic development in a more critical manner than other types of workers. Many of them think workers cannot benefit from economic reform, and decry the party-state's development strategy of letting some people get rich first. They also criticize economic development for creating grave wealth disparity in the country, though a few of them believe that it has raised workers' living standards in comparison to the pre-reform period.

Third, concerning state–labor relations, due to the concealing mechanism of legal hegemony, some affirmative and ambivalent workers believe that the existence of numerous labor laws is evidence of the party-state's pro-labor inclinations. For these workers, the party-state appears to be autonomous from the capitalists because it puts into place a labor law system that is thought to be able to curb economic misdeeds. Furthermore, the decentralized politics in China have contributed to the transmuting mechanism of labor laws. The fact that local governments are largely responsible for capital accumulation, and thus, have not stringently enforced labor laws, whereas the central government is more concerned about political legitimacy, and thus has made many labor laws, has induced many affirmative, ambivalent, and critical workers to attribute the political bias towards businesses to local governments and their officials; and many of them consider the central government good and pro-labor. In contrast, the concealing mechanism and the transmuting mechanism of legal hegemony have little effect on the radical workers. The radical workers see through the intricate relations between the government and businesses, believing that the party-state is not autonomous or neutral from the capitalist class. Some see no essential differences between the central government and local governments, viewing them both as protective shields for the capitalists. Some understand that the legal system is subsumed under the political system, and that legal problems do not simply lie at the implementational level, but are also rooted in a political system that is undemocratic and partial towards capitalists. Some realize that although the party-state should serve the interests of workers and the peoples, in reality, it protects that of the capitalists. Some reject the officially constructed discourses of the rule of law and legal rights defense because they realize how the legal system and the labor law system in reality protect the interests of capitalists.

Finally, it is worth reiterating that despite the hegemonic effects of the labor law system, labor laws should not be simply conceived of as a pure instrument for class rule; it is, in fact, one terrain for class struggle and reflects the balance of forces between the classes. While the ruling class continuously seeks to acquire worker consent to its rule mediated through the labor law system and control their actions with coercive capacities, the working class attempts to carry out resistance in the legal terrain, to constrain the ruling class with the legal logic and rhetoric that it reproduces, and to advance their interests through any means possible, including both legal and extra-legal tactics. In some cases, workers are able to win some rights, laws, and pro-labor policies; laws, in fact, organize 'the structure of the compromise equilibrium permanently imposed on the dominant classes by the dominated' (Poulantzas 2000, 91). However, the legal system is not a level playing field, but merely a sloped terrain of class struggle within which the ruling class and the working class do not have similar access to power because the juridico-political structures in capitalist society have been asymmetrically established as previously explained.

Notes

1. Interview S1.
2. Interview S5.
3. Interview S2.
4. In the past, it was a common practice for factories to keep two months of worker salaries. For example, if a worker started working in a factory in early January, the salary for that month would only be released to the workers at the end of February.
5. See Article 6, http://news.xinhuanet.com/ziliao/2003-09/08/content_1068863.htm, accessed 10th May 2014.
6. See http://www.gov.cn/zwgk/2012-05/07/content_2131567.htm, accessed on 10th May 2014.
7. Interview S6. In 2005, the administrative area of Panyu was reduced, and Guangzhou was restructured to include 10 city-districts (including Panyu) and two county-level cities, see http://www.gz.gov.cn/publicfiles//business/htmlfiles/gzgov/s2768/list.html, accessed on 11th June 2014.
8. For the document issued by the Guangzhou Social Security Bureau see http://www.hrssgz.gov.cn/zwxxgk/xxgkml/gzwj/bmgfxwj/201105/t20110526_163111.htm, accessed on 1st January 2014. For the document issued by the Guangdong province government, see http://www.gdhrss.gov.cn/publicfiles/business/htmlfiles/zwgk/1315/201204/33993.html, accessed on 5th February 2014.
9. See http://www.gov.cn/zwgk/2007-04/24/content_592937.htm, accessed on 1st January 2014.
10. See http://english.people.com.cn/90882/8426667.html, accessed on 11th May 2014.
11. The informants gave me a copy of the Guangzhou Social Security Bureau's reply. Their legal actions have also been reported by a newspaper, see http://www.nfgb.com.cn/NewsContent.aspx?id=27418 and http://right.workercn.cn/c/2012/09/05/120905110244905720755.html, accessed on 3rd May 2014.
12. See http://www.npc.gov.cn/englishnpc/Law/2007-12/12/content_1383912.htm, accessed on 7th May 2014.
13. See http://english.people.com.cn/90882/8426667.html, accessed on 14th April 2014.
14. Interview S4.
15. See http://www.nfgb.com.cn/NewsContent.aspx?id=27418 and http://right.workercn.cn/c/2012/09/05/120905110244905720755.html, accessed on 11th July 2014.
16. Interview S7.

17. See the news report http://nfgb.com.cn/NewsContent.aspx?id=6467, http://gzdaily.dayoo.com/html/2009-05/20/content_574000.htm, http://www.nfgb.com.cn/NewsContent.aspx?id=3794, accessed on 11th March 2014.
18. Interview S8.
19. According to my fieldwork, this is not specific to Mei Xia, and indeed, is a common strategy deployed by the Chinese government to monitor and control labor and political activists.
20. http://gongyi.oeeee.com/zxtj/201205/t20120515_1293812.html, accessed on 1st August 2014.
21. However, the government, the trade union and the factory also tried to tame her with soft tactics, for example, arranging for her to attend Japanese lessons in the factory, granting her a scholarship for her studies after her resignation.
22. http://www.clb.org.hk/en/content/hospital-security-guards-detained-50-days-after-staging-protest, accessed on 2nd July 2014.
23. http://www.clb.org.hk/en/content/trial-labour-activist-wu-guijun-eventually-gets-underway-shenzhen, accessed on 2nd July 2014.
24. China's per capita GDP in 2013 was only 6807 USA dollar, which is lower than many developed countries'. See http://data.worldbank.org/indicator/NY.GDP.PCAP.CD/countries/1W?display=default, accessed on 3rd August 2014.

References

Chan, King-Chi Chris, and Sio-Ieng Elaine Hui. 2012. The Dynamics and Dilemma of Workplace Trade Union Reform in China: The Case of the Honda Workers' Strike. *Journal of Industrial Relations* 54: 653–668.

Chan, Jenny, and Ngai Pun. 2010. Suicide as Protest for the New Generation of Chinese Migrant Workers: Foxconn, Global Capital, and the State. *The Asia-Pacific Journal* 37 (2): 1–50.

Friedman, Eli, and Ching Kwan Lee. 2010. Remaking the World of Chinese Labour: A 30-Year Retrospective. *British Journal of Industrial Relations* 48 (3): 507–533.

Hall, Stuart. 1980. *Drifting into a Law and Order Society*. London: Cobden Trust.

Liebman, Benjamin. 2007. China's Court: Restricted Reform. *China Quarterly* 191: 620–638.

Lubman, Stanley. 1999. Bird in a Cage: Chinese Law Reform after Twenty Years. *Northwestern Journal of International Law & Business* 20: 383–424.

Poulantzas, Nicos. 2000. *State, Power, Socialism*. London: Verso.

Pun, Ngai, and Huilin Lu. 2010. Unfinished Proletarianization: Self, Anger, and Class Action among the Second Generation of Peasant-Workers in Present-Day China. *Modern China* 36 (5): 493–519.

Qiu, J.L. 2009. *Working-Class Network Society: Communication Technology and the Information Have-Less in Urban China*. London: MIT Press.

Thompson, E.P. 1977. *Whigs and Hunters: The Origin of the Black Act*. Harmondsworth: Penguin.

Thompson, E.P. 1980. *The Making of the English Working Class*. Harmondsworth: Penguin.

CHAPTER 7

Conclusion: The Chinese State, the Law, Labor Relations, and Hegemony

1 The Chinese State: From Passive Revolution to Hegemony

As the title of this chapter suggests, this book investigates four cardinal and interrelated subjects: *the Chinese state, the labor law system, labor relations, and hegemony*. This concluding chapter encapsulates the hegemonic mechanisms inherent in the labor law system, the characteristics of legal hegemony, worker vulnerability towards legal hegemony, and the precariousness of legal hegemony. Finally, directions for future research on the hegemonic capacity of the Chinese state are proposed.

The overarching conceptual framework of this book posits that, in an attempt to cope with the socio-political and economic impasse that emerged during the state-socialist era, the Chinese party-state has commenced a top-down capitalist revolution, beginning in 1978. This revolution is in sharp contrast to bottom-up bourgeoisie revolutions that took place in France and other countries. The Chinese passive revolution signifies that the country has started to implement capitalism (be it state capitalism, bureaucratic capitalism, or guanxi capitalism), but with no immediate engagement of the capitalist class as it did not readily exist in the early reform period. Without a dominant capitalist class to exercise moral and ethico-political leadership over the popular masses, the party-state had to navigate the passive revolution with mostly naked power so as to quell social protests and political opposition against the revolution. Therefore, the early reform period witnessed an authoritarian state applying

E.S.I Hui, *Hegemonic Transformation*, Series in Asian Labor and Welfare Policies, DOI 10.1057/978-1-137-50429-6_7

heavy-handed measures (as manifested in the Tiananmen Massacre and the clampdown on independent trade unions and political groups) to secure a stable economic and socio-political environment for the growth of capitalism. Many studies upholding the authoritarian state thesis have already captured this side of the Chinese party-state. Moreover, the passive revolution has dictated that the party-state must play a strong role in planning, organizing, and facilitating the capitalist economic development. Scholars hailing from the developmental state perspective (and similar contending perspectives) have grasped this dimension of the party-state. Furthermore, in order to pre-empt the formation of opposing forces, the party-state has adopted a strategy of trasformismo, maintaining the state corporatist structures laid down in the socialist period to co-opt working class leaders. Studies advocating the state corporatist approach have underscored this characteristic of the party-state. *I argue in this book that these three approaches –authoritarian state, developmental state, and corporatist state– to the Chinese state are not contending or unrelated perspectives, but are different parts of the same whole. It is, thus, more meaningful to comprehend them in juxtaposition with each other against China's broader social, political, and economic transformations.*

Following the commencement of the passive revolution, the party-state has forcefully steered the process of class recomposition in the country. Through affirming private property rights, establishing a labor market, commodifying labor power, adopting a market wage system, and implementing the labor contract system, the party-state has demoted the working class from the country's master to the exploited class that is compelled to sell its labor power to the capitalists. On the other hand, through its legal, economic, and social policies, the party-state has forged the formation of the capitalist class, which consists of foreign capitalists, private domestic capitalists, cadre-turned-capitalists, state capitalists, and the petty bourgeoisie. The rise of the capitalist class has not only been witnessed in the economic realm; the party-state has also bestowed certain political power to it by permitting capitalists to join the CCP, the National People's Congress, and the People's Political Consultative Conference. Having forsaken the working class and peasants in its social class alliance, the post-Maoist party-state has established a regime alliance with this newborn capitalist class.

The implementation of capitalism, the recomposition of class forces, and the formation of a state–capital alliance have triggered escalating social discontent and protests in the reform era, especially in connection with labor relations. While economic reform was a top priority for the second and third generation of Chinese leaders, Deng Xiaoping and Jiang Zemin, social equality and harmony are considered an equally crucial agenda by the fourth generation of leaders, the Hu-wen government, who keenly propagate the hegemonic project of the harmonious society, and have enacted numerous labor laws to pacify the aggrieved workers. The newly inaugurated Xi-Li government has been mobilizing people to pursue 'China's dream' and build up a 'moderately prosperous society'. All these indicate a changing role for the party-state in driving the capitalist economy—after the formation of a dominant class, its rule is no longer merely based on coercion, but also on garnering the subaltern class's consent to the new ruling bloc. That is, the Chinese party-state has been undergoing a hegemonic transformation, and its role has been gradually shifting from forcefully steering the passive revolution into establishing capitalist hegemony in such a way that the popular masses will actively or passively follow the ruling bloc's moral and ethico-political leadership.

2 The Labor Law System and Double Hegemony

2.1 Four Hegemonic Mechanisms

The labor law system is a vital vehicle through which the Chinese party-state has constructed the capitalist hegemony. It has produced *double hegemony*, which seeks to deflect workers' opposition against both the market economy and the party-state. Concerning capital–labor relations, the *normalizing mechanism* embedded in the labor law system has legitimized capitalist principles such as private property rights, surplus value extraction, waged labor, commodification of labor, and so forth. Many workers have taken labor laws as a yardstick for measuring employer behavior. Even though they are not completely happy with their jobs, they consider their bosses to be fair and just as long as they are legally compliant. Moreover, the labor law system upholds labor mediation, arbitration, and litigation as the most appropriate channels for dispute resolution. Stressing individual forms of labor activism amounts to marginalizing and stigmatizing collective forms, such as strikes and protests. Extra-legal actions are thus out of the question for some workers, whereas others, also affected by the norms imposed by the labor law system, try hard to justify extra-legal actions.

The *countervailing mechanism*, incorporated into the labor law system, also buttresses capitalist dominance. Despite its pro-capital essence, the labor law system provides aggrieved workers with a platform for resolving labor disputes. Many workers, therefore, believe that the market economy is not structurally exploitative, and that their hardships are a result of their own inadequate personal qualities (such as being poorly educated or irresolute in rights-defense) or a result of erratic misdeeds from idiosyncratic employers. For these workers, the juridical sphere is autonomous from the capitalist economy, and labor laws are a useful tool for remedying misbehavior occurring in the economic realm. However, in Poulantzas's terms, this perceived autonomy of the juridical is only a relative autonomy as the labor law system is structured to preserve the long term dominance of the capitalist class.

Concerning state–labor relations, the abundance of labor laws, which seemingly try to regulate capitalists, has convinced some workers that the party-state is protective towards workers. They, thus, attribute workers' misfortunes to their own poor psychological and behavioral traits rather than to the state's pro-capital bias. This *concealing mechanism* embedded in the labor law system induces some workers to believe that the political regime is 'autonomous' from the market economy and is willing to curb economic misdeeds. Hence, they do not fundamentally challenge the party-state's legitimacy.

In addition to the concealing mechanism, the *transmuting mechanism* also bulwarks the Chinese party-state from workers' radical challenges. Due to the decentralized politics of China, local governments are delegated the task of capital accumulation, while the central government is preoccupied with maintaining political legitimacy and social harmony. Some workers, therefore, perceive government corruption and its pro-businesses bias as being caused by local governments or individual officials. They do not criticize the central government or the party-state as a whole, which they consider independent from capitalists. Put in another way, the transmuting mechanism shifts the target of workers' contempt from systemic state–capital collusion to individual officials and/or local governments.

Through these four mechanisms, the labor law system has been able to impose double hegemony on some workers. However, it should be highlighted that these mechanisms have not completely eradicated worker discontent towards the market economy or the party-state. In fact, hegemony is not about the complete submission of workers to the ruling class or full elimination of social discontent or opposition. It is only an unstable equilibrium of compromises (Poulantzas 2000, 31) between class opponents at any given historical moment. If worker contestation does not aim to shake the foundation of the market economy and the party-state, and are contained within a capitalist framework, then they are perfectly compatible with capitalism, and thus, are often allowed and tolerated by the ruling bloc.

2.2 *Characteristics of Legal Hegemony*

Based on the discussions of the previous chapters, I summarize the characteristics of legal hegemony and, broadly, capitalist hegemony in China in the following ways. First, *capitalist hegemony has developed concurrently alongside the economic and political lines* in such ways that it has acquired a national-popular appearance. Workers' commonsensical judgment of economic development is often marked by nationalist sentiments actively imbued by the party-state (see Xiao Mei, the affirmative worker from Chap. 4). Although soaring economic growth in China has not benefited them much, some workers endorse it due to the belief that economic prosperity is good for the nation and can increase the nation's power over its rivals. Some workers (such as Chang Shan, the ambivalent worker in Chap. 5) are aware of employers' exploitation, but are willing to 'sacrifice' themselves for the country's economic prosperity. All of this echoes what Gramsci highlights: 'the development and expansion of the particular group are conceived of, and presented, as being the motor force of a universal expansion of a development of all the "national" energies' (Gramsci 1971, 182).

However, the economic should not be understood as simply relying on the political. It is true that the capitalist leadership is bolstered by state-led nationalism, but the Chinese party-state's political legitimacy hinges, consequently, upon economic growth and capital accumulation, especially when democratic elections are absent in the country. The party-state sets goals for economic development and mobilizes the nation to achieve them; afterwards, it propagates throughout the country that these goals have been attained in order to secure its legitimacy. This is what Breslin called 'performance based legitimacy' (2007, 44). The interdependence between the political and the economic contributes to a symbiotic relation between the party-state and capitalists in China. In Anglo-Saxon and Western European countries, satisfactory economic performance may partly contribute to the stability of the political regime, but their legitimacy is largely derived from the political system of representative democracy, which is absent in China. Compared to its Western counterparts, it is imperative for the Chinese party-state to maintain its legitimacy through driving economic development. As a matter of fact, one reason that Deng Xiaoping had to launch the passive revolution was to resolve economic (and political) deadlock facing the CCP at the time (McNally 2008; Gray 2010).

Second, legal hegemony in China *capitalizes on the lingering memories of a socialist legacy and history.* The economic hardship during the state-socialist era has induced some workers who grew up during those times to feel grateful for the greater material benefits, however basic, brought about through economic reform (see Qiang Lai and Ah Rong, the affirmative workers in Chap. 4). Official discourses on economic progress, such as pursuing the China's dream and moderately prosperous society, have struck a responsive chord among the workers exposed to that period of disquieting experiences, especially the first generation of migrant workers; they are, thus, susceptible to the economic and moral worldviews being reproduced by the capitalist class. Moreover, political and social chaos during the Cultural Revolution has left many workers ready to accept the party-state's discourse on social stability (see Ah Kong, the ambivalent worker from Chap. 5). For them, the 'rule of law' is a means by which to prevent social disorder. Their trust in the legal system is the starting point at which the labor law system can exercise double hegemonic effects.

Furthermore, although socialist ideologies have declined in China, the pro-labor image of the party-state lingers in the purview of the minds of some workers. Numerous legal measures that were legislated by the party-state in the reform period to guard against unfair employer treatment of workers continue to reinforce this perception held by some workers. For them, the party-state is autonomous from the capitalists and is able to constrain them. Some scholars have analyzed how socialist legacy was utilized by state workers in their protests (Lee 2007). This book has shed light on the other side of the coin—how the remnants of socialist thoughts are manipulatively invoked to strengthen capitalist leadership over the working class.

The third characteristic of legal hegemony is that it *builds upon legal concessions.* The consent given by the working class is exchanged for concessions made by the hegemonic dominant class. The Chinese labor law system offers workers a certain degree of protection so that more of them do not interpret their miserable experiences as originating from the structurally biased market economy or the pro-capital party-state. However, as Gramsci stresses, the concessions granted by the capitalist class are usually 'of an economic-corporate kind…such sacrifices and such a compromise cannot touch the essential…' (Gramsci 1971, 161). Therefore, in China, legal concessions often take the forms that are compatible with a capitalist-legal framework, rather than ones that essentially alter the asymmetrical capital–labor relations. These legal concessions may contradict the short-term, particular interests of individual capitalists, but in the long run, they will consolidate the general interests of capitalism as a system and of the capitalists as a class.

However, it should be noted that legal concessions, as exemplified in numerous Chinese labor laws, are by no means granted readily or willingly by the ruling class. As Poulantzas underscores, the law 'has inscribed within it the material concessions imposed on the dominant classes by popular struggles' (Poulantzas 2000, 84); and in fact, the legal system is a site for class struggle, as Thompson suggests, though it is an uneven, biased, and partial site. Legal concessions in China are the hard-fought products of working class struggles. The 1995 Labour Laws was legislated not only to guide the labor market and wage labor relations, but also to alleviate the intensifying labor discontent as manifested in the 1989 Tiananmen Democratic Movement, the post-1989 labor protests, and the protests related to the Zhili fire that broke out in 1993 (Ngok 2008).[1] The 2004 Provisions for Minimum Wage were implemented to ameliorate escalating labor unrest subsequent to China's admission to the WTO in 2001. The 2007 Arbitration Laws and the 2008 Labour Contract Law were enacted to further dampen burgeoning labor strikes in the country (Hui and Chan 2012).

The legal concessions won by the Chinese workers have, in turn, led to a minimal degree of economic concession. Prior to the enactment of various labor laws, wages and benefits of workers were determined by race-to-the-bottom competitions among capitalists in the market. Although these laws cannot fully eradicate race-to-the-bottom practices, they set the minimum standards regarding wages, working hours, overtime payment, and so forth, with which employers supposedly must comply. Although weak legal implementation and local protectionism in China imply that not every worker actually benefits from the legally-derived economic concessions, some studies show that employers have become more legally compliant (Chan 2013). It is important to underline that economic concessions given by the capitalist class in China has, thus far, been secured mostly through legal means; it seldom takes the form of regular and institutionalized collective agreements between corporations and workers (as in some Western countries) because collective bargaining has been poorly executed in China.

Fourth, as explicated in Chap. 2, *the ruling class rules with persuasion alongside coercion*, but under normal situations, the latter is often invisible. Poulantzas highlights:

> ...in every State, law is an integral part of the repressive order and of the organization of violence. By issuing rules and passing laws, the state establishes an initial field of injunctions, prohibitions and censorship, and thus institutes the practical terrain and object of violence. (2000, 77)

> And once political power was institutionalized, these States had less recourse to such violence in normal contexts of domination—even though they now enjoyed a monopoly of its legitimate use. (2000, 80)

The role of coercion in securing subordination of the Chinese working class is not so discernible in the worker-interviewees who have run into individual industrial disputes or experienced no disputes at all. However, it is prominent in those who have vigorously championed collective worker interests. The state's coercive activities have taken a number of forms. At the mildest level, with its Great Firewall system, the party-state blocks websites that cover sensitive political and social issues, such as those related to Falungong, the Tiananmen democratic movement, and any information about 'rebellious' organizations and dissidents.[2] For instance, Twitter, Flicker and YouTube were blocked ahead of the 20th anniversary of the Tiananmen movement in 2009.[3] The popular masses (including Wang Ling, the radical worker in Chap. 6) need to utilize a special technique called 'Fanqian' to get around the state's cyber controls. The other state measures to exercise online control include prosecuting vocal 'internet celebrities' from time to time[4] and hacking into internet service providers' databases and servers.[5] In addition, bowing to the state's pressure, many internet companies act as accomplices to internet control. For instance, China Yahoo provided the state with a journalist's email to a US website regarding the 15th anniversary of the Tiananmen movement as evidence for his prosecution; he was later sentenced to 10 years of imprisonment.[6] Google China acceded to filtering out information that is considered unwanted by the state from user search results.[7]

Surveillance over labor activists is the second form of party-state coercion concerning labor relations. According to the fieldwork, many pro-labor NGO staff, rights lawyers, scholars, and worker activists are regularly approached by the party-state's security personnel, who ask them for details on their activities and updates on other activists and organizations. In addition to this, if these labor advocates become directly involved in specific labor actions, the security personnel or government officials may give them covert or overt pressure, warning them not to step out of line. For example, the legal scholar introduced in Chap. 6 was instructed by the government not to raise the issue of trade union reform in the negotiation meetings with Mei Xia's factory; the government tried to constrain Mei Xia's activism through spying on her communications and forbidding her to join high-profile activities; Shao Jiang (the radical worker in Chap. 6) was given pressure through security personnel to halt the campaign about Panyu's legal minimum wage.

The severest form of state coercion is forceful clampdowns on labor activists or organizations that are deemed ungovernable and causing serious trouble. As explicated in Chap. 6, some strike leaders have been detained, prosecuted, or thrown into jail. Also, more than 10 labor NGOs in the PRD suffered from a government crackdown in 2012; they were investigated in a harassing manner by various government departments (such as the Tax Bureau, Fire Bureau, etc.) and accused of breaching different rules and laws; some of them were forcefully evicted from their offices by their landlords, who admitted that they were also under government pressure.[8] And in 2015 seven labor NGO activists from Guangzhou, who were actively involved in workers' strikes, were placed under 'criminal coercive measures'. They were accused of 'disturbing public order, or committing fraud, adultery and embezzlement'.[9]

2.3 Worker Susceptibility to Legal Hegemony

In spite of its hegemonic capacity, not all workers have bought into double hegemony wielded by the labor law system. Endeavoring to examine the degree to which workers have rendered allegiance to capitalist leadership, I have constructed a typology of worker susceptibility towards legal hegemony in Chap. 4. Under this typology, workers are classified into five modes —affirmative, indifferent, ambivalent, critical, and radical—according to three criteria. The first criterion is the level of knowledge regarding labor laws and the level of motivation to gain such knowledge. This reflects whether, and to what degree, workers regard labor laws as relevant to them. The second criterion is the degree to which workers accept or reject the labor law system, which consists of party-state-constructed legal discourses (such as the rule of law and legal rights-defense) and the actual legal practices. This indicates how much workers place trust, or distrust, in the labor law system. The third criterion is whether they identify any defects inherent in the labor law system; if yes, whether they attribute these defects to the faults of individual government officials or employers, or systemic causes lying within the legal system, the state and/or the market economy. This criterion reflects the reasons behind distrust of the labor law system and the degree to which workers are vulnerable to the values and ideologies reproduced therein.

The affirmative workers approve of the official legal discourses and labor law practices, and have readily rendered active consent to capitalist leadership through the mediation of the labor law system. Most of them perceive of capitalist reform and economic growth in a positive light. They endorse the state's development strategy of 'let some people get rich first', which is akin to the liberal 'trickle down' theory, believing that economic progress fuelled by the state's pro-businesses policies will eventually benefit other members of the society. Many of the affirmative workers believe that employers would have been above reproach had they paid workers wages according to labor laws. The market economy and the wealthy class are thought to have created jobs for workers and economic prosperity for the country, rather than exploiting labor. In other words, the capitalist class's interests have been universalized as that of the working class and the nation; the affirmative workers have interpreted their life and work experiences from the perspective of the dominant class.

The indifferent, ambivalent, and critical workers have only rendered passive consent, rather than active consent, to capitalist leadership—they have neither completely assented to it, nor fundamentally challenged it. The indifferent workers are unmotivated to gain legal knowledge and have submitted themselves to the economic and political status quo. The labor and social policies (such as the household registration system) and personal attributes in relation to age, education, and the gender role have tied them to their rural origins. They feel detached from the cities and consider their working life there transitory. Therefore, they see labor laws and socio-economic development as irrelevant to them. Believing in free market ideology, they opt for quitting their jobs when faced with problematic bosses, rather than resorting to the labor law system.

Both the ambivalent and critical workers do not place full trust in the labor law system because of the gap between their work experiences and official legal rhetoric, i.e., the unfulfilled promises of the latter. However, the labor law system is still able to elicit passive consent because their 'spontaneous discontent is contained by the pre-existing categories of the dominant ideology' (Femia 1987, 137). Although the critical workers discredit the labor law system and the ambivalent workers partially disapproved of it, their criticism usually targets implementation issues rather than asymmetrical power relations embedded within the system. Many of them opine that the central government holds good intentions to protect workers with labor laws; they attribute the failing labor law system to the fault of local governments or officials, who either do not enforce labor laws effectively or have strong connections with businesses.

For the radical workers, the hegemonic mechanisms embedded in the labor law system have failed to elicit active or passive consent. They have formulated radical challenges to both the capitalist economy and the party-state. They are relatively immune to the normalizing mechanism of legal hegemony, which seeks to normalize wage labor, surplus value extraction, property rights, and other capitalist practices. In addition, they are not influenced much by the countervailing mechanism; some of them understand that the legal and the economic are not independent of each other, that the law-making process and legal content are biased towards capitalists, and that workers and capitalists are on unequal footing within the legal realm. Moreover, the concealing mechanism and the transmuting mechanism have little effect on them; they see through the intricate relations between government and businesses, and do not construe the party-state, as a whole, as autonomous from the capitalist class. In brief, the radical workers have rejected the labor law system and fundamentally contest the capitalist worldviews it reproduces. They have also refused to follow the ruling bloc's leadership and seek to challenge capitalist domination.

This self-constructed typology allows us to conceptualize the differing degrees of hegemonic effects mediated through the labor law system, rather than comprehending hegemony as a zero-sum phenomenon. Hegemony is a provisionary product and a terrain of continuous class struggles. It is possible for Chinese workers to negotiate, contest, or transgress these hegemonic boundaries. This typology also permits us to understand worker susceptibility to legal hegemony as non-static and ever-changing, thus opening up the way for conceptualizing the possibility of workers to overcome double hegemony and transform the exploitative system.

3 The Fragility of Legal Hegemony

Hegemony is not static or stationary. The ruling bloc needs to continue to strive for reproducing its ideological and moral ascendency over the working class so as to forestall the latter's revolt. Legal hegemony in China must be conceived of as unstable and precarious in nature, rather than as sturdy and stationary. This book has illustrated that double hegemony mediated through the labor law system has influenced Chinese migrant workers in an uneven manner. The affirmative workers have granted active consent to the ruling class's leadership, whereas the indifferent, ambivalent, and critical workers have rendered passive consent. Finally, the radical workers have acceded no consent at all. This exposes the fragility and precariousness of legal hegemony in China.

The critical workers distrust official legal discourses and legal practices because their working experiences have clashed with the legal ideals promoted by the party-state in such ways that they have become disillusioned. They have started to develop criticisms of the labor law system and socio-economic system after witnessing discrepancies between legal ideals and legal reality. In comparison to the affirmative workers that have conferred active consent to legal hegemony, the labor law system imposes weaker hegemonic effects on the critical workers. They do not give any active consent to the ruling class's leadership and disapprove of the labor law system, but only for non-systemic reasons. If the party-state and the capitalist class continue to fail in creating 'legal' working experiences for this type of worker, it is possible that they will increasingly contest legal hegemony, especially as their class consciousness continues to grow in the process of collective struggle. In short, although they are subject to legal hegemony, the critical workers are in a state of acute volatility; they can be transformed into the radical type and take extra-legal actions if external conditions were to provide fertile soil. On the other hand, as these workers believe that the injustices heaped on workers are rooted in the lax implementation of labor laws, they can be changed into the affirmative mode if the party-state is able to create legal working conditions for them.

The ambivalent workers have only partly accepted official legal discourses, realizing that the labor law system is tainted by legal loopholes. Similar to the critical workers, they do not render active consent to the ruling class's leadership because they are sometimes frustrated by the legal reality they witness; yet their world conceptions are still articulated in terms of the capitalist values and ideas. If the ruling class were to create legal working conditions for them, the ambivalent workers would be likely to develop into the affirmative mode. Should the ruling class fail to do so, their contestation of legal hegemony may escalate, and it would be possible for them to transform into critical or even radical workers.

For the indifferent workers, various labor and social policies have bound them to their rural origins, and thus contribute to their sense of alienation, detachment, and resignation in the cities. Even though they receive treatment below legal standards, they perceive of labor laws as irrelevant to them. Their apathy towards the labor law system is not a result of conscious choices, but that of the social alienation created by the state's economic and social policies. In other words, the party-state's failure in securing their active consent to legal hegemony is an outcome of its own making.

Due to their sense of apathy and irrelevancy concerning the labor law system, it is possible that the indifferent workers will take extra-legal means to fight for their interests if they become extremely agitated or if their class consciousness matures. It is because the party-state-constructed legal discourses and legal knowledge have not yet become common sense for them; the belief that legal channels are the most appropriate means for settling disputes has not taken root in their minds. If economic and legal concessions are prerequisite for securing worker allegiance to a capitalist economy, then those workers that do not feel accepted into the cities and benefit little from those concessions are unlikely to confer active consent to legal hegemony. In other words, the state's social and labor policies, which have helped expedite economic accumulation based on blatant exploitation and the separation of production and reproduction, have weakened the foundation for the hegemonic leadership of the capitalist class.

The radical workers have formulated fundamental criticism of the systemic problems connected to uneven economic development, the political regime, and the labor law system. They are aware that the legal system is manipulated by the party-state, and that the capitalists and government have a symbiotic relationship. They do not acquiesce to capitalist leadership and have managed to transcend capitalist hegemony. The radical workers have developed stronger class and political consciousness. Therefore, these workers cannot be placated by merely creating legal working conditions for them or by making employers legally compliant. They do not simply demand legal minimum wages, but wages in fair proportion to the labor that they put in. Hence, they represent a serious threat to capitalist dominance.

The affirmative workers have already conferred active consent to the ruling bloc through the mediation of the labor law system; their endorsement of the system is based on the coherence between what they have been indoctrinated into and the legal reality, and the comparison between a period with and without labor laws. It is likely that they will remain affirmative if the ruling bloc is able to produce legal working experience for them; otherwise, they may shift into the ambivalent, critical, or even radical mode.

Three more points should be noted about the fragility of legal hegemony. First, the unevenly developed economy and growing social inequality has sown seeds for the precarious root of hegemony. In order to acquire a universal appeal, the capitalist class needs to address and incorporate the subaltern class's interests into theirs. Capitalist hegemony should be built upon economic concessions given by the dominant class in such ways that the working class feels 'shared' interests with the former, and as a result render their allegiance to it. In post-war USA and Britain, one of the key pillars for capitalist hegemony was the politics of mass production and mass consumption (Rupert 1995; Rhiannon 2000). This economic model turned class conflicts into class compromise and cooperation. Politicians and businesses in these countries propagated the idea that class conflict could be ameliorated through increasing production, productivity, and economic growth, and that if businesses did well, workers would also benefit. As a matter of fact, during the post-war period, worker wages were on the rise and could 'share' in the fruits of economic growth. They thus gave their consent to capitalist leadership.

Such a concessionary mechanism has not been built into the Chinese economic model, which has relied immensely on export-oriented, low-technology, and labor intensive manufacturing industries. Under this model, Chinese employers seek to increase surplus value through adopting super-exploitative measures rather than motivating workers to raise their productivity with a growth-sharing ideology. As a result, labor share in the country's economy has declined to a level of less than 50% since the late 1990s (see Graph 1). Although the Chinese party-state has implemented a minimum wage system, it has only secured minimal economic concessions from employers. The minimum wage as a proportion of average wages in the country has dropped from close to 50% in 1994 to below 25% in 2009 (see Graph 2).

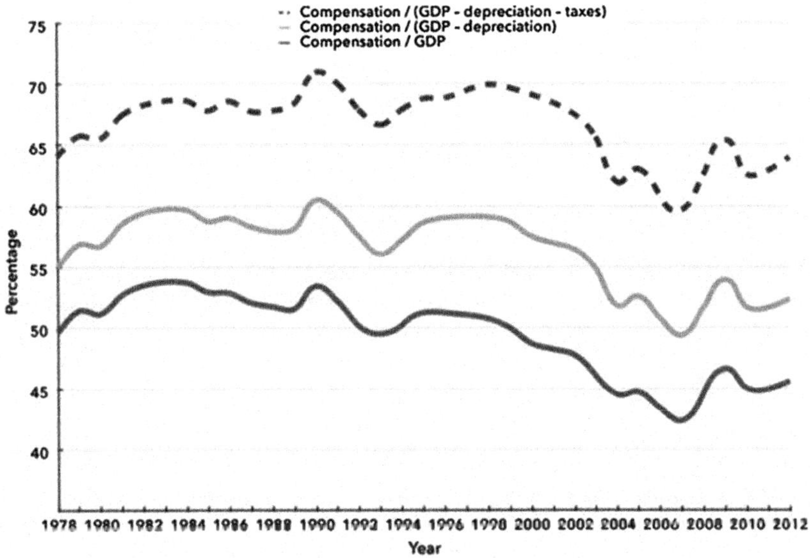

Graph 1 Labor share of GDP in China. *Source*: Hao (2014)[16]

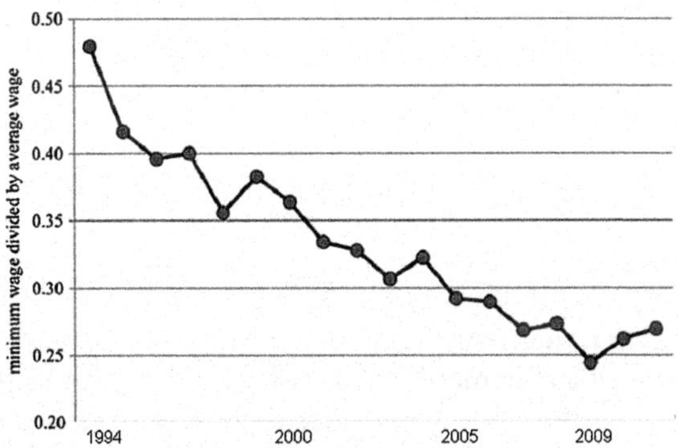

Graph 2 Minimum wage as a proportion of the average wage in China. *Source*: Li and Sicular (2014)

Capitalist hegemony in China has not been sturdily built upon economic concessions or legal concessions. Although many of the worker-informants see economic development in a positive light, they are not without complaints about rising social inequality, skyrocketing inflation, and a widening income gap. The material seeds for their discontent towards the market economy have already been sown; the super-exploitative economic model pursued by the party-state has ironically endangered the foundation of capitalist hegemony and, thus, the model itself. It is possible that latent worker dissatisfaction with the economy will burst into overt resistance against the ruling bloc's leadership should enabling conditions emerge in future.

The second point to underscore about the fragility of legal hegemony is related to the role of Chinese trade unions. Trade unions in the Western capitalist societies have played a crucial role in reproducing capitalist hegemony. In both the post-war USA and Britain, trade unions were incorporated into the production politics of mass production. Acting as the 'partners' to capitalists, they abandoned the goal of radical social and economic reform, and sought to defend worker interests within the capitalist framework. By concentrating on collective bargaining and agendas compatible with capitalism, they were able to, on the one hand, wrest a certain degree of short-term material gains from employers. On the other, they helped strengthen capitalist hegemony by endorsing private property rights, wage labor, employer authority over production processes, and the ideology of individual rights (Rupert 1995; Rhiannon 2000). The Chinese trade unions have not performed such functions. They have failed to secure worker acquiescence to the state–capital nexus through advancing immediate worker interests through wage bargaining or other effective means. On the contrary, they are commonly seen by workers as supportive and subordinate to the party-state and businesses; in many cases, they intensify worker discontent rather than ameliorate it. All in all, Chinese trade unions have not developed a hegemonic capacity in the same way as their Western counterparts; they basically have failed to absorb labor unrest into state-sanctioned legal channels, that is, contain it within the capitalist-legal framework. They, therefore, have become a key factor in contributing to the precariousness of capitalist hegemony in China.

The third point to highlight about the precariousness of legal hegemony is related to the role of labor NGOs in China. As elaborated in this book, when facing disputes, some worker-informants have sought aid from labor NGOs. Most of them opine that labor NGOs were helpful to their rights-defense and they have shown vast appreciation for the NGOs' support. However, due to the labor NGOs' legalistic approach and their emphasis on workers' legal rights, some scholars criticize the labor NGOs for individualizing labor disputes and channeling them into legally sanctioned procedures (Chan and Siu 2012; Friedman and Lee 2010). Moreover, the labor NGOs were criticized for participating in the party-state's project of the rule of law (Friedman and Lee 2010), and for acting like 'anti-solidarity machines' (Lee and Shen 2011, 173). This kind of criticism is partly, but not completely, valid. It is important to note that these NGOs are not homogenous. They differ in objectives, values, and operational arrangements. It is true that some NGOs have confined themselves within capitalist-legal boundaries and help, maybe unconsciously, atomize workers' activism, keep them within the legal sphere, and reproduce capitalist values embedded into the labor law system. However, some labor NGOs have transcended capitalist-legal boundaries. As elaborated from Chaps. 4 to 6, some NGOs work under legal pretexts, but they aim to heighten workers' awareness of labor rights (not only legal rights) and foster their class collectivity through organizing focus group discussions, encouraging the sharing of workplace grievances among workers, facilitating the discussion of social and labor policies, and engaging in action-planning on issues that concern workers. Due to the encounters with workers facing similar situations and the consciousness-raising activities of NGOs, some of the worker-interviewees have developed class empathy for and a class identification with other workers, realizing that their plight is not specific to themselves and that other workers also suffer from unfair situations This prompts them to take steps to question the commonsense about capital–labor relations. Some workers' class identification is so strong that they have dedicated themselves to helping fellow workers in need. While the ruling class attempts to fragmentize and decompose the working class, and the official trade unions have acted as its accomplice, some NGOs have helped to establish class connections and solidarity among workers and raise their class consciousness. This in turns has made legal hegemony precarious and fragile.

In brief, the precariousness and fragility of legal hegemony in China are the results of a number of factors: (1) the party-state has failed to consistently uphold the legal ideals it has reproduced; the discrepancies between legal ideals and legal reality have disillusioned some workers; (2) labor laws still have not turned into commonsensical knowledge for a segment of workers; (3) the party-state's social and labor policies, which have triggered workers' sense of apathy and irrelevancy concerning labor laws, have paradoxically hindered its elicitation of the active consent of some workers; (4) unbalanced economic development and growing social inequality have laid the material foundation for worker contestation to capitalist leadership; (5) the party-led trade unions are unable to secure short-term material concessions for workers and, hence, worker allegiance to the ruling bloc; and (6) some labor NGOs have helped raise workers' class consciousness, which, to a certain extent, aids workers to overcome legal hegemony.

4 Future Research

This book sheds light on the hegemonic capacity of the Chinese party-state during the course of its hegemonic transformation. Due to space limitations, it only explores embryonic hegemony in China by concentrating on the labor law system and capital–labor relations at the point of production. The other aspects, however, are worthy of further attention in the future.

First, certain developments occurring in China may alter the quality and characteristics of its incipient hegemony. At the economic level, China has been trying to carry out industrial upgrades and create a domestic consumption-based economy. Li (2011) estimates that the latter goal would be possible if corporate profits were cut by 15% and redistributed as wages. Furthermore, the party-state has made greater efforts to improve the social insurance system, as exemplified by implementation of the Social Insurance Law in 2011. The hukou system is also under reform, however minimal. In 2014, the CCP Political Bureau adopted the Opinion on Further Reforming the Hukou System, suggesting, among other things, granting residential status to migrant workers who have lived in the cities for a long time.[10] And under the 2011–2015 Five-Year-Plan, the party-state was seeking to raise the minimum wage rate by 13% annually.[11] If all of these are achieved successfully, they may help transform the super-exploitative economic model in China and reduce the income gap. If that is the case, what will be the impact on worker vulnerability to hegemony?

At the level of class organizations, it is foreseeable that the party-state will continue to allow the ACFTU to monopolize the organizations of trade unions, but may push for reforms such as democratic trade union elections and effective collective wage bargaining. These policies, if implemented meaningfully, may persuade some workers that the party-led trade unions can, somehow, represent them and fight for their interests; this in turn may strengthen the role of trade unions in manufacturing worker consent at the point of production (Burawoy 1979).

At the social level, the party-state has adopted a dual-track approach towards civil society. First, although civil society organizations remain closely monitored by the state, there are signs that it may loosen its grip. For example, innovative social administration (*shehui guanli chuangxin*) has been widely promoted in Guangdong province since 2012; registration for civil organizations at the Bureau of Civil Affairs has been made easier; increasingly, more government agencies subcontract social services to social organizations. Second, the party-state has become extremely harsh with vocal labor NGOs, as illustrated by its crackdown on labor NGOs and NGO activists in 2012 and 2015. What are the influences of these new trends on the development of Chinese civil society, and thus on its role in cultivating capitalist hegemony?

Second, alongside workplace issues, social concerns over environmental security, land expropriation and housing demolition have provoked grave discontent from the popular masses. As a matter of fact, protests related to these issues have been multiplying in China and are sometimes larger in scale than labor protests. For example, in 2011, the villagers in Wukan in Guangdong province staged protests against corrupt government officials that illegally appropriated their farmland and sold it to developers.[12] In 2013, some residents in Beijing drank pesticide to protest against the demolition of their homes by the government.[13] In 2014, in Maoming, Guangdong, several hundred people staged serious protests against the government for planning to build a paraxylene (PX) plant in the city.[14] Also, in the same year, thousands of people from the county of Boluo in Guangdong took to the streets to protest against the construction of a trash incinerator.[15] Like labor, nature is a fictitious commodity (Polanyi 2001), which is one of the indispensable production factors in capitalism. How has the ruling bloc organized its moral and ethico leadership over the subaltern class on these key issues?

Third, the Chinese party-state is continuously being contested by political activists and dissidents. Its governing strategies for dealing with political challenges still depend heavily on coercion. For instance, shortly ahead of the 25th Anniversary of the Tiananmen Massacre in 2014, it launched a large-scale detention and prosecution of political activists, including the seasoned reporter Gaoyu, rights-lawyers Pu Zhiqiang and Xu Zhiyong, a Hong Kong book publisher working on a politically sensitive book and so forth. Has political suppression by the party-state offset its hegemonic attempts in other dimensions, such as industrial relations? If yes, in what ways and to what extent?

In summary, this book illuminates the ways in which the Chinese party-state has developed an embryonic hegemonic capacity through the labor law system during its hegemonic transformation. A thorough understanding of the above-elaborated issues would help us further grasp the hegemonic capacity of the Chinese party-state and the developmental path of embryonic hegemony in the country.

Notes

1. The Zhili Fire took place in Zhili Toy Factory, which produced for an Italian brand. It was the normal practice of the factory to lock all doors and windows in the factory premises and dormitories so as to keep the workers inside of the factory. When the fire broke out, the workers were locked inside and could barely escape. As a result, 87 workers died in the fire (Ngok 2008, 62). The Zhili fire provoked many overseas social groups to protest against the employer and government for the maltreatment of the workers.
2. http://www.theguardian.com/technology/2012/dec/14/china-tightens-great-firewall-internet-control, accessed on 1st January 2014.
3. http://news.bbc.co.uk/2/hi/asia-pacific/8460129.stm, accessed on 11th July 2014.
4. http://www.scmp.com/news/china/article/1299281/chinese-american-venture-capitalist-charles-xue-taken-away-beijing-police?page=all.
5. http://www.theguardian.com/technology/2011/may/13/china-cracks-down-on-vpn-use, accessed on 5th May 2014.
6. http://www.amnestyusa.org/our-work/cases/china-shi-tao, accessed on 12th July 2014.
7. http://www.theguardian.com/technology/2011/may/13/china-cracks-down-on-vpn-use, accessed on 12th July 2014.
8. Interview D1, D3, D6 and D12.
9. http://www.wsj.com/articles/china-details-accusations-against-detained-labor-activists-1450807379, accessed on 4th March 2016.
10. http://finance.sina.com.hk/news/-33452-6821719/1.html, accessed on 11th August 2014.
11. http://www.china.org.cn/opinion/2012-02/13/content_24624457.htm, accessed on 15th September 2014.
12. http://www.scmp.com/topics/wukan, accessed on 13th September 2014.

13. http://www.foxnews.com/world/2013/12/11/china-residents-drink-pesticide-to-protest-bulldozing-homes/, accessed on 15th September 2014.
14. Paraxlyene is a dangerous chemical that can damage abdominal organs and the nervous system if inhaled or absorbed into body. For the protest, see http://www.scmp.com/news/china/article/1465140/people-maoming-and-shenzhen-stage-fresh-protest-over-planned-px-plant, accessed on 11th August 2014.
15. http://www.washingtonpost.com/world/asia_pacific/chinese-protesters-march-against-trash-incinerator/2014/09/13/17646b78-3b2a-11e4-a023-1d61f7f31a05_story.html, accessed on 15th September 2014.
16. Hao (2014) argues that the apparent rise of the labor share after 2007 was a result of an increasing number of worker struggles against deteriorating employment conditions in the aftermath of the global economic crisis.

References

Breslin, Shaun. 2007. *China and the Global Political Economy*. New York: Palgrave Macmillan.

Burawoy, Michael. 1979. *Manufacturing Consent: Changes in the Labor Process Under Monopoly Capitalism*. Chicago: University of Chicago Press.

Chan, King Chi Chris. 2013. Contesting Class Organization: Migrant Workers' Strikes in China's Pearl River Delta, 1978–2010. *International Labor and Working-Class History* 83: 112–136.

Chan, Anita, and Kaxton Siu. 2012. Chinese Migrant Workers: Factors Constraining the Emergence of Class Consciousness. In *China's Peasants and Workers: Changing Class Identities*, ed. Beatriz Carrillo and David S.G. Goodman. Cheltenham: Edward Elgar Publisher.

Femia, Joseph V. 1987. *Gramsci's Political Thought: Hegemony, Consciousness, and the Revolutionary Process*. Oxford: Clarendon Press.

Friedman, Eli, and Ching Kwan Lee. 2010. Remaking the World of Chinese Labour: A 30-Year Retrospective. *British Journal of Industrial Relations* 48 (3): 507–533.

Gramsci, Antonio. 1971. *Selections from the Prison Notebooks*, trans. and ed. Q. Hoare and G.N. Smith. New York: International Publishers.

Gray, Kevin. 2010. Labour and the State in China's Passive Revolution. *Capital and Class* 34 (3): 449–467.

Hao, Qi. 2014. The Labor Share Question in China. *Monthly Review* 65 (8).

Hui, Sio-Ieng Elaine, and King Chi Chris Chan. 2012. The "Harmonious Society" as a Hegemonic Project: Labour Conflicts and Changing Labour Policies in China. *Labour, Capital and Society* 44 (2): 153–183.

Lee, Ching Kwan. 2007. *Against the Law: Labor Protests in China's Rustbelt and Sunbelt*. Berkeley: University of California Press.

Lee, Ching Kwan, and Yuan Shen. 2011. The Anti-Solidarity Machine?: Labor Nongovernmental Organizations in China. In *From Iron Rice Bowl to Informalization: Markets, Workers, and the State in a Changing China*, ed. Sarosh Kuruvilla, Ching Kwan Lee, and Mary Elizabeth Gallagher. Cornell University Press.

Li, Minqi. 2011. The Rise of the Working Class and the Future of the Chinese Revolution. *Monthly Review* 63 (2): 38.

Li, Shi, and Terry Sicular. 2014. The Distribution of Household Income in China: Inequality, Poverty and Policies. *China Quarterly* 217: 1–41.

McNally, Christopher A. 2008. The Institutional Contours of China's Emergent Capitalism. In *China's Emergent Political Economy: Capitalism in the Dragon's Lair*, ed. Christopher A. McNally. London: Routledge.

Ngok, Kinglun. 2008. The Changes of Chinese Labor Policy and Labor Legislation in the Context of Market Transition. *International Labor and Working-Class History* 73: 45–64.

Polanyi, Karl. 2001. *The Great Transformation: The Political and Economic Origins of Our Time Author*. Boston: Beacon Press.

Poulantzas, Nicos. 2000. *State, Power, Socialism*. London: Verso.

Rhiannon, Vickerss. 2000. *Manipulating Hegemony: State Power, Labour and the Marshall Plan in Britain*. Hampshire: Macmillan Press Ltd.

Rupert, Mark. 1995. *Producing Hegemony: The Politics of Mass Production and American Global Power*. Cambridge: Cambridge University Press.

Appendix 1: Details of Informants

E.S.I Hui, *Hegemonic Transformation*, Series in Asian Labor and Welfare Policies, DOI 10.1057/978-1-137-50429-6

In-depth interviews with workers

Numbering	*Date of interview (DD-MM-Year)*	*Gender*	*Experience of labor dispute*	*Work in which city*	*Industries*	*Years of work experience*	*Position*	*Age*	*Education level*	*Relations with trade union*
Affirmative mode										
Q1	15-12-2012	Male	No experience	Guangzhou	Car industry	Over 5 years	Engineer	Over 30	University	Enterprise trade union official
Q2	22-11-2012	Female	No experience	Guangzhou	Car industry	Over 3 years	Rank and file	Early 20s	Vocational secondary school	Enterprise trade union official
Q3	15-12-2012	Male	No experience	Panyu	Electronics industry	Over 11 years	Engineer	Late 20s	University	N/A
Q4	15-12-2012	Male	No experience	Shenzhen	Electronics industry	Over 7 years	Skilled worker	Early 30s	University	Enterprise trade union official
Q5	16-01-2013	Male	No experience	Shenzhen	Electronics industry	Over 2 years	Rank and file	Early 20s	Vocational secondary school	N/A
Q6 Qiang Lai	16-01-2013	Male	No experience	Shenzhen	Electronics industry	Over 20 years	Rank and file	Over 40s	Primary school	N/A
Q7 Zhi Hui	19-01-2013	Male	No experience	Guangzhou	Car industry	5 years	Rank and file	23	Vocational secondary school	Trade union member
Q8	15-12-2012	Female	No experience	Shenzhen	Electronics industry	Over 7 years	Team leader	Late 20s	University	Trade union member
Q9	16-01- 2013	Female	No experience	Shenzhen	Electronics industry	2 years	Rank and file	20	Junior high school	N/A
Q10 Xiao Mei	16-01-2013	Female	No experience	Shenzhen	Electronics industry	Over 5 years	Team leader	Early 20s	Senior high school	N/A
Q11	06-01-2013	Female	No experience	Guangzhou	Electronics industry	2 years	Rank and file	Early 20s	Junior high school	Trade union member
Q12 Ah Wen	24-03-2013	Male	Individual disputes	Dongguan	Molding industry	29 years	Rank and file	Mid 40s	Primary school	N/A
Q13	24-03-2013	Male	Individual disputes	Dongguan	Furniture industry	Over 5 years	Rank and file	Over 30s	Primary school	N/A
Q14 Qing Fa	14-10-2012	Male	Individual disputes	Shenzhen	Warehouse logistics	6 years	Rank and file	28	Vocational secondary school	N/A

(continued)

(continued)

Numbering	*Date of interview (DD-MM-Year)*	*Gender*	*Experience of labor dispute*	*Work in which city*	*Industries*	*Years of work experience*	*Position*	*Age*	*Education level*	*Relations with trade union*
Q15	14-10-2012	Male	Individual disputes	Shenzhen	Furniture industry	12 years	Rank and file	Over 40	Primary school	N/A
Q16	17-11-2012	Male	Individual disputes	Shenzhen	Electronics industry	7 years	Rank and file	Over 40	Primary school	N/A
Q17	17-11-2012	Male	Individual disputes	Shenzhen	Electronics industry	8 years	Rank and file	Over 40	Primary school	N/A
Q18 Ah Rong	21-10-2012	Male	Individual disputes	Shenzhen	Logistics	14 years	Rank and file	Over 40	Junior high school	N/A
Q19 Liu Chi	1-12-2012	Male	Collective disputes	Guangzhou	Auto industry	5 years	Technician	Early 30s	University graduate	Enterprise trade union official
Q20 Cai Lin	22-11-2012	Female	Collective disputes	Shenzhen	Electronics industry	4 years	Rank and file	Early 30s	Primary school	N/A
Q21	14-03-2013	Male	Collective disputes	Guangzhou	Auto industry					Enterprise trade union chair
Indifferent mode										
T1 Ah Qing	11-09-2012	Female	No experience	Shenzhen	Shoe industry	3 years	Rank and file	36	Primary school	N/A
T2 Ah Ying	08-12-2012	Female	No experience	Shenzhen	Electronics industry	9 years	Rank and file	34	Primary school	N/A
T3	15-10-2012	Female	No experience	Huizhou	Textile industry	2 years	Rank and file	28	Junior high school	N/A
T4	11-11-2012	Male	No experience	Dongguan	Furniture industry	5 years	Rank and file	30	Primary school	N/A
T5	12-11-2012	Female	No experience	Huizhou	Electronics industry	3 years	Rank and file	26	Primary school	N/A
T6	18-12-2012	Female	No experience	Shenzhen	Furniture industry	4 years	Rank and file	Over 30s	Primary school	N/A
T7	18-12-2012	Male	No experience	Shenzhen	Electronics industry	6 years	Rank and file	Over 40	Did not go to school	N/A
T8	03-01-2013	Female	No experience	Guangzhou	Electronics industry	5 years	Rank and file	30	Junior high school	N/A

(continued)

(continued)

Numbering	*Date of interview (DD-MM-Year)*	*Gender*	*Experience of labor dispute*	*Work in which city*	*Industries*	*Years of work experience*	*Position*	*Age*	*Education level*	*Relations with trade union*
Ambivalent mode										
P1 A Kong	13-01-2013	Male	No experience	Shenzhen	Electronics industry	1.5 year	Warehouse logistics	Mid 20s	College graduate	N/A
P2 Ah Xi	13-01-2013	Male	No experience	Shenzhen	Electronics industry	Over 10 years	Rank and file	Over 40	Primary school	N/A
P3 Jian Hua	16-12-2012	Male	Individual disputes	Dongguan	Electronics industry	11 years	Rank and file	Late 20s	Vocational secondary school	N/A
P4	16-12-2012	Male	Individual disputes	Dongguan	Furniture industry	4 years	Rank and file	Over 30s	Primary school	N/A
P5 Gui nan	13-01-2013	Male	Individual disputes	Shenzhen	Logistic company	9 years	Rank and file	Late 20s	Junior high school	N/A
P6	12-12-2012	Female	Individual disputes	Huizhou	Textile industry	5 years	Rank and file	Late 20s	Primary school	N/A
P7	13-12-2012	Female	Individual disputes	Huizhou	Electronics industry	3 years	Rank and file	24	Junior high school	N/A
P8 Chang Shan	4-11-2012	Male	Collective disputes	Foshan	Auto industry	5 years	Deputy line leader	Mid 20s	Vocational secondary school	Enterprise trade union branch chair
P9	4-11-2012	Female	Collective disputes	Foshan	Auto industry	3 years	Rank and file	Early 20s	Vocational secondary school	Trade union member
P10	25-11-2012	Male	Collective disputes	Shenzhen	Electronics industry	8 years	Delivery assistant	Mid 20s	Junior high school	N/A
P11	13-01-2013	Male	Collective disputes	Shenzhen	Textile industry	5 years	Driver	Mid 30s	Junior high school	N/A
Critical mode										
R1	13-01-2013	Female	No experience	Shenzhen	Electronics industry	6 years	Rank and file	Mid 30s	Primary school	N/A
R2 Zhang Lin	16-01-2013	Female	No experience	Shenzhen	Electronics industry	Over 3 years	Team leader	22	Vocational secondary school	N/A

(continued)

(continued)

Numbering	*Date of interview (DD-MM-Year)*	*Gender*	*Experience of labor dispute*	*Work in which city*	*Industries*	*Years of work experience*	*Position*	*Age*	*Education level*	*Relations with trade union*
R3 Chen Fei	19-01-2013	Male	No experience	Guangzhou	Auto industry	5 years	Rank and file	Early 20s	Vocational secondary school	Trade union member
R4 Shu Ren	16-12-2012	Male	Individual disputes	Dongguan	Furniture industry	Over 20 years	Rank and file	Over 40s	Primary school	N/A
R5	11-11-2012	Male	Individual disputes	Shenzhen	Security guard company	12 years	Security guard	Over 40s	Primary school	N/A
R6 Fu Shan	13-01-2013	Female	Individual disputes	Shenzhen	Electronics industry	7 years	Rank and file	Late 20s	Vocational secondary school	N/A
R7	18-10-2012	Female	Individual disputes	Shenzhen	NGO	8 years	Worker-tunred NGO staff	Over 30s	Junior high school	N/A
R8	21-10-2013	Male	Individual disputes	Shenzhen	NGO	6 years	Worker-turned NGO staff	Late 20s	Senior high school	N/A
R9	12-03-2013	Male	Individual disputes	Dongguan	NGO	4 years	Worker-turned NGO staff	Mid 20s	Junior high school	N/A
R10 Xin Xin	25-11-2012	Female	Individual disputes	Shenzhen	Electronics industry	7 years	Rank and file	Early 20s	Junior high school	N/A
R11	03-04-2013	Male	Individual disputes	Guangzhou	Electronics industry	12 years	Rank and file	Over 40s	Primary school	N/A
R12	01-02-2013	Female	Individual disputes	Huizhou	Printing industry	4 years	Rank and file	Early 30s	Primary school	N/A
R13 You Yang	01-12-2012	Male	Collective disputes	Shenzhen	Molding industry	Over 10 years	Technician	Early 40s	Vocational secondary school	N/A
R14	18-03-2013	Male	Collective disputes	Shenzhen	Garment industry	6 years	Rank and file	Early 30s	Junior secondary school	N/A
R15	13-02-2013	Male	Collective disputes	Shenzhen	Electronics industry	6 years	Rank and file	27	Junior high school	N/A

(continued)

(continued)

Numbering	*Date of interview (DD-MM-Year)*	*Gender*	*Experience of labor dispute*	*Work in which city*	*Industries*	*Years of work experience*	*Position*	*Age*	*Education level*	*Relations with trade union*
R16	11-02-2013	Female	Collective disputes	Shenzhen	Electronics industry	6 years	Rank and file	Late 20s	Primary school	Trade union member
R17	10-02-2013	Female	Collective disputes	Shenzhen	Electronics industry	6 years	Rank and file	Early 30s	Primary school	N/A
R18	06-01-2013	Male	Collective disputes	Guangzhou	Auto industry	5 years	Team leader	Mid 20s	Vocational secondary school	Trade union members' representative
R19	23-03-2013	Male	Collective disputes	Shenzhen	Electronics industry	7 years	Division leader	Early 30s	University	Trade union executive committee
Radical mode										
S1 Wang Lin	06-01-2013	Female	No experience	Guangzhou	Auto industry	Over 2 years	Assistant to department head	25	University	Trade union member
S2 Xiao Bao	20-05-2013	Female	Individual disputes	Shenzhen	NGO	9 years	Worker-turned NGO staff	under 30	Vocational secondary school	N/A
S3	11-04-2013	Female	Individual disputes	Shenzhen	NGO	8 years	Worker-turned NGO staff	Over 30s	Junior high school	N/A
S4	19-11-2012	Male	Individual disputes	Shenzhen	NGO	9 years	Worker-turned NGO staff	34	Junior high school	N/A
S5 Lin xia	04-11-2012	Female	Individual disputes	Foshan	Auto industry	3 years	Rank and file	Early 20s	Vocational secondary school	Trade union member
S6 Zhi Wan	11-10-2012	Male	Collective disputes	Panyu	Jewelry industry	Over 10 years	Facility management	Mid 30s	Junior high school	N/A
S7 Shao Jiang	11-10-2012	Male	Collective disputes	Panyu	Jewelry industry	Over 10 years	Line leader	Mid 30s	Junior high school	N/A
S8 Mei Xia	01-12-2012	Female	Collective disputes	Foshan	Auto industry	3 years	Rank and file	Early 20s	Vocational secondary school	Trade union member

(continued)

(continued)

Numbering	*Date of interview (DD-MM-Year)*	*Gender*	*Experience of labor dispute*	*Work in which city*	*Industries*	*Years of work experience*	*Position*	*Age*	*Education level*	*Relations with trade union*
S9	23-02-2014	Male	Collective disputes	Guangzhou	Auto industry	8 years	Division leader	Mid 30s	College level	Enterprise trade union chair
S10	24-02-2014	Male	Collective disputes	Guangzhou	Auto industry	7 years	Division leader	Mid 30s	Vocational secondary school	Enterprise trade union chair
S11	24-02-2014	Male	Collective disputes	Guangzhou	Auto industry	5 years	Division leader	Early 30s	Vocational secondary school	Enterprise trade union chair
S12	25-02-2014	female	Collective disputes	Panyu	Jewelry industry	6 years	Rank and file	Mid 30s	Primary school	N/A
S13	11-12-2012	Male	Collective disputes	Shenzhen	Electronics industry	7 years	Rank and file	Early 30	Junior high school	N/A
S14	13-12-2012	Female	Collective disputes	Foshan	Auto industry	3 years	Rank and file	Over 20s	Vocational secondary school	Trade union member
S15	14-12-2012	Male	Collective disputes	Foshan	Auto industry	3 years	Deputy line leader	Mid 20s	Vocational secondary school	Trade union member
S16	22-11-2012	Male	Collective disputes	Guangzhou	Auto industry	8 years	Division leader	Early 30s	Vocational secondary school	Enterprise trade union chair

Interviews with labor NGO staff

Numbering	*Date of interview*	*Based in which city*
D1	11-12-2012	Shenzhen
D2	14-10-2012	Shenzhen
D3	14-04-2013	Shenzhen
D4	15-04-2013	Shenzhen
D5	15-03-2013	Dongguan
D6	10-10-2012	Hong Kong
D7	11-02-2013	Hui Zhou
D8	01-03-2013	Hong Kong
D9	01-03-2013	Hong Kong
D10	24-03-2013	Shenzhen
D11	12-12-2012	Hong Kong
D12	14-12-2012	Dongguan
D13	18-02-2012	Shangdong
D14	06-12-2012	Hong Kong
D15	15-12-2012	Guangzhou
D16	15-12-2012	Guangzhou
D17	04-02-2012	Panyu
D18	04-02-2012	Panyu
D19	29-03-2012	Dongguan

Interviews with scholars

Numbering	*Date of interview*	*Based in which city*
H1 (also a registered lawyer)	13-12-2012	Shenzhen
H2 (also a registered lawyer)	29-12-2012	Guangzhou
H3 (also a registered lawyer)	14-01-2013	Guangzhou
H4	04-02-2013	Guangzhou
H5	13-04-2013	Hong Kong
H6	29-11-2012	Guangzhou
H7	28-10-2012	Shenzhen

Interviews with lawyers and judges

Numbering	*Date of interview*	*Based in which city*
F1 Lawyer	14-11-2012	Shenzhen
F2 Lawyer	20-11-2012	Shenzhen
F3 Lawyer	15-12-2012	Shenzhen
F4 Legal practitioner	15-12-2012	Shenzhen
F5 Lawyer	04-02-2013	Hong Kong
F6 Judge	03-03-2013	Dongguan
F7 Judge	24-02-2013	Dongguan
F8 Judge	19-10-2012	Dongguan

Interviews with government officials

Numbering	*Date of interview*	*Based in which city*
J1	13-11-2012	Retired government official at the town level
J2	16-12-2012	Official from CCP Politics and Law Commission
J3	18-12-2012	Official from CCP Politics and Law Commission
J4	03-02-2013	Government official at town level

Interviews with trade unionists

Numbering	*Date of interview*	*Based in which city*
G1	27-12-2012	Cadre from Guangdong provincial trade union
G2	07-12-2012	Cadre from Guangdong provincial trade union
G3	23-04-2013	Cadre from Guangdong provincial trade union
G4	21-04-2013	District level cadre in Shenzhen
G5	13-03-2013	Cadre from Shenzhen city trade union

Interviews with employers

Numbering	*Date of interview*	*Based in which city*
E1	14-11-2012	Electronics factory in Shenzhen
E2	15-11-2012	Electronics factory in Shenzhen
E3	13-12-2012	Furniture factory in Shenzhen
E4	13-02-2013	Watch factory in Dongguan

Index

E.S.I Hui, *Hegemonic Transformation*, Series in Asian Labor and Welfare Policies, DOI 10.1057/978-1-137-50429-6

J

L

M

N

O

P

R

CPSIA information can be obtained
at www.ICGtesting.com
Printed in the USA
LVOW13*1842141117
556262LV00017B/249/P

9 781349 700196